OXFORD ENGLISH MONOGRAPHS

General Editors
CHRISTOPHER BUTLER   VINCENT GILLESPIE
DOUGLAS GRAY   EMRYS JONES
ROGER LONSDALE   FIONA STAFFORD

Hazlitt and the Reach of Sense

Criticism, Morals, and the Metaphysics of Power

UTTARA NATARAJAN

CLARENDON PRESS · OXFORD
1998

Oxford University Press, Great Clarendon Street, Oxford OX2 6DP
Oxford New York
Athens Auckland Bangkok Bogotá Buenos Aires Calcutta
Cape Town Chennai Dar es Salaam Delhi Florence Hong Kong Istanbul
Karachi Kuala Lumpur Madrid Melbourne Mexico City Mumbai
Nairobi Paris São Paolo Singapore Taipei Tokyo Toronto Warsaw
and associated companies in
Berlin Ibadan

Oxford is a registered trade mark of Oxford University Press

Published in the United States
by Oxford University Press Inc., New York

© Uttara Natarajan 1998

First published 1998

All rights reserved. No part of this publication may be reproduced,
stored in a retrieval system, or transmitted, in any form or by any means,
without the prior permission in writing of Oxford University Press.
Within the UK, exceptions are allowed in respect of any fair dealing for the
purpose of research or private study, or criticism or review, as permitted
under the Copyright, Designs and Patents Act, 1988, or in the case of
reprographic reproduction in accordance with the terms of the licences
issued by the Copyright Licensing Agency. Enquiries concerning
reproduction outside these terms and in other countries should be
sent to the Rights Department, Oxford University Press,
at the address above

British Library Cataloguing in Publication Data
Data available

Library of Congress Cataloging in Publication Data
Natarajan, Uttara.
Hazlitt and the reach of sense: criticism, morals, and the
metaphysics of power/Uttara Natarajan.
(Oxford English monographs)
Includes bibliographical references (p.   ) and index.
1. Hazlitt, William, 1778-1830–Knowledge–Literature.
2. Literature–History and criticism–Theory, etc.   3. Criticism-
-England–History–19th century.   4. Metaphysics in literature.
5. Literature and morals.   6. Ethics in literature.   7. Power
(Philosophy)   I. Title.   II. Series.
PR4773.N38   1998   824'.7–dc21   I   98-24839
ISBN 0-19-818437-9

1 3 5 7 9 10 8 6 4 2

Typeset by J&L Composition Ltd, Filey, North Yorkshire
Printed in Great Britain on acid-free paper by
Biddles Ltd,
Guilford and King's Lynn

For my Parents,

*in deep gratitude for their
unflagging support over the years*

Acknowledgements

ROY PARK has been the most important single influence on the writing of this book; its argument is addressed to him and the book has taken the shape it has because he has been its auditor. Paul Hamilton has provided support and critical commentary on which I have drawn throughout. Jonathan Wordsworth supervised the work in its early stages. Philip Davis, Tom Paulin, and Gillian Rudd have offered encouragement and advice when I was badly in need of both. James Morley has seen me through the ups and downs of writing. I am indebted to the Department of English Language and Literature at the University of Liverpool for the research fellowship which enabled me to complete this work. I am also grateful to the library staff at Saint Joseph College, Connecticut, who generously allowed me free access to their library resources while I was living in America. For permission to reproduce material that has already appeared in print, I am grateful to the editors of *New Blackfriars Review*, *Philological Quarterly*, *Romanticism*, and *Studies in Romanticism*.

Contents

ABBREVIATIONS   xi

INTRODUCTION   1

1 THE SHAPES OF POWER:
   HAZLITT'S METAPHYSICS OF DISCOURSE   11
   - Hazlitt and Horne Tooke: A Philosophy of Grammar   11
   - The Real Language of Poetry   20
   - The Power Principle   27
   - The Palace of Thought: Hazlitt and Berkeley   31
   - Two Worlds   36

2 THE SECRET SOUL OF HARMONY:
   IMAGINATION, ASSOCIATION, AND UNITY   40
   - Unitarianism and Coleridge   41
   - Hazlitt and Associationism   51
   - Association and Necessity   64
   - Unity of Design   72

3 THE MIGHTY INTELLECT:
   THE SELF AS FOCUS IN HAZLITT'S THEORY   78
   - Hazlitt and Butler   78
   - Hazlitt and Coleridge: The Divergent Positions   84
   - The Artistic Ideal   88
   - The Bias of Genius   93
   - The Egotistical Sublime   96
   - On Diction   102
   - Hazlitt, Keats, and Shakespeare   107

4 A LONG-CONTESTED FREEDOM: METAPHYSICS AND MORAL THEORY	120
Alterity and the Moral Question	120
The Moral Ideal	127
Particular and Universal	131
Epistemological Background: Hazlitt's Theory of Abstraction	136
Hazlitt's 'Romantic' Morality	141
Liberty and Necessity	146
Hazlitt and Kant	154
5 ESSAYS POLITICAL AND FAMILIAR: TWO ASPECTS OF HAZLITT'S IDEAL	166
Abstracting Passion: The Ideal of Power	166
His Own Interpreter: The Essayist as Artist	179
BIBLIOGRAPHY	191
INDEX OF HAZLITT'S WORKS	199
GENERAL INDEX	203

Abbreviations

CLB	*Charles Lamb Bulletin*
ELH	*Journal of English Literary History*
KSMB	*Keats–Shelley Memorial Bulletin*
PMLA	*Publications of the Modern Languages Association of America*
PQ	*Philological Quarterly*
PS	*Prose Studies*
RES	*Review of English Studies*
SEL	*Studies in English Literature, 1500–1900*
SIR	*Studies in Romanticism*
WC	*Wordsworth Circle*

Whatever is placed beyond the reach of sense and knowledge, whatever is imperfectly discerned, the fancy pieces out at its leisure . . .

Introduction

THIS book asks for the recognition of Hazlitt's stature as a philosophical critic. Coleridge remarked that 'No man was ever yet a great poet, without being at the same time a profound philosopher.'[1] Perhaps the same can be said of the critic. Certainly Hazlitt is both a great critic and a profound philosopher, and he is one because he is the other. The 'only pretension, of which I am tenacious,' he tells us in *The Plain Speaker*, 'is that of being a metaphysician' ('On Envy'; xii. 98).[2] In *A Letter to William Gifford*, he writes, 'I have been called "a writer of third-rate books." For myself, there is no work of mine which I should rate so high, except one, which I dare say you never heard of—An Essay on the Principles of Human Action' (ix. 51).

An Essay on the Principles of Human Action: Being an Argument in favour of the Natural Disinterestedness of the Human Mind. To which are added, Some Remarks on the Systems of Hartley and Helvetius (1805) is Hazlitt's early metaphysical treatise, written, as its title indicates, in the style of the eighteenth century, and outlining a theory of the imagination that is the philosophical ground of the whole corpus of his work. As that theory is expanded and amplified, it leaves behind its generic origins to find a more felicitous, if less conventional expression in literary criticism and the autobiographical intimacy of Hazlitt's conversational prose. Hazlitt's philosophical endeavour is inextricably involved with the enterprise of writing itself; the range of his writings gives us his philosophy as a totality.

Simply put, Hazlitt's philosophical thesis is of a domain of intellectual power, located beyond the reach of the senses. In that domain, the human being is transformed from mechanism

---

[1] S. T. Coleridge, *Biographia Literaria or Biographical Sketches of my Literary Life and Opinions*, ed. W. J. Bate and J. Engell, vol. vii of *The Collected Works of Samuel Taylor Coleridge*, Bollingen series no. 75, 2 vols (Princeton, NJ: Princeton University Press, 1983), vol. ii, ch. xv, pp. 25–6.
[2] All quotations from Hazlitt are taken from *The Complete Works of William Hazlitt*, ed. P. P. Howe, 21 vols (London and Toronto: J. M. Dent, 1930–4). References are by volume and page.

into free agent, controlling, rather than controlled by, the material world outside. By releasing the mind from its dependence on the senses, Hazlitt constructs a metaphysics of power; every aspect of his thought and writing is grounded in that metaphysics.

'Power' is a fashionable term in current literary discussion and has become something of a catchword in Hazlitt scholarship. John Kinnaird's study is subtitled 'critic of power'; Bloom's formula for Hazlitt, in the *Modern Critical Views* series, is 'poetics of power'.[3] My own study also deals with the concept of power as central to Hazlitt, but unlike Kinnaird and Bloom, my concern is with the metaphysical origin of that concept and its implications for Hazlitt's thought. To Hazlitt, power signifies the mind's independence of the senses. The love of power, familiar to the philosophers of self-interest as part of the habitual mechanism of the self, is given, in his metaphysics, an altogether different status; it is the manifestation of an innate principle of power that attests to an autonomy of the intellect the reverse of mechanical. The commitment to such a principle persists from Hazlitt's early philosophical writings through to the later conversational prose. Where Kinnaird finds that the essayist of 'the *Table-Talk* phase' has suffered 'a lapse from his former convictions,' of 'an essentially transcendent power—that is, a power of mind communicably free of its source in a conditioned self',[4] I assert a continuity between the metaphysician and the essayist, contained in the lasting conviction, not of a transcendent, but of a self-conditioned power of the mind. The belletrist of the *Table-Talk* period shares with the theoretician of the *Essay* an understanding of power as epistemological: power is the mind's formative ability.

By adopting Hazlitt's approach to power as a metaphysical rather than a political construct, I have found myself running counter not only to the dominant trends in Hazlitt criticism, but also to a more general critical trend. The historicizing of Romanticism has become the index of critical validity recently, so much so that we are in some danger of forgetting that the history of events may not take precedence over the history of ideas. Nor is the second simply conflatable with the first. Perhaps it is no

---

[3] John Kinnaird, *William Hazlitt: Critic of Power* (New York: Columbia University Press, 1978); Harold Bloom, 'Introduction', in Bloom (ed.) *Modern Critical Views: William Hazlitt* (New York: Chelsea House, 1986), 3 ff.
[4] Kinnaird, *William Hazlitt*, 286–7.

more than timely, then, that my formulation of Hazlitt's metaphysics of power reopens the field of enquiry outlined by that tired old phrase 'Romantic idealism'. Within this field, Hazlitt stands out in two important respects. The first is his consistency. I write this, conscious that to the modern critical mind, intellectual complexity has become increasingly synonymous with paradox and discontinuity, especially in the warring of the political against the aesthetic.[5] I believe, none the less, that the true complexity of Hazlitt's thought is to be found in its quite astonishing consistency, in the way in which a single metaphysical principle—power—brings politics, philosophy, and poetics into a unity that rises above the local ambiguities and apparent contradictions in his writings. Or to borrow his own way of putting it, 'I have been accused of inconsistency, for writing an essay, for instance, on the Advantages of Pedantry, and another, on the *Ignorance of the Learned*, as if ignorance had not its comforts as well as knowledge' ('On the Causes of Popular Opinion', *Uncollected Essays*; xvii. 313).

The ability to occupy, without contradiction, two contradictory positions, is the hallmark, not of a fractured, but of a comprehensive intellect; such an ability is Hazlitt's peculiar gift, and must be accountable, in some measure, for the second distinguishing feature of his idealist philosophy. Hazlitt's idealism is rendered unique by the form in which it is manifested, the product of a mind that is *without contradiction* radical and conservative all at once. Coleridge's engagement with German idealism is notorious, but Hazlitt is a proponent of what we must call British idealism. Where Coleridge is absorbing and propagating the ideas of Kant and his followers, Hazlitt's idealism is evolving, not from the Germans, but from the empiricist tradition dominant in Britain. His reading is of his own compatriots, among them, Hobbes, Locke, Hartley, Burke, and Hume. His metaphysics is the product of a polemical engagement, a process of refuting and undermining

---

[5] See for example J. Whale, 'Hazlitt on Burke: The Ambivalent Position of a Radical Essayist', *SIR* xxv, no. 4 (winter 1986), 465–81, which assumes that the global or unified view of Hazlitt is reductive. To Whale, 'Given the urgency and contingency of Hazlitt's journalistic productions, resolving contradictions in order to construct a coherent system of thought would seem dubious, not least because it destroys a sense of dynamic exploration' (ibid. 465).

the philosophies that he perceives as at once the most influential and the most invidious: the philosophies closest to home.

Hazlitt's close involvement with the empiricist tradition in Britain makes his philosophical theory a particularly rich hybrid, never breaking entirely away from the tradition that it seeks to refute, but achieving rather a symbiosis of the experiential and the ideal, the particular and the abstract. His dealing with the figures, great and small, of British empiricism is marked by a profound understanding and respect as much as by antagonism. At his most effective, indeed, what Hazlitt offers us is not just a refutation, but a transformation, a kind of colonizing of empiricist ideas and terminology by his own idealistic agenda. This is nowhere more apparent than in his redefinition of experience itself. It is, he observes, 'a wrong interpretation of the word *experience*,' that confines it 'to a knowledge of things without us; whereas it in fact includes all knowledge relating to objects either within or out of the mind' ('On the Writings of Hobbes', *Lectures on English Philosophy*; ii. 124). In his attention to that experiential province, of objects within the mind, we find Hazlitt's ideal philosophy.

The process of colonizing brings to the fore philosophers who are no longer regarded as central to the empiricist tradition, and some who have never been so regarded, but whose terms and concepts are used by Hazlitt to destabilize the tradition from which they emerge. 'Without pretending to much originality,' he writes in his *Prospectus of a History of English Philosophy*, 'I believe it possible to deduce from preceding writers all the materials of a sound philosophy' (ii. 119). The prominence that this book gives to philosophers who will be perceived by many today as minor, and who will be almost unknown to many more, is due to the extent to which Hazlitt draws on them for the materials of his 'sound philosophy'. David Hartley's principle of the association of ideas (1749), at one time one of the most influential doctrines of the eighteenth century and the foundation of Hartley's mechanistic model of the mind, becomes, for Hazlitt, the evidence of the mind's active, anti-mechanical tendency. From the empiricist and grammarian John Horne Tooke (1736–1812), he borrows the linguistic thesis that severs signifier from signified, and, handling with a considerable degree of sophistication terms and issues that are still focal to modern linguistic theories, turns that thesis, again, into an argument for the mind's formative power. Edmund Burke's *A Philosophical Enquiry into the Origins of our Ideas of the Sublime and Beautiful* (1759), which defines the sublime as a 'mode of terror' and grants pain a greater efficacy than pleasure in determining the intensity of human responses, is absorbed into Hazlitt's refutation of the pleasure principle of the Utilitarians, while Abraham Tucker (1705–74), a self-professed Lockian, is presented as an 'arrant truant' from Locke's school ('Preface to an Abridgement of Abraham Tucker's Light of Nature Pursued'; i. 130). Hazlitt calls attention to Tucker's theory of the unity of consciousness, and in so doing admits more fully than anywhere else his own sympathy with Kantian thought.

The language that Hazlitt uses is often recognizably the language of the British empiricists; his concepts are startlingly close to those of their German adversaries. In discussing his idealism, it becomes almost impossible not to draw the comparison with Schiller, say, or Schlegel, and finally, Kant himself. But unlike the British philosophers with whom Hazlitt is closely and actively engaged, his reading of the Germans in translation is limited and even cursory. What we have here is analogy, never perfect, but close enough to confirm a strong intellectual affinity that has so far been largely ignored.

In the essay 'On Tooke's "Diversions of Purley"', Hazlitt alludes to Kant in support of his key premiss that nature, or the external world, is rendered legible only by means of the innate mental impulse towards whole-making, ultimately an impulse of self-affirmation that is independent of empirical process: '*The mind alone is formative*, to borrow the expression of a celebrated German writer, or it is that alone . . . that constructs the idea of the whole' (*Lectures on English Philosophy*; ii. 280). The allusion is glib enough, but it indicates Hazlitt's awareness that Kant's supposition, 'that objects must conform to our knowledge,'[6] corroborates his own case for an empowered self, a self that participates actively in the construction of that which it perceives,

---

[6] Immanuel Kant, *Immanuel Kant's Critique of Pure Reason*, trans. Norman Kemp Smith (London: Macmillan, 1929), 22. Cited by Hazlitt from Willich's translation: 'The objects of experience are regulated according to these ideas; and not, *vice versâ*, our ideas according to the objects' ('Madame de Staël's Account of German Philosophy and Literature', *Morning Chronicle*, 17 February 1814; xx. 19).

rather than one whose perceptions are passively dependent on the impressions of sense impinging upon it.

By attending to the idealistic aspect of Hazlitt's thought, we recover an epistemology in which, like Kant's, although knowledge may begin with experience, it does not arise out of experience. Yet Hazlitt does not marginalize, but reinterprets experience ('all knowledge relating to objects either within or out of the mind') in order to achieve what I have called his symbiosis of the experiential and the ideal. His emphasis on experience, however redefined, is the evidence of his abiding commitment to his philosophical origins and prevents us from treating as absolute any analogy with the German idealists. If I appear sometimes to have leaned too far towards the ideal half of the symbiotic relation, I have done so in response to the tyranny of a certain assumption that has coloured almost every approach to the philosophical Hazlitt to date, and that first occurs in Elisabeth Schneider's *The Aesthetics of William Hazlitt* (1933). Schneider makes the categorical distinction between Coleridge as an 'idealist' and Hazlitt as a 'realist', which has permeated most subsequent accounts of Hazlitt.[7] While her recognition of Hazlitt's independence from Coleridge as critic and theorist marks an important new departure in Hazlitt scholarship, that categorical distinction has obscured the idealistic elements in Hazlitt's thought. Over the years, Hazlitt's 'realism' has formed the backdrop to the extensive and detailed attention given to the particular and the concrete in his writing, most cogently, in Roy Park's account of Hazlitt as a critic of abstraction, and prior to Park, by Schneider, O'Hara, and Bullitt.[8] Such attention has been at the expense of the larger theoretical framework of his writing. The emphasis on the concrete has led to our overlooking Hazlitt's commitment to an ideal, a 'truth' that is contained in the symbiosis of particular and abstract. Hazlitt rejects alike the merely particular and the merely abstract. His ideal is an 'aggregate' of particulars, and abstraction is the process of aggregation, the bringing together of particulars

---

[7] E. W. Schneider, *The Aesthetics of William Hazlitt: A Study of the Philosophical Basis of his Criticism* (Philadelphia: University of Pennsylvania Press, 1933), 94, 168.
[8] Roy Park, *Hazlitt and the Spirit of the Age: Abstraction and Critical Theory* (Oxford: Clarendon Press, 1971); J. D. O'Hara, 'Hazlitt and the Functions of the Imagination', *PMLA* lxxxi, no. 1 (1966), 73–85; J. M. Bullitt, 'Hazlitt and the Romantic Conception of the Imagination', *PQ* xxiv, no. 4 (October 1945), 343–61.

into a unified whole. Poetry for him is just such an ideal, a form of abstraction, embodying the symbiosis.

The reluctance to attribute an idealism to Hazlitt appears in great measure to arise from the difficulty of reconciling philosophical idealism in any form whatsoever with the portrait of a truculent and down-to-earth Hazlitt to which recent scholars have become so attached. Thus Harold Bloom, in his introduction to the volume on Hazlitt in the *Modern Critical Views* series, finds that 'Hazlitt, like Johnson, refuses to carry philosophical aesthetics into the pragmatic realms of criticism.'[9] Similarly, David Bromwich, whom Bloom cites as 'Hazlitt's best critic',[10] contends that 'his early appeal to the Kantian motto, "the mind alone is formative" . . . intended only a summary recognition of some organizing faculty for associations, in every kind of human activity'.[11] I argue, on the contrary, that that recognition, far from being 'summary', is at the heart of Hazlitt's thinking about the imagination.[12]

When we understand Hazlitt as participating in the idealistic enterprise of the Romantic period, his common ground with Coleridge becomes immediately apparent, to an extent that will perhaps be something of a surprise to many readers. But if Hazlitt's is an idealizing philosophy, it is also a secular philosophy, and it is the secularizing tendency that divides him from Coleridge. I have sidestepped both that critical viewpoint which, insofar as it acknowledges that he is at all theoretical, treats Hazlitt's theory simply as derivative of Coleridge's, and that other viewpoint which, defending his intellectual autonomy, cuts him off altogether from what are perceived as typically Coleridgean concerns and so obscures the philosophical idealism, closely similar to Coleridge's, at the heart of his critical theory. Hazlitt is neither merely derivative of nor merely isolated from Coleridge, but is grappling (in my view, more successfully than Coleridge) with just those issues that place Coleridge at the heart of our

---

[9] Bloom, *William Hazlitt*, 9.   [10] Ibid. 1.
[11] David Bromwich, *Hazlitt: The Mind of a Critic* (New York and Oxford: Oxford University Press, 1983), 239.
[12] Robert Ready also notes the centrality to Hazlitt's thought of the 'relational, formative power of the understanding', and finds that the main tenet of his lectures on philosophy is 'the action of a formative mind perceiving relations'—Robert Ready, *Hazlitt at Table* (London and Toronto: Associated University Presses, 1981), 16. Ready's discussion of the effect of this tenet is confined to the *Table-Talk* volume.

reconstructions of Romantic philosophy. The recognition of his achievement and autonomy as a thinker can leave us in no doubt about why we must treat him as no less central to our understanding of the Romantic period, to any attempt to define, analyse, or even historicize, what Romanticism means.

If Hazlitt's relation with Coleridge must be rewritten, then so too must his relation with another great Romantic figure, by whom he has been overshadowed in a different way. If he has been misunderstood as a follower of Coleridge, he has been misunderstood also as a precursor of Keats. In the light of Keats's canonical standing, Keats's Hazlitt, the Shakespeare critic to whom we trace some of Keats's most memorable pronouncements on poetry and poethood in the letters, has remained paramount and is inevitably considered representative. The protean nature embodied in Keats's phrase 'camelion Poet'[13] has been taken to stand also for Hazlitt's ideal of poethood, in which personality is consistently minimized. We can cite Bromwich's analysis, 'the poet not confined to his own personality has the . . . advantage over the poet thus confined', or John Mahoney's study of Hazlitt, 'Poetry—and literature in general . . . seeks to minimize personality'.[14]

The protean construct that emerges from Hazlitt's Shakespeare criticism is less than compatible, however, not only with his own very distinctive and non-protean authorship, but also with the egotism that he repeatedly describes as the condition of poetry and of art in general. David Bromwich, who fully acknowledges this lack of compatibility, describes it in terms of paradox and apology: 'Hazlitt's metaphors have led him where he might have preferred not to go,' 'Hazlitt was a critic of egotism in theory but an adept of it in practice,' the closeness of 'solitary power' and 'self-reliant egotism' shows 'the one movement of Hazlitt's mind that he failed to treat consistently in "a true metaphysical spirit."'[15] Yet the paradox is easily removed when we separate Hazlitt from Keats to decipher his theory of genius as a theory of

---

[13] To Woodhouse, 27 October 1818—John Keats, *The Letters of John Keats: 1814–1821*, ed. H. E. Rollins, 2 vols (Cambridge, Mass.: Harvard University Press, 1958), i. 387.
[14] Bromwich, *Hazlitt*, 131; John L. Mahoney, *The Logic of Passion: The Literary Criticism of William Hazlitt*, 2nd edn (New York: Fordham University Press, 1981), 104. [15] Bromwich, *Hazlitt*, 145, 187, 322.

power, that is, a theory not of self-annihilation, but of self-affirmation. So deciphered, Shakespeare becomes the glorious exception to that theory, not its rule: 'Shakespear (almost alone) seems to have been a man of genius, raised above the definition of genius' ('On Genius and Common Sense', *Table-Talk*; viii. 42). Poetic egotism, absent in Shakespeare, but present in all other genius, is the manifestation of an innate power that is the governing notion of Hazlitt's metaphysics and literary criticism alike. The creations of genius, equally as the exercise of 'disinterestedness' in the *Essay on the Principles of Human Action*, are enabled by a powerful self, an egotistical sublime that Hazlitt does not apologize for, but celebrates throughout his writing.

I have said that Hazlitt's theoretical principles are held with an unusual degree of consistency, but it is important to recognize that 'consistency' does not mean 'system' in his perjorative sense of the term. Our experience of reading Hazlitt is quite different from our experience of reading Coleridge, and it is partly his vociferous opposition to systems that has led to the privileging of the 'pragmatic', the 'real', and the 'particular' at the expense of the theoretical or abstract in Hazlitt's work. The range and fluidity of his writings resist systematizing, and the critique that elicits the unifying theory secreted within that range, however well intentioned, must take the risk of running counter to the spirit of its subject. The *Essay* itself communicates the power of the imagination in the sheer speed of its operation as it flashes beyond the instant into the future; that speed and its excitement are also captured in Hazlitt's famous term 'gusto' and re-enacted in the brilliance of a prose that appears to defy fixity or containment. Yet at the same time, Hazlitt invariably recognizes the distinction, now made explicit in our modern vocabulary, between the systematic and the systemic. The imagination, to him, is naturally systemic: 'The imagination is an *associating* principle; and has an instinctive perception when a thing belongs to a system' ('On Reason and Imagination', *The Plain Speaker*; xii. 51). His model, of imaginative synthesis by the systemic association of an array of particulars, may serve as our model in bringing together the different aspects of Hazlitt's thought.

By understanding the metaphysician, we gain our most illuminating insights into the mind of the critic. But what Hazlitt offers us—a passionate and stable commitment to a certain vision of the human, and especially the imaginative, mind—cannot be confined within the metaphysical forum; it gains its force and intensity, indeed, achieves its success, from its refusal so to be confined. The truth of his vision is demonstrated rather than defined in his work. As he says of Abraham Tucker, so we may say of Hazlitt, that 'he convinces the reader oftener by shewing him the thing in dispute, than by defining its abstract qualities; as the philosopher is said to have proved the existence of motion by getting up and walking' ('Preface to An Abridgement of Abraham Tucker's Light of Nature Pursued'; i. 124).

I

The Shapes of Power
Hazlitt's Metaphysics of Discourse

In his *Letter to William Gifford*, Hazlitt attributes the fidelity to truth in his literary criticism to his early discovery of metaphysical truth, offering, in explication of that truth, a lengthy summary of the *Essay on the Principles of Human Action* (ix. 51–8). We are invited, then, to look to the *Essay* for the origins of Hazlitt's critical position, and of the understanding of poetic language which informs that position. It will be found that the entire metaphysical basis of the *Essay on the Principles of Human Action* may be summarized as the subordination of the senses to the mind. Every later development of Hazlitt's thought is rooted in that subordination. In the independence of the mind from sensory manipulation, or equivalently, from manipulation by the objects of an external material reality, we may identify his concept of 'power'.

The affirmation of innate power is the subtext of Hazlitt's theory of discourse in general, and of poetic discourse in particular. Ordinary language, in his view, is an index to the mind of the speaking subject, rather than the expression of an external objective reality. In poetry, however, the mind's power is so magnified as to elide that distinction; thus, inspired language inheres with reality. The common ground of poetic and linguistic philosophy is Hazlitt's understanding of the structure of language, in which he finds evidence of the formative power of the mind.

Hazlitt and Horne Tooke: A Philosophy of Grammar

In 1809 Hazlitt's *New and Improved Grammar of the English Tongue* was published.[1] The project of the book, as proclaimed

---
[1] The title-page bears the date 1810, although the work actually appeared in late 1809 (see Howe's bibliographical note, ii. 2).

in its opening paragraph, would seem to bear out the mundane appearance of its title; the work is announced simply as a practical and updated grammar, necessitated by the shortcomings of its predecessors: 'there has hitherto been no such thing as a real English Grammar. Those which we have are little else than translations of the Latin Grammar into English' (ii. 5). For the most part indeed, the bulk of Hazlitt's *Grammar* is little more than a scientific and routinely descriptive listing of nine parts of speech and their functions, together with an equally matter-of-fact analysis—contained in twenty-one 'rules'—of syntax, constituting, in a standard format familiar from any number of grammars available to us today, an account of English linguistic structure considered *per se* and not primarily in relation to other languages. The intention of following convention—what 'is expected in a grammar'—in the plan of the work is explicitly declared by Hazlitt in his introduction (ii. 12).

The character of this kind of text is necessarily impersonal, entailing as it does a degree of objectivity that leaves little room for a subjective authorial voice. Nevertheless, seizing upon loopholes—'to explain the principles of the English language, *such as it really is*;' 'to instruct others in *the nature and origin of language*' (ii. 5, 6; my italics)—such a voice does in fact appear in Hazlitt's book. In the Preface, in the introductory sections of chapters, and in occasionally inserted remarks in the body of its text, there emerges a purposive theory of language that enunciates a definite metaphysical position, placing the work itself in the genre and traditions of a 'philosophical grammar'.

Perhaps no stronger evidence is required of the philosophical standing of Hazlitt's *Grammar* than the authorship of a companion text, appended to it in the first edition. William Godwin's *New Guide to the English Tongue* is published in the same volume in the form of an addition to Hazlitt's *Grammar*; the association brings Hazlitt together with one of the foremost philosophers of his time. In the *New Guide*, Godwin emphatically asserts the philosophical purpose of the study of grammar. The English language, he writes, offers 'as salutary a lesson of philosophy and system, as any that is to be learned from the disquisitions of Priscian and Lily.'[2]

---

[2] William Godwin, *A New Guide to the English Tongue. In a Letter to Mr. W. F. Mylius, Author of the School Dictionary. By Edward Baldwin, Esq.*, in *A New and*

Both the *New Guide* and Hazlitt's *Grammar* secrete a philosophical project; at the same time, and despite their joint appearance, the theoretical interests of the two grammarians are not concurrent. For Godwin, the philosophy of language tends to the strictly rational end of a systematic clarity of thought and expression.[3] His philosophical concern is with the purpose and efficacy of language; Hazlitt's with its epistemological bearing. *A New and Improved Grammar of the English Tongue* explores the epistemological insights afforded by the rules of language. That exploration is charged with the presence of a strong precursor figure and dialogic 'other', chief influence, but also chief adversary: not Godwin, but John Horne Tooke, author of the *Diversions of Purley* (1798).

In the *Diversions of Purley*, Tooke articulates a theory of knowledge which has a direct relevance to Hazlitt, starting from the very statement of his grounds: 'Grammar ... as absolutely necessary in the search after philosophical truth,' or at least, 'philosophical Grammar (to which only my suspected compliment was intended) to be a most necessary step towards wisdom and true knowledge.'[4] By making the connection between grammar and epistemology, Tooke provides Hazlitt with the platform on which his own version of that connection is evolved. The *Diversions* reappraises the history of grammatical ideas so as to ratify a particular philosophy of mind.

Tooke summarizes the work of traditional grammarians as proceeding from thing to word, or signified to sign. Since words are the signs of things, grammarians assume that the different sorts of words must correspond exactly to the different sorts of things in reality. Four sorts or categories of things are identified and, correspondingly, four sorts or categories of words are defined; these are the four parts of speech. Having arrived at this classification, however, grammarians are forced to confront words which do not match any of the four defined categories of

---

Improved Grammar of the English Tongue: For the Use of Schools. By William Hazlitt. To which is Added, A New Guide to the English Tongue, In a Letter to Mr. W. F. Mylius, Author of the School Dictionary. By Edward Baldwin, Esq. (London: M. J. Godwin, 1810), 166.

[3] Ibid. 201–2.
[4] John Horne Tooke *EπEA πTEPOENTA or, the Diversions of Purley,* 2nd edn, 2 vols (London, 1798), i. 5, 10.

things. In order to accommodate such words, rather than questioning their first assumption (that sorts of words correspond to sorts of things), they merely reverse their route. Instead of working from signified to sign as before, they now attempt to proceed from sign to signified, multiplying categories in reality to match the multiplicity in the sorts of the words describing that reality. Tooke perceives both approaches as identically fallacious. He finds, too, that those grammarians of his own time who seek to resolve the fallacy by treating words as the signs of 'ideas', rather than 'things' only perpetuate the error. Even if we treat the relation between sign and signification as a relation between word and idea, rather than word and thing, we simply transfer the fallacy to another area of discussion, assuming a multiplicity in the operations of the mind, if not in the categories of real things.

Tooke locates the heart of the grammatical fallacy in the first assumption of an immediately correspondent or referential basis for language, which he undertakes to refute by a single linguistic principle: 'the errors of Grammarians have arisen from supposing all words to be *immediately* either the signs of things or the signs of ideas: whereas in fact many words are merely *abbreviations* employed for dispatch, and are the signs of other words.'[5] Hence, different words that have a common root may be treated as referring to the single absolute meaning signified by that root.

From the principle that multiple words have a common root, Tooke develops, through an etymological argument, his metaphysical position of 'no abstract ideas'. His 'proof' is a process of synonymizing. By collapsing the terms for abstract concepts, which he calls 'abbreviations' (e.g. *right, wrong, just, true*), into their etymological roots, which he treats as the originals for which these abbreviations substitute (respectively, *to order, to wring, to command, to believe*), he denies the concepts themselves independent existence.[6] In other words, since it is possible to reduce any abstract term to its root, by Tooke's account, that abstract term is no more than its root; it does not own an independent meaning. If every abstract term is meaningless, then its signification, the idea

---

[5] Ibid. 26–7.
[6] Ibid. ii. 7–14, 18–20, 89, 402–8, etc. Cited by Hazlitt in 'On Tooke's "Diversions of Purley"', *Lectures on English Philosophy* (ii. 272–4, 275–8).

for which that term stands, is necessarily non-existent. There are no abstract ideas.

The implications of Tooke's thesis of synonymity are powerfully highlighted when we compare it with Coleridge's famous argument for *desynonymizing* language in the fourth chapter of *Biographia Literaria*:

> in all societies there exists an instinct of growth, a certain collective, unconscious good sense working progressively to desynonymize those words originally of the same meaning, . . . The first and most important point to be proved is, that two conceptions perfectly distinct are confused under one and the same word, and (this done) to appropriate that word exclusively to one meaning, and the synonyme (should there be one) to the other. But if (as will be often the case in the arts and sciences) no synonyme exists, we must either invent or borrow a word.[7]

For Coleridge, it is language which is simple and meaning composite; he locates the route to knowledge in discarding the notion of synonymity in language. According to him, the number of words available to us is limited as compared to the complexity of thought, since multiple meanings are often comprehended under a single word. Conversely, by treating language as characterized by extensive synonymity, Tooke refers a multiplicity of words to a single meaning. Exactly opposite to Coleridge, he exposes the composite character of language in order to claim that thought is simple, 'and consequently that it was as improper to speak of a *complex idea*, as it would be to call a constellation a complex star'.[8]

By denying a complexity in the operations of the mind, Tooke is asserting that the mind can be no more than simply receptive; it is a purely passive receiver of external impressions. His conclusion, of 'no abstract ideas', is used to refute Locke's view of abstraction as a complex operation of the mind. Tooke insists on a rigorous confinement of the mind to the passive or physical model posited by Locke, a model that is belied, in his view, by Locke's own theory of abstraction. 'The business of the mind, . . . extends no farther than to receive Impressions, that is, to have Sensations or Feelings. What are called its operations, are merely the operations of the Language.'[9]

---

[7] Coleridge, *Biographia*, vol. I, ch. iv, pp. 82–4.   [8] Tooke, *Diversions*, i. 37.
[9] Ibid. 51. Cited by Hazlitt in 'On Tooke's "Diversions of Purley"' (*Lectures on English Philosophy*; ii. 278).

It is the heightened emphasis of the passivity implied in the Lockian model of the mind that brings Hazlitt into opposition with Tooke. In the lecture 'On Mr. Tooke's "Diversions of Purley"', he writes, memorably, 'I would class the merits of Mr. Tooke's work under three heads: the etymological, the grammatical, and the philosophical. The etymological part is excellent, the grammatical part indifferent, and the philosophical part to the last degree despicable; it is downright, unqualified, unredeemed nonsense' (*Lectures on English Philosophy*; ii. 270). Elsewhere, more mildly, he deplores the reduction of thought to simple sensation in an observation that is very much in the spirit of Coleridge's desynonymizing remarks:

We are too apt, both from the nature of language and the turn of modern philosophy, which reduces every thing to simple sensations, to consider whatever bears one name as one thing in itself, which prevents our ever properly understanding those *mixed modes* and various clusters of ideas, to which almost all language has a reference. ('Definition of Wit'; *Miscellaneous Writings*; xx. 359)

The denial of the composite signification of language is a denial of the complexity of ideas and of the role played by the mind in achieving that complexity. By contrast, in Hazlitt's own account of language as the manifestation of an innate formative ability in the mind, we begin to perceive the concept, central to his epistemology, of an active and empowered mind.

In the *Grammar*, Hazlitt adopts Tooke's first principle as containing an important theoretical insight, but rejects his metaphysics as embroiled, after all, in the identical confusion of which he indicts his predecessors—the confounding of words with things, whereby the structure of language is allowed to define reality, although the pattern of correspondence, by Tooke's own first principle, is demonstrably fallacious. 'Mr. Tooke's whole object is to show that the different parts of speech do not relate to the differences in ideas or things, and yet he would make the difference in the one, the test of the difference in the other' (ii. 6n.). Hazlitt's *Grammar*, by contrast, uses grammatical distinctions to dissever linguistic classifications from immediate correspondence to an absolute reality. His method is simple, and consists merely in enumerating the different linguistic forms capable of being assumed by a single word;

for instance, snow (substantive), snowy (adjective); white (adjective), whiteness (substantive):

So if we say that snow is white, snow, the name of the subject of discourse, is a substantive, and white, the name of the quality we attribute to it, is an adjective, not because snow is a substance, and white a quality, for we may speak of a snowy mountain, or say that whiteness is hurtful to the eyes, when these words will change their character, though the things themselves cannot. (ii. 7)

This proves, then, 'that the grammatical distinctions of words do not relate to the nature of the things or ideas spoken of, but to our manner of speaking of them' (ii. 6).

This is a focal point of Hazlitt's *Grammar*; it finds support, incidentally, in a philosophical argument elsewhere cited by him with considerable admiration.[10] In *An Essay towards a New Theory of Vision* (1709), George Berkeley uses human language as a model to explain the universal language of nature; this model, emerging as a subtext used merely to illustrate Berkeley's larger observations on nature and reality, becomes the core of Hazlitt's linguistic analyses. Berkeley treats the relation between visible objects (objects as perceived by the sight) and tangible objects (objects as manifested to the touch) as composing a language, which can be compared to ordinary language and the relation, between words and their signification, of which ordinary language is composed.[11] The link, according to Berkeley, between signifier and signified is one of association, and association between two ideas does not suggest a necessary, but only a habitual connection

---

[10] See, for instance the qualification in his praise of Butler's *Sermons* in a note to the *Remarks on the Systems of Hartley and Helvetius*: 'After Berkeley's Essay on Vision, I do not know of any work better worth the attention of those who would learn to think' (i. 50 n.). Again: 'the "Essay on Vision," [is] the greatest by far of all his works, and the most complete example of elaborate analytical reasoning and particular induction joined together that perhaps ever existed' ('On Locke's "Essay on the Human Understanding"', *Lectures on English Philosophy*; ii. 180); also, 'his *Essay on Vision* [is] . . . a masterpiece of analytical reasoning' ('My First Acquaintance with Poets', *Uncollected Essays*; xvii. 113).

[11] 'And the manner wherein they [objects of vision] signify and mark unto us the objects which are at a distance is the same with that of languages and signs of human appointment, which do not suggest the things signified by any likeness or identity of nature, but only by an habitual connexion that experience has made us to observe between them' (section 147).—George Berkeley, *An Essay Towards a New Theory of Vision*, in *The Works of George Berkeley, Bishop of Cloyne*, ed. T. E. Jessop and A. A. Luce, 9 vols (London: Nelson, 1948–57), i. 231.

between those ideas.[12] Words, then, are not *like* things, and 'a word pronounced with certain circumstances, or in a certain context with other words, hath not always the same import and signification that it hath when pronounced in some other circumstances or different context of words.'[13]

It is exactly this point, apparently merely commonsensical, that Hazlitt makes regarding grammatical distinctions, reiterating it with a wealth of illustration in every possible context in the second and main part of his *Grammar* ('Of the Parts of Speech'), in order to assert a larger philosophical position: that language pertains, not to an objective material reality, but to the mind's perception of the relation between things. Consequently, words cannot be treated as 'abbreviations' that ultimately refer to a single and absolute meaning, and therefore to a simple sensation received by the mind. The seemingly innocuous project of listing and describing the different parts of speech potentially undermines, in fact, Tooke's theory of abstract ideas, by attacking the doctrine of synonymity on which it is founded.

At the same time, the *Grammar* constructs a model of common discourse, of which the identifying characteristics are twofold, first, that language implies a selfhood; second, corollary to this first and developed from it, that linguistic structure is a question of choice, and therefore arbitrary.

Although by definition, 'Words, considered nakedly in themselves, are the names or signs of certain things; words, as parts of speech, *i.e.* as component parts of a sentence, are the names or signs of certain things, accompanied with an intimation in what manner they are joined together in the mind of the speaker, and made the subjects of discourse' (ii. 20). In other words, every intelligible use of language refers to a self. Grammar, which describes the use of words, is not a key to their meaning (substance or reality), but only to the possible points of view of the speaking or writing subject. Grammatical categories express some one or the other of these points of view. Hazlitt fastens on Tooke's more casual use of the word 'consider' in his definition of the noun to foreground the instrumentality of the speaking subject in shaping linguistic structure. In Tooke's account, 'A consideration

---

[12] Section 25, Berkeley, *An Essay Towards a New Theory of Vision*, 176
[13] Section 73 (ibid. 198).

of *Ideas*, or of the *Mind*, or of *Things* . . . will lead us no farther than to *Nouns:* i.e. the signs of those impressions, or names of ideas.'[14] Hazlitt draws upon this definition in his own account of the parts of speech, deliberately emphasizing the verb 'consider' so as to accentuate the role played by the mind in the construction of meaning. Thus, a substantive 'is not the name of a thing really subsisting by itself (according to the old definition), but of a thing *considered* as subsisting by itself' (ii. 7), and 'Any idea or thing, considered as a circumstance belonging to or connected with another, may be an adjective' (ii. 8).

The importance of 'considered' is that it denies 'necessary connection' between signs and their signification; 'considered' refers to the possibility of choice given to the user of language, which he exercises in the formulation of his text. Hence, for example, 'the notion of agency or passiveness has no necessary connection with the active and passive forms of verbs' (ii. 9–10), and more generally, 'There is no essential or necessary difference in the ideas expressed by adverbs, prepositions, or conjunctions, and by the other parts of speech' (ii. 22). This idea, of linguistic *choice*, will later be evoked by Hazlitt to emphasize the contrast between ordinary language, composed of 'voluntary signs', and the involuntary language of poetry ('On Poetry in General', *Lectures on the English Poets*; v. 12).

Finally, by referring grammatical structure to the point of view of the speaking subject, Hazlitt posits that the construction of language not only merely indicates ideas in the mind, but also reflects the manner in which these ideas are assembled into a whole in order to produce any given expression. The observation, that the structure of language represents the organization of discrete linguistic units into a single sense or meaning, is the rationale of his section on syntax:

> The words so combined are said to make a *complete sense*, because the end of speech is then answered.—Any number of words thrown together by accident, convey a distinct sense or meaning in themselves, or separately excite certain ideas in the mind, but they do not inform us of the intention and views of the speaker in using them . . . (ii. 73)

Syntactical structure, from the above, is a holistic expression of the mind; thus, it is also the index of its formative ability. 'It is

---

[14] Tooke, *Diversions*, i. 51.

chiefly by the regular combination of words that we become intelligible to one another; or can mark not only the ideas which are passing in our minds, but the manner in which we connect them together, or are affected by them' (ii. 20). Taken in conjunction with the previous passage, we have here, in a deceptively casual guise, a point of far-reaching philosophical significance, that language has not only a utilitarian connective function—the communication between individuals—but also a philosophical and reflexive one. As the index of an innate formative ability of a mind, it becomes the instrument to the analysis, hence knowledge, of a self.[15]

The model of common discourse constructed in Hazlitt's *Grammar* can be taken to provide a frame for his theory of imaginative or inspired language. It will be found that he recognizes in such language the primary general attribute of common discourse, that it is the manifestation of a selfhood invested with an original capacity to generate wholes. In poetry, however, the power of the speaking subject is so magnified that it bridges the gulf between word and thing, and so wipes out the arbitrariness of connection between signifier and signified. In other words, Hazlitt claims for poetic discourse exactly what he denies for common speech: that the manner in which the poet speaks of a thing is so much more expressive of the nature of that thing itself, that inspired language approximates to reality.

The Real Language of Poetry

In order to reconstruct Hazlitt's approximation of word to thing in poetry, I will begin with his great poetic 'Defence' in the introduction to the *Lectures on the English Poets*. The lecture 'On Poetry in General' is the obvious starting-point for an analysis of Hazlitt's poetics. Its object is definition, the determination, as Hazlitt puts it in *A Letter to William Gifford*, of 'what *poetry* is'

---

[15] Hazlitt appears very close to Coleridge here; his observation on syntax is almost replicated, for instance, in the letter of 22 October 1826 from Coleridge to the younger James Gillman: 'the legitimate Order 38; Connection of words [correspond] to the *Laws* of Thinking and to the acts and affections of the Thinker's mind.'—S. T. Coleridge, *Collected Letters of Samuel Taylor Coleridge*, ed. E. L. Griggs, 6 vols (Oxford: Clarendon Press, 1956–71), vi. 630.

(ix. 44). The word poetry, he declares, 'has these three *distinct* meanings in the English language, that is, it signifies the composition produced, the state of mind or faculty producing it, and, in certain cases, the subject-matter proper to call forth that state of mind. . . . I have endeavoured to define that common something which belongs to these several views of it' (*A Letter to William Gifford*; ix. 44–5). The lecture undertakes so to define poetry, broadening the applicability of the term, as to vindicate the activity of the poet; by so doing, it falls into a genre of poetic 'Defence' to which, following the pattern set by Aristotle's *Poetics*, Sidney's *A Defence of Poetry*, and closer to Hazlitt's own time, Shelley's *Defence of Poetry* belong. By generic necessity, then, the lecture is probably the most cogent and forceful statement of Hazlitt's poetics, conveniently drawing together the various assumptions about poetry and poetic composition that recur throughout his work.

'On Poetry in General' contains a surprisingly technical account of poetic composition as a physical process, 'surprising' in view of the antithetical relation of poetry to science that is often assumed elsewhere in Hazlitt's writings, not least in the latter part of this essay itself (v. 9). Nonetheless, the definition with which it begins, and which may be said, therefore, to mark the point of departure for the entire series of *Lectures on the English Poets*, presents a theory of stimulation and response that appears to be modelled upon Locke's quasi-scientific hypothesis—itself akin to the 'corpuscular' theories of Newton—of impulses received upon the senses by particles travelling from external objects; there is something here too, of Hume's 'first principle' of human nature, that an *idea* (object of thought) always presupposes an *impression*:[16] 'The best general notion which I can give of poetry is, that it is the natural impression of any object or event, by its vividness exciting an involuntary movement of imagination and passion, and producing, by sympathy, a certain modulation of the voice, or sounds, expressing it' (v. 1).

The postulate of musical sounds produced by sympathetic vibration contains the characteristically empirical notion of a

---

[16] John Locke, *An Essay Concerning Human Understanding*, ed. P. H. Nidditch (Oxford: Clarendon Press, 1975), Bk II, ch. viii, sections 11–12, pp. 135–6; David Hume, *A Treatise of Human Nature*, ed. L.A. Selby-Bigge, 2nd edn revised P. H. Nidditch (Oxford: Clarendon Press, 1978), 6–7.

keyboard, with the 'object or event' being the hammer, the imagination, the instrument itself, and poetry, the sounds produced by the instrument. Such a description of poetry, in terms of concepts borrowed from the physics of sound, appears to offer a peculiarly material idea of the imagination, as a faculty directly responsive to the impression of an external reality ('object' or thing) that is then transferred associatively to the actual sense organ producing the physical effect of 'voice, or sounds'. Harmony—the fittedness of each sound to the other, such that together they constitute a whole—is produced involuntarily by the excitement of the imagination. The epithet 'involuntary' seems to imply an instinctive or necessary reaction and so enhances the sense of an almost physiological operation of the imagination.

The domination of the physiological element in Hazlitt's account of an intellectual process provided ample room for the derision of the *Quarterly*'s reviewers:

The impression, of which Mr. Hazlitt talks, is an impression producing by sympathy a certain modulation of sounds. The term sympathy. . . [in] a physiological sense . . . is used to denote the fact, that the disorder of one organ produces disorder in the functions of certain other parts of the system. Does Mr. Hazlitt mean, that the impression produces the modulation of sound essential to poetry, in a mode analogous to that in which diseases of the brain affect the digestive powers?[17]

The reviewers' sarcasm is heavy-handed; nonetheless, it highlights a characteristic of Hazlitt's description of creative language that recurs throughout in his writing. In the introductory essay to the *Lectures on the English Comic Writers*, the effect of wit or humour is similarly described in terms which combine intellectual stimulation with physiological effect:

The transition . . . from one impression to another that we did not at all expect, . . . this alternate excitement and relaxation of the imagination, the object also striking upon the mind more vividly in its loose unsettled state, and before it has had time to recover and collect itself, causes that alternate excitement and relaxation, or irregular convulsive movement of the muscular and nervous system, which constitutes physical laughter. The *discontinuous* in our sensations produces a

---

[17] E. S. Barnett and William Gifford, 'Hazlitt's *Lectures on the English Poets*', *Quarterly Review* xix (1818), 426. Countered by Hazlitt in *A Letter to William Gifford*; ix. 45–6.

correspondent jar and discord in the frame. The steadiness of our faith and of our features begins to give way at the same time. ('On Wit and Humour'; vi. 7)

Again, it is a sense of the physical impact of language that must at least partially influence Hazlitt's recourse to a scientific, often recognizably Newtonian terminology, in order to describe imaginative composition. We can cite, for instance, his comment on Godwin's novels—'The impression made upon the reader is the exact measure of the strength of the author's genius' ('On the English Novelists', *Lectures on the English Comic Writers*; vi. 130)—or more conclusively, the third of his closing remarks to the essay on *Lear*, 'That the greatest strength of genius is shewn in describing the strongest passions: for the power of the imagination, in works of invention, must be in proportion to the force of the natural impressions, which are the subject of them' ('Lear', *Characters of Shakespear's Plays*; iv. 271). This seems to carry an echo of Newton's second law of motion, 'The rate of change of momentum is directly proportional to the impressed force . . .'. In fact, Newton's formulation of momentum as proportionate to mass actually reappears in the lecture 'On Poetry in General', in the analysis of the style of the Old Testament: 'Things were collected more into masses, and gave a greater *momentum* to the imagination' (v. 17).

Even in the process of exposing its affinity with the corpuscular theories of contemporary science, however, Hazlitt's 'keyboard' model in the lecture 'On Poetry in General' has already begun to deviate from the prevalent empiricist epistemology in one important respect. By Locke's corpuscular hypothesis, since the real essence of things consists of 'particles' which are imperceptible, the real nature of things is unknowable. The implications for language are clear:

Sure I am, that the signification of Words, in all Languages, depending very much on the Thoughts, Notions, and *Ideas* of him that uses them, must unavoidably be of great uncertainty, to Men of the same Language and Country. . . . Nor is it to be wondred, that the Will of GOD, when cloathed in Words, should be liable to that doubt and uncertainty, which unavoidably attends that sort of Conveyance, . . .[18]

[18] Locke, *Human Understanding*, Bk III, ch. ix, sections 22–3, pp. 489–90.

By contrast, the curiously technical aspect of Hazlitt's account of the poetic process seems to emphasize the strength or substance of the language he describes in such graphically material terms. In his usage, the term 'impression' forcefully repudiates 'doubt and uncertainty' to assert the impact of inspired language (which would include the Word of God). Opposite to Locke, Hazlitt *identifies* inspiration with the language in which it is expressed, in the single term 'poetry' applied to both. As inspiration, poetry is substance itself, the immanent spirit within the dead letter of life: 'it is "the stuff of which our life is made." The rest is "mere oblivion," a dead letter' (v. 2). The non-poetic is lifeless, but in poetic language we find being itself, a life and a truth that does not rely on external or objective meaning: 'This language is not the less true to nature, because it is false in point of fact; but so much the more true and natural, if it conveys the impression which the object under the influence of passion makes on the mind' (v. 4).

Earlier, I categorized the essay 'On Poetry in General' as emerging from a tradition of poetic 'Defence' that began with Aristotle's *Poetics*. Common to all of these works is the subordination of factual narrative, history, to the imaginary narrative, poetry. Directed by the criteria of probability and necessity, and at the same time, freed from the constraints of fact, poetry surmounts the particular to offer, instead, universal truth.[19] In his observation regarding the distinction between truth and fact, Hazlitt offers his own corroboration of a standard premiss of the 'Defence' genre. Implicitly, Locke's thesis of the unknowability of things-in-themselves is circumvented here by the location of 'truth' and 'nature' in objects as they are moulded by the mind's recreation of the factual world. Poetry is both real and natural, as well as ideal, because the truth or substance of poetic language pertains to an ontological reality that is independent of the factual. Imaginative creation is authenticated by the feeling or 'passion' in which it originates, and not by the tyranny of conformity to fact.

Hazlitt's poetic theory is resonating here with the poetics of his favourite literary icon, Edmund Burke. Burke's *Philosophical*

---

[19] 'Hence poetry is something more philosophic and of graver import than history, since its statements are of the nature rather of universals, whereas those of history are singulars.'—Aristotle, *Poetics*, trans. I. Bywater in *The Complete Works of Aristotle*, ed. Jonathan Barnes, Bollingen series no. 71.2, 2 vols (Princeton, NJ: Princeton University Press, 1984), ii. 2323.

Enquiry into the Origins of our Ideas of the Sublime and Beautiful (1759) argues persuasively against the strictly mimetic view of language and poetry. The pictorial quality of words, Burke contends, is limited and cannot account for the greatest part of their effect; i.e. the power of words does not consist primarily in raising visual images of the things represented by them. The original object having long been lost to view, words do indeed suggest that object, but without raising a visual image of it. This establishes that the basis of verbal communication is the associative weight carried by the sounds of words, by their 'having from use the same effect on being mentioned, that their original has when it is seen.'[20] Consequently, Burke observes (as does Hazlitt in his *Grammar*), that 'words undoubtedly have no sort of resemblance to the ideas for which they stand;' they convey not so much a description of things, as the particular point of view of the speaking subject: 'The truth is, all verbal description, merely as naked description, though never so exact, conveys so poor and insufficient an idea of the thing described, that it could scarcely have the smallest effect, if the speaker did not call in to his aid those modes of speech that mark a strong and lively feeling in himself.'[21]

From the notion that the effect of language does not reside in its evocation of visual images, Burke concludes that words, however exact, are hopelessly inadequate as the representation of things, except as they are authenticated by feeling. The true province of language is not things as they are, but things as they are felt, and the highest expression of things as they are felt is in poetry. 'In reality poetry and rhetoric do not succeed in exact description so well as painting does; their business is to affect rather by sympathy than imitation; to display rather the effect of things on the mind of the speaker, or of others, than to present a clear idea of the things themselves.'[22] Hence poetry is not, strictly speaking, an imitative art, nor is this its limitation, but the reverse. Having sympathy rather than imitation as its basis, poetry is 'more capable of making deep and lively impressions than any other arts, and even than nature itself in very many cases.'[23]

---

[20] Edmund Burke, *A Philosophical Enquiry into the Origins of our Ideas of the Sublime and Beautiful*, 2nd edn (1759; repr. Menston: The Scolar Press, 1970), part V, section 4, p. 321. [21] Ibid., part V, sections 6, 7, p. 333, pp. 339–40.
[22] Ibid., section 5, p. 332. [23] Ibid., section 7, p. 334.

Burke's thesis, that language achieves the communication of things as they are felt, is captured in Hazlitt's term 'impression', imbued as it is with the weight of feeling. The 'natural impression of any object' describes that object, not as it is in itself, but as it is felt, 'feeling' referring to the intellectual or imaginative rather than the sensory response. Where Burke's substitution of 'impression' for 'image' transfers the mimetic relation of poetry from 'the things themselves' to 'the effect of things on the mind', Hazlitt more explicitly elevates the effect above the thing so as to validate the imagination, 'that faculty which represents objects, not as they are in themselves, but as they are moulded by other thoughts and feelings, into an infinite variety of shapes and combinations of power' (v. 4). In this light, the 'involuntary movement of imagination' that he describes as the origin of poetry is not a mere passive receptivity, but refers to the inevitable tendency of the imagination to react upon and remould the objects that are impressed upon it. By Hazlitt's own definition, this tendency characterizes the imagination as active. 'Any thing is so far active as it modifies and re-acts upon the original impulse' ('On Liberty and Necessity', *Lectures on English Philosophy*; ii. 268). The apparent passivity of the imaginative process that might otherwise be inferred from the keyboard model is hence belied.

Hazlitt's definition of poetry, then, actually converts a standard empirical model into an emblem of non-empirical process. His keyboard is revealed as akin to Shelley's lyre in *A Defence of Poetry*, also a stock empirical image vitally transformed by its investment with an innate active attribute:

Man is an instrument over which a series of external and internal impressions are driven like the alternations of an ever-changing wind over an Aeolian lyre which move it by their motion to ever-changing melody. But there is a principle within the human being, and perhaps within all sentient beings, which acts otherwise than in a lyre and produces not melody alone but harmony, by an internal adjustment of the sounds and motions thus excited to the impressions which excite them.[24]

By virtue of the instrumentality of the imagination in producing truth or substance from the external world, the stimulation and

---

[24] P. B. Shelley, *Shelley's Prose, or, the Trumpet of a Prophecy*, ed. David Lee Clark, 2nd corr. edn (1966; repr. London: Fourth Estate, 1988), 277.

response definition or keyboard model of the lecture 'On Poetry in General' does not represent for Hazlitt what he himself prosecutes in Locke, 'the considering the mind as a physical thing,' i.e. a thing purely determined by external material impulses ('On Tooke's "Diversions of Purley"', *Lectures on English Philosophy*; ii. 279). The non-physical operation of the mind occupies the lacuna between the physical receptivity to sensation, and its product in the form of perception or expression. In this space, the mind displays its constructive ability, 'that alone which by its pervading and elastic energy unfolds and expands our ideas, that gives order and consistency to them, that assigns to every part its proper place, and that constructs the idea of the whole' ('On Tooke's "Diversions of Purley"'; ii. 280). Meaning originates in an intellectual process that surpasses sensory response. Poetry, in particular, 'does not define the limits of sense, or analyze the distinctions of the understanding, but signifies the excess of the imagination beyond the actual or ordinary impression of any object or feeling' ('On Poetry in General'; v. 3). The prime mover in the process of poetry is not the object but the imagination, and it is Hazlitt's confidence that the forms of the imagination are substantial that results in his description of imaginative process in material terms. In the 'excess of the imagination beyond the actual or ordinary impression of any object or feeling' is embodied in its highest degree the power of human perception; that concept of 'power' is at the very core of Hazlitt's celebration of all intellectual activity as the vindication of an innate self-directing principle with which the mind is endowed.

The Power Principle

In order to understand the concept of 'power' that emerges directly from Hazlitt's view of the mind's formative ability, it becomes necessary to turn to his metaphysics. 'Power' is the identifying attribute of the mind and is *innate*; its characteristic is *activity*. Throughout his work, Hazlitt makes free and recurrent use of the term in varying contexts, but always with this twofold sense, of innateness and activity, constant in, and inseparable from, his usage. It will be found, in fact, that the two qualities have an implication far beyond mere verbal convention. 'That the idea of power is inseparable from activity,' is listed by Hazlitt as one of his fundamental metaphysical principles in the *Prospectus of a History of English Philosophy*; also, that this idea derives from the innate exertion of the powerful faculty, and not, as in Locke, from the observation of external objects: 'We do not get this idea from the outward changes which take place in matter, but from the exertion of it in ourselves' (ii. 119).[25]

'Power' comprehended in Hazlitt's twofold sense of the term is at the heart of his metaphysics. The *Essay on the Principles of Human Action* is governed by the notion of a mind innately active; thus, by Hazlitt's usage, an empowered mind. The argument of the *Essay* runs as follows: to account for action at all, we must presume an object of volition. Any object of volition is always an object that we have not yet attained; it has future being only, and is therefore wholly imaginary. Because it is wholly imaginary, it cannot be directly or immediately apprehended by the senses. Ergo, sensory response cannot account for action at all. On the contrary, since the object of volition is always imaginary, all action is the product of imaginative exercise. The *Essay* establishes that the impulse to action is produced from within the mind, rather than stimulated from without, or that there exists an innate tendency to action within the mind that is independent of its

---

[25] Bromwich writes that although Hume 'could discard the idea of power ... Hazlitt did find the idea of power in Locke. It is only by making power "an original idea derived from within, like the sense of pleasure and pain, and quite distinct from the visible composition and decomposition of other objects," that Hazlitt believes "we can avoid being driven into an absolute scepticism with regard to cause and effect." And this Locke had done' (Bromwich, *Hazlitt*, 30). On the contrary, Hazlitt's account of the origin of power is antithetical to Locke's, since it is Locke who derives the idea of power from the observation of external objects rather than from our innate intellectual operations. It is true that in his essay on Locke in the *Lectures on English Philosophy*, Hazlitt writes that Locke, despite himself, 'seems to have been upon the point of discovering' that the mind's perception of relation, i.e. its innate active or formative tendency, 'is at the bottom of all our ideas whatever' ('On Locke's "Essay on the Human Understanding"'; ii. 155). But Locke did not make this explicit: 'It is thus that the inquiring mind seems to be always hovering on the brink of truth, but that timidity or indolence, or prejudice, which is both combined, makes us shrink back, unwilling to trust ourselves to the fathomless abyss' (ii. 155). Both here and in the essay 'On Liberty and Necessity' cited by Bromwich, Hazlitt remains clearly critical of the actual account that Locke gives of the origin of our idea of power: 'It were to be wished that he had given it as simple a source as possible, *viz.* the feeling we have of it in our own minds, which he sometimes seems half inclined to do, instead of referring it to our observation of the successive changes which take place in matter' (*Lectures on English Philosophy*; ii. 260).

receptivity to sense impressions. By freeing the mind from a dependence on the senses, Hazlitt releases its potential to constitute its own objects; this is 'power'.

The innate tendency to activity in the mind, as posited in the *Essay on the Principles of Human Action*, is elsewhere described by Hazlitt as 'the love of power', and characterized as an independent 'principle' of the mind. 'The love of power or action is another independent principle of the human mind, . . . Our passions in general are to be traced more immediately to the active part of our nature, to the love of power' ('Mind and Motive', *The Examiner*, 9 April 1815; xx. 47–9). The same 'principle' is alluded to in the essay 'On the Love of Life': 'Our notions with respect to the importance of life, and our attachment to it, depend on a principle, which has very little to do with its happiness or its misery' (*The Round Table*; iv. 1) and again in the lecture 'On Poetry in General': 'The sense of power is as strong a principle in the mind as the love of pleasure' (*Lectures on the English Poets*; v. 7).

In the last of these statements, Hazlitt traces the 'sense of power' to 'the common love of strong excitement' (v. 7), citing an illustration from Burke's *Philosophical Enquiry into the Origins of our Ideas of the Sublime and Beautiful* in support of his point. In the observation that follows, 'Objects of terror and pity exercise the same despotic control over it [the mind] as those of love or beauty' (v. 7), it is still Burke's two categories of sublime ('terror and pity') and beautiful ('love or beauty') that are uppermost in his thought. I have remarked already the relevance of Burke to Hazlitt's term 'impression' in describing the transformative process of the imagination in the lecture 'On Poetry in General'. The assertion in the same lecture of a new principle that diminishes the pleasure principle of human behaviour now begins to suggest a further connection with Burke.

Burke's formulation of the 'mode of terror' in his definition of the sublime contains a modification of the pleasure principle which complexifies the nature of our responses to that principle. In his theory, the passions concerning self-preservation are the most powerful of all passions, and revolve around the ideas of pain and danger.[26] Whatever excites such ideas is a source of the sublime; the sublime is a mode of terror, 'that is, it is productive of

---

[26] Burke, *Philosophical Enquiry*, part I, section 6, pp. 57–8.

the strongest emotion which the mind is capable of feeling.'[27] The power of the sublime, originating in its association with pain and danger, categorizes it as an idea belonging to self-preservation.[28] By taking the view that the passions belonging to self-preservation are the strongest of which we are capable, Burke reinforces the assumption of self-love that underlies the pleasure principle. At the same time, his affirmation that pain, not only actual pain, but even its mere idea, excites our sense of selfhood more strongly than any that stems from 'positive pleasure', must qualify the notion that the tendency of the self is the mere or mechanical pursuit of pleasure alone.[29] For Burke, 'pleasure' as it pertains to varying degrees of sensory gratification marks the passive attribute of the mind; the passions of self-preservation pertain to something other than such gratification. Terror and hence the sublime rather rouse the mind to activity. 'As common labour, which is a mode of pain, is the exercise of the grosser, a mode of terror is the exercise of the finer parts of the system.'[30] It is in this context, with reference to our being formed to an 'active purpose', that he offers the illustration cited by Hazlitt in support of the power principle: the sense of delight that arises when we are confronted with spectacle of any kind, even if it is a spectacle of distress.[31]

Burke's philosophical position is ultimately empiricist. In the introductory essay of the *Philosophical Enquiry*, entitled 'On Taste', he describes the imagination or 'creative power' as absolutely dependent on the senses.[32] The fourth part of the *Philosophical Enquiry* is devoted to an empirical explication of the corporal or sensory reactions that are both productive of and produced by the sublime. Nonetheless, his awareness of the active character of the passions, his emphasis on the superior strength of activity to gratification and, in the section on 'Words', his exaltation of things as they are felt by the mind over things as they are seen by the eye, seem, by lifting the intellectual above the sensory perception, to undermine his own mechanistic assumptions.

It is this aspect of Burke which Hazlitt retains in his own adoption of a 'power principle' as the counterpart of Burke's 'mode of terror'. The principle of power is Hazlitt's answer to

---

[27] Burke, *Philosophical Enquiry*, section 7, pp. 58–9.
[28] Ibid., part II, section 22, p. 160. [29] Ibid., part I, section 3, pp. 48–9.
[30] Ibid., part IV, section 7, p. 256. [31] Ibid., part I, section 14, p. 74.
[32] Ibid. 15–16.

the Utilitarian 'pleasure principle' that governs the mechanical systems based on self-love; it becomes the polemical tool by which he replaces the mind or imagination for the senses as the seat of action. 'In short, the question, whether life is accompanied with a greater quantity of pleasure or pain, may be fairly set aside as frivolous, and of no practical utility' ('On the Love of Life', *The Round Table*; iv. 3). Hazlitt's targets are Locke and Hartley, as well as Bentham, whose 'matter-of-fact' philosophies (i. 70 n.) carry an emphasis upon immediate sensory reaction that seems to assume a fundamental passivity in the human condition. His power principle, on the other hand, which is manifested in mental activity, restores emphasis to the will and the objects of volition; it raises man above the machine, by asserting his agency.

The Palace of Thought: Hazlitt and Berkeley

Hazlitt's doctrine of intellectual empowerment, which foregrounds the perceptual process in the construction of reality, calls also for the comparison with Berkeley. Hazlitt's admiration for Berkeley is expressed in a number of contexts, and acts as a pointer to the strong presence of the Berkeleian philosophy in the development of his critical theory.[33] In *The Principles of Human Knowledge*, Berkeley undertakes to refute Locke's thesis that the substance of the material world is unknowable, by a counter-argument that it is the mind's perception of external objects which gives these objects being. He argues that 'things', which are the objects of the sense, ought therefore to be renamed 'ideas'. 'If it be demanded why I make use of the word *idea*, and do not rather in compliance with custom, call them things, I answer, . . . because the term *thing*, in contradistinction to *idea*, is generally supposed to denote somewhat existing without the mind'.[34] The contention that 'things'—material objects—are 'ideas'—conceptions of the mind—is the logical inference to be drawn from Berkeley's basic premiss that

---

[33] Such admiration is expressed chiefly in relation to *An Essay Towards a New Theory of Vision* (see n. 10 above) with which he appears in closest theoretical agreement; however, Hazlitt's general respect for Berkeley's abilities as a metaphysician is also clearly expressed in the *Lectures on English Philosophy* (ii. 180 n., 199).

[34] George Berkeley, *A Treatise Concerning the Principles of Human Knowledge*, Part I, section 39 (Berkeley, *Works*, ii. 57).

'*esse* is *percipi*.'[35] The philosophy of immaterialism, which treats matter (the external objective reality) as spirit (mental perception), approached from the other end provides Hazlitt with a rationale whereby spirit (the forms of the imagination) assumes a material character. One of his favourite descriptions of poetry is Theseus' version in *A Midsummer Night's Dream*: 'And as imagination bodies forth | The forms of things unknown, the poet's pen | Turns them to shapes, and gives to aery nothing | A local habitation and a name' (v. i. 14–17). This passage is frequently invoked in Hazlitt's own accounts of literary composition, not so much to emphasize that the product of the poet's art is reducible to airy nothing, but rather that the poet has the power to embody, or make real and specific, that nothing.[36] The best paintings also manifest such a power: 'So much do Rembrandt's pictures savour of the soul and body of reality, that the thoughts seem identical with the objects' ('Whether Genius is Conscious of its Powers?', *The Plain Speaker*; xii. 120). The savour of reality in the imagination's product is expressed in Hazlitt's habitual characterization of imaginative creation as 'substantial'. Describing, for instance, his collection of Elizabethan authors in one of the *Lectures on the Age of Elizabeth*, he quotes from Wordsworth's 'Personal Talk': 'books, we know, Are a substantial world' ('On Marston, Chapman, Deckar, etc.'; vi. 247). Later on in the same *Lectures*, he laments that the characters of Beaumont and Fletcher 'do not take a substantial form' ('On Beaumont and Fletcher, etc'; vi. 249). Such instances, conflating the imaginary and the substantial, may be multiplied from other of Hazlitt's works. So 'vivid were his impressions,' he observes of Cosway, 'that they included the substances of things in them' ('On the Old Age of Artists', *The Plain Speaker*; xii. 96). In 'A Farewell to Essay-Writing', he declares, 'I have brooded over an idea till it has become a kind of substance in my brain,' and again, 'my ideas, from their sinewy texture, have been to me in the nature of realities' (*Uncollected Essays*; xvii. 317, 320).

[35] Part I, section 3, Berkeley, *A Treatise Concerning the Principles of Human Knowledge*, 42.
[36] For example, in the following: *The Life of Thomas Holcroft*, Bk IV, ch. i (iii. 129); 'Macbeth' and 'The Tempest', *Characters of Shakespear's Plays* (iv. 186, 238); 'On Shakspeare and Ben Jonson' and 'On the Works of Hogarth: On the Grand and Familiar Style of Painting', *Lectures on the English Comic Writers* (vi. 37, 146); 'On a Landscape of Nicholas Poussin', *Table-Talk* (viii. 170).

Hazlitt's strong sense of the mind's ability to turn thought to substance unmistakably manifests the influence of an immaterialist philosophy. The mind creates that which it perceives, literally so in art—the 'palace of thought'—even if not, as according to Berkeley, in reality. 'A fine gallery of pictures is a sort of illustration of Berkeley's Theory of Matter and Spirit. It is like a palace of thought—another universe, built of air, of shadows, of colours. Every thing seems "palpable to feeling as to sight"' ('The Dulwich Gallery', *Sketches of the Principal Picture Galleries in England*; x. 19). Art is the paradigm of Berkeley's vision of reality for Hazlitt, in whom we find not so much a theoretical concurrence with the Berkeleian hypothesis, as a deep-seated empathy with its formulation of the power with which the mind is invested. In the early *Essay on the Principles of Human Action*, Hazlitt's strong sense of such a power feeds into the philosophical claim for the existence of a thinking or intellectual principle in the mind that is beyond the receptivity to sense impressions. In the later expounding of his poetic theory in the lecture 'On Poetry in General', it takes the form of an argument for the authenticity of the mind's creation.

'If poetry is a dream, the business of life is much the same. If it is a fiction, made up of what we wish things to be, and fancy that they are, because we wish them so, there is no other nor better reality' ('On Poetry in General'; v. 3). There is a Berkeleian awareness here, even if it is rather figurative than literal, of the immaterial character of life, whence Hazlitt puts poetry and life on the same footing and suggests that the true or 'better' reality is in the mind's creation. By the same token, the ideal beauty of portraiture, in the essay 'On Sitting for One's Picture', reverses the relation of nature to art. It is the portrait, the intellectual reality, that appears alive, while the living face, the material or factual reality, fades into a picture, 'a mere object of sight'. Similarly, in creating his art, the sculptor himself is turned into stone (*The Plain Speaker*; xii. 113).

So far, indeed, is Hazlitt from a literal concurrence with Berkeley, that we find him expressly discounting the philosophy of immaterialism for its inability to stand the test of common sense ('On Locke's "Essay on the Human Understanding"', *Lectures on English Philosophy*; ii. 181). But without any formal or rigorously literal adherence to Berkeley's theory, Hazlitt preserves, in his formulation of 'power', Berkeley's sense of the control exercised by the mind over the objects of perception. Hence his preference for the ill-defined or partially comprehended, as offering a release from the passivity of relation to objects more inescapably defined to the senses. Such a preference is articulated in different contexts in the essays; for instance, in Hazlitt's setting the *Tatler* over the *Spectator* as leaving more to the understanding of the reader ('On the Tatler', *The Round Table*; iv. 8) as well as in his feeling for the 'undefined and infinite' character of the untranslated Scriptures ('On Pedantry', *The Round Table*; iv. 82); also in his criticism of the French tragedy's lack of the 'obscure, distant, imperfect' ('Schlegel on the Drama', *Contributions to the Edinburgh Review*; xvi. 89) and of the neo-classical drama's denial of the view of life as 'a strange and romantic dream, long, obscure, and infinite' ('Anthony and Cleopatra', *Characters of Shakespear's Plays*; iv. 231). Each of these judgements is based on the knowledge that the mind's ability to constitute its own objects is strongest in that area of experience which is least governed by immediate sensation, and which therefore affords the maximum scope for mental activity.

In this way, a familiar Romantic position—that the sublime is approached through the dimly apprehended—takes on a particular metaphysical significance for Hazlitt. The association of the sublime with indistinctness of apprehension is theorized in Burke's *Philosophical Enquiry,* which lists obscurity as an attribute of the sublime.[37] When we are unable to perceive the bounds of an object or image, Burke argues, such an image strikes the mind with its greatness by suggesting infinity. Hence poetry, which affects us through the unrepresentable, by obscure images, is more powerful than the visual arts, which affect us by representations that are in their nature determinate.[38] Burke's theory suggests a link between sensory deprivation and imaginative power that is integral to Hazlitt's view of the imagination.

'Whatever is placed beyond the reach of sense and knowledge, whatever is imperfectly discerned, the fancy pieces out at its leisure; and all but the present moment, but the present spot, passion claims for its own, and brooding over it with wings outspread, stamps it with an image of itself' ('Why Distant

---

[37] Burke, *Philosophical Enquiry,* part II, section 3, p. 99.
[38] Ibid., section 4, pp. 107–8.

Objects Please', *Table-Talk*; viii. 255–6). Hazlitt's affinity with Berkeley is revealed in his idea of an immaterial creation 'beyond the reach of sense and knowledge' projected from within the mind, 'an image of itself'. The allusion to the Holy Ghost brooding dovelike over the abyss presents the imagination as spirit; consequently, its creation may be taken to be endowed with a vital principle. The present alone, in which, according to the *Essay on the Principles of Human Action*, we are absolutely subject to immediate sensation, contains a factual reality; while 'all but the present moment, but the present spot,' which 'passion claims for its own, and . . . stamps . . . with an image of itself', embodies another—the imaginative or 'better'—reality.

The association of distant objects with perception that is independent of immediate sensory response may also be referred to Berkeley's *Essay towards a New Theory of Vision*. Here, by establishing that the mind's apprehension of objects at a distance is an act of judgement rather than a direct sensory reaction, Berkeley logically extends this thesis to apply to nearby objects, and hence to all objects of our vision. 'Distant objects' constitute the starting-point of Berkeley's argument; given Hazlitt's knowledge of the work, the title of his own essay in *Table-Talk* can itself be taken as sufficiently evocative of Berkeley.

Conversely, too, the indifference to the pleasure afforded by distant objects signifies a confinement to the present, or synonymously, a lack of perspective, that always represents the unimaginative for Hazlitt, the condition of enslavement to the factual world of the senses. This is the subtext of his description of the Cockney as 'confined to one spot, and to the present moment' ('On Londoners and Country People', *The Plain Speaker*; xii. 67) and of his equally damning account of the French: 'they have no idea either of mental or aerial perspective. Every thing must be distinctly made out and in the foreground' ('Madame Pasta and Mademoiselle Mars', *The Plain Speaker*; xii. 333). Remarks such as these are only apparently arbitrary; they secrete the same theoretical view that is suggested by Coleridge in the second chapter of *Biographia*, when he connects the 'reliance on the immediate impressions of the sense' with 'a debility and dimness of the imaginative power': the view that the imagination offers a release from sensory limitation.[39]

Two Worlds

The evocation of poetry as a world apart from the workaday world of fact is a stock literary convention; Hazlitt's recourse to this convention is illuminated by his vision of the transformative power of the imagination. The notion of intellectual transformation sets up a dualism, consisting of the material and the imaginative realities, and this dualism, brought about by the imagination's tendency to idealize, persistently informs Hazlitt's sense of poetic composition. According to the essay 'On People of Sense', 'grosser feelings, by passing through the strainers of . . . imaginary, wide-extended experience, acquire an involuntary tendency to higher objects' (*The Plain Speaker*; xii. 245). These 'grosser feelings' are sensory and belong to a factual reality; their transformation is imaginative, composing the 'better reality'. An interesting sidelight on Hazlitt's sense of poetry as an actual, if alternative, world is given in the introduction to the *Lectures on the Age of Elizabeth*, where he posits that the discovery of the New World and the general burgeoning of travel literature, brought a credibility to poetry by realizing the visions of the imagination in the historic fact of alternative existence ('General View of the Subject'; vi. 187–8). The lecture 'On Miscellaneous Poems etc.' in the same series, offers another, more conventional version of the dualism of poetry and life, where poets are described as enjoying an unending afterlife in their verse (vi. 297).

For Hazlitt, 'poets see nature, veiled to the sight, but revealed to the soul in visionary grace and grandeur!' (*Liber Amoris*; ix. 130). It is the inability to elicit the 'visionary' from the factual reality that constitutes, according to him, the limitation and defect of Hogarth's art—by reproducing the external world too literally, he precludes ideal existence. 'He had an intense feeling and command . . . of nature, as it fell within his own observation, or came within the sphere of his actual experience; but he had little power beyond

---

[39] Coleridge, *Biographia*, vol. I, ch. ii, p. 30.

that sphere, or sympathy with that which existed only *in idea*. He was "conformed to this world, not transformed"' ('On the Works of Hogarth', *Lectures on the English Comic Writers*; vi. 146). In this view of Hogarth, Hazlitt expressly opposes Lamb's account in the essay 'On the Genius and Character of Hogarth', where Lamb argues against categorizing Hogarth as belonging to the familiar rather than the grand style in painting. Lamb claims for Hogarth precisely what Hazlitt denies: a transformation of his subject by a 'quantity of thought' and a 'poetical and almost prophetical conception in the artist,' into 'permanent abiding ideas. Not the sports of nature, but her necessary eternal classes.'[40] Notwithstanding the difference of opinion about example, however, the theoretical conception and language of both writers correspond almost perfectly. For Hazlitt, as for Lamb, the identifying characteristic of the imagination is the idealization of the subject. Mere factual observation imposes the limitation of the senses on the mind, ratifying the Lockian dichotomy of thought and thing, where the perception of the inspired eye removes it. In *Characteristics*, Hazlitt observes, 'Every one would rather be Raphael than Hogarth;' 'Raphael's figures are sustained by *ideas*: Hogarth's are distorted by mechanical habits and instincts' (CCVI, CCVII; ix. 198, 199). Like Raphael and opposite to Hogarth, Milton frees us from the subjugation to the senses by the power of his poetic or intellectual transformation:

Milton has got rid of the horns and tail, the vulgar and physical *insignia* of the devil, and clothed him with other greater and intellectual terrors, reconciling beauty and sublimity, and converting the grotesque and deformed into the *ideal* and classical. Certainly Milton's mind rose superior to all others in this respect, on the outstretched wings of philosophic contemplation, in not confounding the depravity of the will with physical distortion, or supposing that the distinctions of good and evil were only to be subjected to the gross ordeal of the senses. ('On Miscellaneous Poems, etc.', *Lectures on the Age of Elizabeth*; vi. 316)

The imaginative ideal shows the truth that rises above the material or matter-of-fact. 'In Spenser,' for instance, 'we wander in another

---

[40] Charles Lamb, *The Works of Charles and Mary Lamb*, ed. E. V. Lucas, 7 vols (London: Methuen, 1903–5), i. 73, 74, 78.

world, among ideal beings' ('On Chaucer and Spenser', *Lectures on the English Poets*; v. 35). In the essay on Scott in *The Spirit of the Age*, 'there is a power in true poetry that lifts the mind from the ground of reality to a higher sphere' (xi. 59). Even when, in another and more politicized context, the validity of poetic idealization is questioned, the poetic ideal remains lifted above the matter-of-fact, 'dwells in a perpetual Utopia of its own' ('On Poetical Versatility', *The Round Table*; iv. 151).

In the best case, however, the dualism of factual and imaginative reality contains not a dichotomy, but a transformation, of sensory into imaginative perception; the former limited and passive, the latter empowered and constitutive. The imagination's working is a manifestation of the power principle, and that which it creates constitutes an immaterial reality, fashioned after the Berkeleian vision of the immaterial forms of life itself. It is this reality that is embodied in poetic discourse, and it is to imaginative language that Hazlitt refers, when he writes, 'It is words that constitute all but the present moment, but the present object . . . they alone answer in any degree to the truth of things' ('Sir Walter Scott, Racine and Shakespear', *The Plain Speaker*; xii. 337). If the province of imaginative reality, from the essay 'Why Distant Objects Please', is 'all but the present moment, but the present object', then, from the above, that reality—'the truth of things'—is embodied in 'words', the language of the imagination. The substantiality of poetic language, as containing the 'better reality' created by the imagination, is thus confirmed.

The understanding of Hazlitt's power principle enables us to reconcile his unequivocal rejection of the physical analogy for mental activity (*Prospectus of a History of English Philosophy*; ii. 124) with the preponderance of the terms from Newtonian mechanics in his critical usage, where 'power', 'impress', 'force', 'momentum', etc. are applied to intellectual activity in a manner that does appear closely analogous to their operation in the physical world. Such usages do not in fact vindicate the physical analogy, but its opposite, termed by Hazlitt 'the philosophy of consciousness' or the 'intellectual' philosophy ('Preface to An Abridgement of Abraham Tucker's Light of Nature Pursued'; i. 127). His habitual recourse, not only to Newtonian terms, but to an apparently sense-oriented vocabulary, a vocabulary pertaining to 'feeling' of various kinds, does not imply the sensory origin of intellectual activity. Rather, it grants to the purely intellectual a degree of actuality equal to, if not greater than, the impressions of the sense.

2

The Secret Soul of Harmony
Imagination, Association, and Unity

FROM Elisabeth Schneider onwards, scholars of Hazlitt have been at some pains to distinguish his philosophical position and principles of criticism from those of Coleridge. In the words of René Wellek, 'While it would be rash to deny that Hazlitt learned something from Coleridge, enough has been said to show that Hazlitt's rejection of Coleridge went far beyond politics into the fundamentals of philosophy and criticism.'[1] It is no part of my argument for Hazlitt to deny such a conclusion; at the most, this chapter will pay a greater degree of attention than is now deemed necessary to the fact that 'Hazlitt learned something from Coleridge'. Roy Park, also protesting against the assimilation of Hazlitt's thought to Coleridge's, reminds us that 'Fancy and imagination, the psychology of artistic creation, the organic metaphor, symbol and the antithesis between mechanism and dynamism are not the sum of Romantic critical theory.'[2] Yet it has more often been the case that in the anxiety to identify a distinctive voice in Hazlitt's criticism, the extent to which the familiar Romantic issues enumerated by Park are very often Hazlitt's issues, is bypassed. In this respect, David Bromwich's comments, 'on the popular critical theme of *unity*, his writings contain nothing markedly graver than the passage . . . on Fielding's physiognomy' and 'The organic metaphor . . . held comparatively little interest for Hazlitt' are typical of the current critical view.[3] It can be shown, on the contrary, that while critical 'themes' of any kind are rarely addressed as such by Hazlitt, unity is thematic in his criticism,

---

[1] René Wellek, *A History of Modern Criticism* 1750–1950, vol. ii: *The Romantic Age* (New Haven and London: Yale University Press, 1955), 189.
[2] Park, *Hazlitt*, 77.   [3] Bromwich, *Hazlitt*, 191, 239.

The Secret Soul of Harmony

and an adherence to a principle of organic unity—often simply presented as the desirability of 'keeping', or that all parts of a composition or character should 'tell'—is fundamental to his discussions of art and literature. This criterion of unity, underlying much of Hazlitt's writing about the imagination, has been mistakenly ignored. It is as a counter to readings like Wellek's, that 'we must not seek in Hazlitt analytical skill or even deep interest in the structure of a work of art,'[4] that this chapter will locate in the context of his notion of power Hazlitt's associationism and the development of his theory of imaginative structure.

Unitarianism and Coleridge

Hazlitt's assertion of the authenticity of the imagination's creation is rooted in his recognition of the freedom of the mind from dependence on the senses and hence the freedom of the imagination from the limitations of factual reality. In his *New and Improved Grammar of the English Tongue*, language manifests the innate formative ability—'power'—of the speaking subject; his theory of poetry affirms that it is through that power alone that we are enabled to reach beyond material limitation to arrive at the knowledge of the true or 'better reality'. Hazlitt's understanding of imaginative creation as authentic and original, brings into play the familiar analogy between poet and God. Following a long tradition in poetics, he points to the etymological significance of the word 'poet'. 'A poet is essentially a *maker*; that is, he must atone for what he loses in individuality and local resemblance by the energies and resources of his own mind' ('Sir Walter Scott', *The Spirit of the Age*; xi. 60). Poetry is original because it is self-constituted. It surpasses material limitation, 'individuality and local resemblance', to manifest instead the 'energies and resources' of the poet's mind. The revelation of the author through his works is relevant in particular to the Unitarian and deistic views of creation, both of which uphold natural religion: the belief that the order of creation leads us to

---

[4] Wellek, *The Romantic Age*, 204.

the understanding of the Creator.[5] For Hazlitt, analogously, poetry leads us to the human imagination; in poetic language, we find 'the infinite variety of shapes and combinations of power' (v. 4) assumed by the imagining mind.

Hazlitt's own religious background is Unitarian; his father was a Unitarian minister, and he himself attended the Unitarian New College at Hackney. It was his early association with Unitarianism that first brought Hazlitt into contact not only with Coleridge, but also with figures such as Joseph Priestley, a friend of his father's and one of Hazlitt's tutors at Hackney. Hazlitt's familiarity with the great Unitarian thinkers is indicated throughout his writings; the *Lectures on English Philosophy*, especially, are dotted with references to Priestley and Jonathan Edwards, both of whom he names in a note to the essay 'On the Tendency of Sects' as the 'two remarkable men' produced by the dissenting tradition (*The Round Table*; iv. 49 n.).

With such a background in view, it can be shown that the language in which Hazlitt describes the power or spirit of imaginative creation is frequently evocative of the Unitarian deity, a single and indivisible presence that unifies the entire order of creation.[6] At the same time, this critical language, even as it manifests the influence of Hazlitt's dissenting background, often undermines its orthodoxy. 'It would be in vain', he remarks wryly towards the conclusion of the essay 'On the Tendency of Sects', 'to strew the flowers of poetry round the borders of the Unitarian controversy' (*The Round Table*; iv. 51). The permeation of Unitarian themes into his own critical usage amounts, in effect, to a displacement by the human of the divine.

Hazlitt's theorizing upon the formative power of the imagination contains two key Unitarian premises, each corroborative of the other: the oneness or indivisibility of the creator and the unity of his design. According to Joseph Priestley, 'the philosopher admits the belief of *one God*, in opposition to a multiplicity of

[5] The deists, however, absolutely reject revealed religion, the revelation of God through the Scriptures. By contrast, the writings of Hartley and Priestley accommodate both; see, for instance, David Hartley, *Observations on Man, his Frame, his Duty, and his Expectations*, 2 vols (London, 1749), ii. 48–52, for Hartley's account of natural religion and revealed religion as mutually corroborative.

[6] John Kinnaird has demonstrated some of the ways in which Hazlitt's critical themes reflect leading ideas in his father's Unitarian writings (Kinnaird, *William Hazlitt*, 1–36, especially p. 20).

The Secret Soul of Harmony

Gods, on account of the *unity of design* apparent in the universe.'[7] Similarly, Coleridge observes in the first of his Lectures on Revealed Religion: 'This admirable and beautiful structure of things that carries irresistible Demonstration of intending Causality, exalts our idea of the Contriver—the Unity of the Design shews him to be *one*.'[8] Like the Unitarian God, Hazlitt's innate intellectual principle is one and indivisible. Thus he writes, refuting Dr Spurzheim's theory of the plurality of the thinking organs, 'the principle of thought and feeling in man is one, whereas the present doctrine supposes it to be many. The mind is one, or it is infinite' ('On Dr. Spurzheim's Theory', *The Plain Speaker*; xii. 139). This is to say that the mind is both one and infinite or, since the intellectual faculty is one, it is also infinite.[9] Since it is infinite, it appears to carry a divine attribute.

The unity of the imagination is identical with the unity of thought or consciousness which is a fundamental tenet of Hazlitt's epistemology. By virtue of this identity, both 'reason' and 'imagination' belong to the same intellectual principle; it is 'sensation' and not 'reason' from which imagination must be contradistinguished (i. 19n.). Accordingly too, although Hazlitt appears frequently to treat 'understanding' and 'imagination' as distinct— the essay on Coriolanus in *Characters of Shakespear's Plays* distinguishes the two as analytic and synthetic, or in Hazlitt's words, 'distributive' and 'monopolising' faculties respectively (iv. 214)—the process of the understanding is ultimately inseparable from the imaginative activity of the poet. In the essay 'On Dr. Spurzheim's Theory', as elsewhere in Hazlitt's philosophical writings, the attributes of each are more or less exchangeable with those of the other (xii. 150–1). It appears, consequently, that 'imagination' is to 'understanding' as, in another context, 'genius' is to 'common sense': the first a kind of intensification of the

---

[7] Joseph Priestley, *Disquisitions Relating to Matter and Spirit* (London, 1777), section 12, p. 151.

[8] S. T. Coleridge, *Lectures 1795: On Politics and Religion*, ed. L. Patton and P. Mann, vol. i of *The Collected Works of Samuel Taylor Coleridge*, Bollingen series, no. 75 (Princeton, NJ: Princeton University Press, 1971), 93–4.

[9] The association of infinity (and, hence, by implication, of divinity) with unity is put simply by Burke in the *Philosophical Enquiry*. Since when the eye or mind contemplates a great uniform object, it is unable to determine its bounds, 'every thing great by its quantity must necessarily be, one, simple and entire' (Burke, *Philosophical Enquiry*, part IV, section 10, p. 264).

ordinary operations performed by the second, 'the same principle exercised on loftier ground and in more unusual combinations' ('On Genius and Common Sense', *Table-Talk*; viii. 32).

In finding the traces of a Unitarian background in Hazlitt's language for the imagination, the comparison with Coleridge becomes inevitable. It can be argued that Coleridge's lifelong preoccupation with 'that ultimate end of human Thought, and human Feeling, Unity' is a persistent reminder of his own Unitarian background.[10] Certainly it was Coleridge the professed Unitarian, who 'came to Shrewsbury, to succeed Mr. Rowe in the spiritual charge of a Unitarian Congregation there,' who was so much the object of the young Hazlitt's admiration ('My First Acquaintance with Poets', *Uncollected Essays*; xvii. 106). In the period of Coleridge's Unitarianism, we can identify in his writings a vision of the imagination as participating in the divine Unity of existence: 'The whole one Self! Self, that no alien knows!' ('Religious Musings', l. 154).[11] This focus upon unity emerges also in Hazlitt's theory of the imagination.

In the memorable account of his encounter with Coleridge, in what is now one of the best known of Hazlitt's essays, he remarks, 'that my understanding . . . found a language to express itself, I owe to Coleridge' ('My First Acquaintance with Poets'; xvii. 107). In the essay 'On the Causes of Popular Opinion', he writes, again, 'Till I began to paint, or till I became acquainted with the author of *The Ancient Mariner*, I could neither write nor speak' (*Uncollected Essays*; xvii. 312). It is possible to multiply instances from Hazlitt's writings, taken from a variety of subjects and from widely separated chronological contexts, that support these contentions. We have, for example, his comments on Burke's style: 'Burke most frequently produced an effect by the remoteness and novelty of his combinations, by the force of contrast, by the striking manner in which the most opposite and unpromising materials were harmoniously blended together' ('Character of Mr. Burke', *Political Essays*; vii. 310). This bears a close resemblance to Coleridge's description of the imagination in

---

[10] S. T. Coleridge, *Lectures 1808–1819: On Literature*, ed. R. A. Foakes, vol. v of *The Collected Works of Samuel Taylor Coleridge*, Bollingen series no. 75, 2 vols (Princeton, NJ: Princeton University Press, 1987), i. 68.

[11] S. T. Coleridge, *The Complete Poetical Works of Samuel Taylor Coleridge*, ed. Ernest Hartley Coleridge, 2 vols (Oxford: Clarendon Press, 1912), i. 115.

chapter xiv of *Biographia Literaria:* 'balance or reconciliation of opposite or discordant qualities,' 'the sense of novelty and freshness, with old and familiar objects,' 'blends and harmonizes'.[12] The resemblance extends to several other examples, such as Hazlitt's remarks on Milton, 'The fervour of his imagination melts down and renders malleable, as in a furnace, the most contradictory materials' ('On Shakspeare and Milton', *Lectures on the English Poets*; v. 58), and again on Burke as the exemplar of great writing: 'The most rigid fidelity and the most fanciful extravagance meet, and are reconciled in his pages' ('On the Prose-style of Poets', *The Plain Speaker*; xii. 12).[13]

The closeness of Hazlitt's language for the imagination to Coleridge's stems from a criterion of unity that is common to both and is grounded in the thesis that the works of the imagination are produced from a single and indivisible first cause, however defined. We find, from Hazlitt's observations, that Caravaggio's work is 'an emanation of pure thought' ('Whether Genius is Conscious of its Powers?', *The Plain Speaker*; xii. 119) and that there is a 'divine mind within' Raphael's art ('On Egotism', *The Plain Speaker*; xii. 158). In his invariable use of a certain set of adjectives—'spirited', 'lively', 'vivid'—with reference to imaginative composition, we can trace the assumption, of a vital principle, that is more than merely conventional. The terms in which the concept of gusto is explicated is another case in point. 'As the objects themselves in nature would produce an impression on the sense, distinct from every other object, and having something divine in it, which the heart owns and the imagination consecrates, the objects in the picture preserve the same impression, absolute' ('On *Gusto*', *The Round Table*; iv. 77). The Unitarian understanding of divine purpose manifested in the order of nature reappears here in Hazlitt, producing a unity-in-multeity configuration very much after the manner of Coleridge's 'Parts and proportions of one wondrous whole!' ('Religious Musings', l. 128).[14] Every natural object is recognized to contain 'something

---

[12] Coleridge, *Biographia*, vol. II, ch. xiv, pp. 16–17.
[13] Comments such as these contradict David Bromwich's observation (in which he seeks, like Park, to distinguish Hazlitt's principles in criticism from Coleridge's) that '*Hazlitt sees no reason why opposites should be reconciled, and never leads us to expect this as a formal property of great works*' (Bromwich, *Hazlitt*, 233–4).
[14] Coleridge, *Poems*, i. 114.

divine', yet distinct from every other, so that each is a separate and vital link in the unified chain of creation. Its divinity is granted by the imagination ('consecrates'), which unifies thereby the whole order of nature.

Hazlitt appears to write occasionally as if divinity is actually inherent in nature, and in this, too, he reflects some aspects of his Unitarian background. In Priestley, especially, the sense of the active presence of God in the world is so strong as to suggest the immanent deity of pantheism, where God and his works are identical. Coleridge makes this a criticism of Priestley in his letter to the Reverend John Edwards of 20 March 1796: 'Quere—How is it that Dr Priestley is not an atheist?—He asserts in three different Places, that God not only *does*, but *is*, every thing.'[15] Mindful of his vulnerablity to such accusations, Priestley himself explicitly disclaims pantheism:

for the same reason that the *maker* of the *table*, or of the *watch*, must be different from the table or the watch, it is equally manifest that the maker of *myself*, of the *world*, and of the *universe* (meaning by it all the worlds that we suppose to exist) must be a being different from myself, the world, or the universe; which is a sufficient answer to the reasoning of Spinoza, who, making the *universe itself* to be God, did, in fact, deny that there was any God.[16]

In the 'Illustrations' of his *Disquisitions* he writes further, 'upon no system whatever, is the great Author of Nature more distinct from his productions, or his presence with them, and agency upon them, more necessary. In fact, the system now held forth to the public, taken in its full extent, makes the Divine Being to be of as much importance in the *system*, as the apostle makes him, when he says, *In him we live, and move, and have our being*.'[17] It will be perceived, however, that despite the disclaimer in 'distinct from his productions', Priestley's profound awareness of 'his presence with them, and agency upon them' bridges and almost elides the separation of creator and created. This elision may be perceived in a number of passages in his writings; for instance, 'We shall have a kind of *union with God* himself; his will shall be our will, and even his power our power; being ever employed to execute our wishes and purposes, as well as his; because they will be, in all

---

[15] Coleridge, *Letters*, i. 192.   [16] Priestley, *Disquisitions*, section 12, p. 149.
[17] Ibid. 354.

respects, the same with his.'[18] There is also his citation of Hartley's conclusion to the *Observations on Man*, which asserts that in the progress of being, created is transformed into creator: 'the Progress of every Individual in his Passage through an eternal Life is from imperfect to perfect, particular to general, less to greater, finite to infinite, and from the Creature to the Creator.'[19] Priestley's Unitarian deity occupies, then, a middle ground between the wholly transcendent God of the deists in which the creator is utterly distinct from the created, and the wholly immanent God of the pantheists, in which the creator is absolutely one with the created.

The resemblances to pantheistic thought in Priestley's account of deity is paralleled in the language of immanence in which Hazlitt sometimes describes the imagination, strengthening the analogy between the Priestleian deity and Hazlitt's imagination. It must be emphasized that 'analogy' is the operative term in understanding Hazlitt's relation both to Priestley and to the pantheists; it is the imagination, not deity, that Hazlitt perceives as unifying the order of nature. The distinction in the essay 'On *Gusto*' between 'the objects themselves in nature' and 'the objects in the picture' is not the conventional distinction between nature and art, but between the imaginative perception of nature and the imaginative expression of nature in art; the imagination is the source of 'something divine' in both. This 'something divine', then, that is expressed in the pictorial arts, is the manifestation, not of deity, but of what Hazlitt calls 'gusto' in the artistic imagination; elsewhere, it is referred to as 'nature' or 'truth'.

'Nature is the soul of art. There is a strength in the imagination . . . where one spirit, that of truth, pervades every part, brings down heaven to earth, mingles cardinals and popes with angels and apostles, and yet blends and harmonises the whole' ('Why the Arts are not progressive: a Fragment', *The Round Table*; iv. 162). The imagination is identical with the 'nature' or 'truth' that is the 'soul of art'; it is the 'one spirit' unifying its own creation. Again, the connection with Coleridge is irresistible. We need only recall

---

[18] Joseph Priestley, 'Dedication' in *The Doctrine of Philosophical Necessity Illustrated; Being an Appendix to the Disquisitions relating to Matter and Spirit* (London, 1777), p. xiii.
[19] Hartley, *Observations*, ii. 439; cited by Priestley, *Philosophical Necessity*, section 10, p. 129.

the phrases 'blends and harmonizes the natural and the artificial' (*Biographia Literaria*) or 'consubstantial with the truths' (*Lay Sermons*), to establish the verbal parallels between this passage and the Coleridgean language of unity and divine presence, as employed with respect to the poetic imagination.[20] Hazlitt read and reviewed the *Lay Sermons* in December 1816 and *Biographia Literaria* in August 1817; the fragment on the Arts is dated to 1814 (iv. 390 n.), and actually anticipates the phrases that I have quoted from these works. But where Coleridge's 'one Self' invariably carries a numinous import, Hazlitt's 'one spirit' or 'something divine' has a more matter-of-fact interchangeability with 'nature' and 'truth'. Coleridge's purpose is theological; Hazlitt's, secular: where Coleridge is concerned with the nature of the divine imagination, it would be truer of Hazlitt to say that he calls attention to the divine nature of the imagination.[21] His review of Schlegel's *Lectures on Dramatic Art and Literature*, for example, contains the following:

In the Heathen mythology, form is everywhere predominant; in the Christian, we find only unlimited, undefined power. The imagination alone 'broods over the immense abyss, and makes it pregnant.' There is, in the habitual belief of an universal, invisible Principle of all things, a vastness and obscurity which confounds our perceptions, while it exalts our piety. A mysterious awe surrounds the doctrines of the Christian faith: the Infinite is everywhere before us, whether we turn to reflect on what is revealed to us of the Divine nature or our own. ('Schlegel on the Drama', *Contributions to the Edinburgh Review*; xvi. 66)

That the Christian myths display 'the habitual belief of an universal, invisible Principle of all things', and that the contemplation of our own nature, equally as the Divine, leads to the revelation of the Infinite, makes complete Unitarian sense. Locke, also writing on scriptural discourse and invariably associating human understanding with human limitation, arrived at the inadequacy of the

---

[20] Coleridge, *Biographia*, vol. II, ch. xiv, p. 17; S. T. Coleridge, *Lay Sermons*, ed. R. J. White, vol. vi of *The Collected Works of Samuel Taylor Coleridge*, Bollingen series no. 75 (Princeton, NJ: Princeton University Press, 1972), 29.

[21] Elisabeth Schneider, probably the first critic who demonstrates Hazlitt's philosophical position and principles of criticism to be independent of Coleridge, writes that 'The greatest difference between the approach of Coleridge and of Hazlitt to philosophy lies in the fact that the former's was fundamentally religious and the latter's was not' (Schneider, *Aesthetics*, 15). This difference is true not only of their approaches to philosophy, but also holds good more generally.

Bible as a revelation of truth, because it is conveyed through a human agency, language:

> The Volumes of Interpreters, and Commentators on the Old and New Testament, are but too manifest proofs of this. Though every thing said in the Text be infallibly true, yet the Reader may be, nay cannot chuse but be very fallible in the understanding of it. Nor is it to be wondred, that the Will of GOD, when cloathed in Words, should be liable to that doubt and uncertainty, which unavoidably attends that sort of Conveyance, when even his Son, whilst cloathed in Flesh, was subject to all the Frailties and Inconveniences of humane Nature, Sin excepted.[22]

For Hazlitt, by contrast, the divinity inhering in scriptural text is *confirmed* precisely because it is deciphered through the product—language—of the mind's 'power' or innate formative capacity. Spirit is conflated with power. The extract from 'Why Distant Objects Please' (viii. 255–6) cited in the previous chapter appears to posit a similitude between spirit and Spirit. In the abyss image of the review of Schlegel, Hazlitt goes further, actually naming the divine presence in the biblical text—the Holy Spirit of Christian tradition—'imagination', thus merging into one what might otherwise have remained merely comparable entities. The revelation of God is identified as a revelation of the imagination's working. By the construction of the passage extracted above from the Schlegel review, a synonymity is implied between the three phrases 'unlimited, undefined power', 'imagination', and 'universal, invisible Principle of all things', whereby the universal Principle is unequivocally recognized as the powerful imagination. Hence its attribute is an obscurity that confounds our sensory perceptions. In the remarks immediately preceding this extract, the Christian is explicitly associated with imaginative belief, and the 'Heathen', by contrast, with material limitation:

> The religion, or mythology of the Greeks, was nearly allied to their poetry: it was material and definite. . . . All was subjected to the senses. The Christian religion, on the contrary, is essentially spiritual and abstract; it is 'the evidence of things unseen.' In the Heathen mythology, form is everywhere predominant; in the Christian, we find only unlimited, undefined power . . . (xvi. 65–6).

---

[22] Locke, *Human Understanding*, Bk III, ch. ix, section 23, pp. 489–90.

The distinction between the 'Heathen' and the Christian mythology is that the one belongs to the senses, the other, to the imagination, the 'unlimited, undefined power' pervading Christian myth.

Writing to Sotheby on 10 September 1802, Coleridge makes the distinction, fourteen years prior to Hazlitt's review of Schlegel, between the Greek and Hebrew poets, in a passage that is remarkably similar to Hazlitt's in both tone and content:

> It must occur to every Reader that the Greeks in their religious poems address always the Numina Loci, the Genii, the Dryads, the Naiads, &c &c—All natural Objects were *dead*—mere hollow Statues—but there was a Godkin or Goddessling *included* in each—In the Hebrew Poetry you find nothing of this poor Stuff—as poor in genuine Imagination, as it is mean in Intellect—/ At best, it is but Fancy, or the aggregating Faculty of the mind—not *Imagination*, or the *modifying*, and *co-adunating* Faculty. This the Hebrew Poets appear to me to have possessed beyond all others—& next to them the English. In the Hebrew Poets each Thing has a Life of it's own, & yet they are all one Life. In God they move & live, & *have* their Being—. . .[23]

Both descriptions find in the Greek literature, in contrast to the vitality of the scriptural text, the predominance of the outward shell of poetry over its substance; both describe the divine in Unitarian terms as a single and indivisible presence independent of material limitation; in Coleridge, 'one Life', or 'God', in Hazlitt, 'unlimited, undefined power', 'an universal, invisible Principle of all things'. Yet the comparison, which convincingly attests to the similarity of thought between the two writers, also highlights the characteristic divergence of their perspectives. In Coleridge's view of the Hebrew poetry, the working of the imagination originates in, and is therefore a revelation of, the deity: 'In God they move & live, & *have* their Being'. For Hazlitt, it is the imagination that charges the Christian text with divinity: 'The imagination alone "broods over the immense abyss, and makes its pregnant."' There is no presupposed 'God', but only a 'habitual belief' in the 'Principle of all things'; the

---

[23] Coleridge, *Letters*, ii. 865–6. In spite of his criticism of Priestley's tendencies to pantheism, Coleridge here describes the relation between creator and created using the same quotation from Acts that Priestley cites in the *Disquisitions* (see above), which suggests that God is both immanent and transcendent in the universe.

'Infinite' is brought before us by our own innate process of thought, reflection.

Among his reminiscences of the year 1799, Crabb Robinson notes that Hazlitt, whose acquaintance he first made in that year, had studied at 'the Unitarian New College, Hackney, and he was one of the first students who left that college an avowed infidel.'[24] By evoking the Unitarian deity in his description of the human imagination, Hazlitt is at once acknowledging and undermining his own religious background. The Unitarian view of the relation between the creator and his works informs his own understanding of imaginative composition, yet unlike Coleridge, it is not deity, but the human imagination that he seeks to exalt. The indivisibility of imaginative power leads Hazlitt to an associationist theory from which is developed in turn a demand for an innate unity in artistic creation.

Hazlitt and Associationism

The Unitarian argument for a single and indivisible godhead leads directly to the associationist notion of a 'chain of being', signifying the link between the various forms of the natural world by virtue of the unity of the design in which they participate. In Priestley's *Doctrine of Philosophical Necessity Illustrated*, 'We ourselves, complex as the structure of our minds, and our principles of action are, are links in a great connected chain, parts of an immense whole.'[25] It will be found that Hazlitt's associationism is based, similarly, on his strong sense of a single first cause from which all other ideas and feelings develop and take their tone. The Unitarian 'chain of being' reappears in his view of poetic composition as a process of cumulative linking. Poetry 'suggests what exists out of it, in any manner connected with it,' it begins where 'one idea gives a tone and colour to others, where one feeling melts others into it' ('On Poetry in General'; v. 10, 12). Hazlitt's description echoes Lamb's account of the imagination in the essay 'On the Genius and Character of Hogarth':

---

[24] H. C. Robinson, *Henry Crabb Robinson on Books and their Writers*, ed. E. J. Morley, 3 vols (London: J. M. Dent & Sons Limited, 1938), i. 6.
[25] Priestley, *Philosophical Necessity*, p. viii.

'that power which draws all things to one,—which makes things animate and inanimate, beings with their attributes, subjects and their accessories, take one colour, and serve to one effect.'[26] Lamb himself is a reader of Priestley, retaining a Unitarian leaning through most of his life, and both he and Hazlitt express the unity achieved by the imagination with a strong flavour of associationism. 'The poetical impression of any object is that uneasy, exquisite sense of beauty or power that cannot be contained within itself; that is impatient of all limit; that (as flame bends to flame) strives to link itself to some other image of kindred beauty or grandeur' ('On Poetry in General'; v. 3). 'Power' resides not within the object, but is a quality of the faculty which perceives it poetically and which, by transferring its own attribute to the object of perception, assimilates that object into itself as an 'image'. Such an image is then situated in relation to (associated with) other images that are instinct with an identical quality; by this relation, it is rendered poetic.

Hazlitt's theory of association does not seek to construe the imagination's working through a mechanistic model based on sensory receptivity, but rather the reverse: it is the creative imagination that is seen to construct an associated chain of images, or more accurately, 'symbols'. The essay 'On the Past and Future' in *Table-Talk*, in fact, explicitly depicts the opposite condition, when association directs intellectual activity instead of vice versa, as a denial of the imagination and a trap: 'The chain of habit coils itself round the heart, like a serpent, to gnaw and stifle it' (viii. 29). In the imaginative operation, the imagination is the cause, not the effect of the associative process. The associative operation of the imagination is further described in 'The Indian Jugglers':

Nature is also a language. Objects, like words, have a meaning; and the true artist is the interpreter of this language, which he can only do by knowing its applications to a thousand other objects in a thousand other situations. . . . art is the seeing nature through the medium of sentiment and passion, as each object is a symbol of the affections and a link in the chain of our endless being. (viii. 82–3)

---

[26] Lamb, *Works*, i. 73. This quotation is also incorporated by Wordsworth into the *Preface* to the 1815 edition of his poems. See William Wordsworth, *The Prose Works of William Wordsworth*, ed. W. J. B. Owen and J. W. Smyser, 3 vols (Oxford: Clarendon Press, 1974), iii. 34.

The turnaround, by which nature is made to approximate to language, rather than language delineated as natural, testifies to Hazlitt's belief in the 'better reality' of the mind's creation. We recall his comments on the Elizabethan dramatists: 'Nature lies open to them like a book' ('On Lyly, Marlow, Heywood, etc.', *Lectures on the Age of Elizabeth*; vi. 213). In 'The Indian Jugglers', natural 'objects' (things) can be interpreted as words when they are invested with significance by imaginative power, here, 'sentiment and passion'. The ability to interpret nature as text testifies to the associative capacity of the artist, his capacity to know an object in 'its applications to a thousand other objects in a thousand other situations'. Association, then, is the process whereby the imagination projects itself into the order of nature so as to produce its own immaterial creation. In the *Remarks on the Systems of Hartley and Helvetius*, Hazlitt asserts that the unity of the different forms of nature could only be apprehended through the internalization of nature by a single and innate faculty of the mind (i. 71). It is this idea that reappears in 'The Indian Jugglers', modified to a less formal and less rigorously philosophical context. So too in the essay 'On the Love of the Country':

There is, generally speaking, the same foundation for our love of Nature as for all our habitual attachments, namely, association of ideas. . . . For there is that consent and mutual harmony among all her works, one undivided spirit pervading them throughout, that, if we have once knit ourselves in hearty fellowship to any of them, they will never afterwards appear as strangers to us, but, which ever way we turn, we shall find a secret power to have gone out before us, moulding them into such shapes as fancy loves, informing them with life and sympathy, . . . (*The Round Table*; iv. 18–20)[27]

[27] The contention that it is the ideas associated by us with the objects of nature, rather than the objects themselves, which give us our love for nature is made rather more explicitly by Schiller in the essay *On the Naive and Sentimental in Literature* (1795). Like Hazlitt in the essay 'On the Love of Country', Schiller posits that our feeling for nature is a kind of recollection, grounded in the organic unity pervading the forms of nature, of which, in a time past, we too have been a part.–Friedrich Schiller, *On the Naive and Sentimental in Literature*, trans. H. Watanabe-O'Kelly (Manchester: Carcanet New Press, 1981), 22.
 On the basis of Hazlitt's remarks in the essay 'On the Love of Country', Schneider remarks that 'he did occasionally tend toward a kind of pantheism which partly unified external phenomena by a feeling that there is "one undivided spirit" pervading nature's works' (Schneider, *Aesthetics*, 42). In fairness to Schneider, the suggestion is both cursory and much qualified; it is she, in the first place, who finds that the difference

It need not be laboured that the 'secret power' is the imagination, which is the source of the inner 'life' of its creation: nature moulded into 'such shapes as fancy loves'. The recognition of 'one undivided spirit' pervaded throughout the works of nature, which can be made continuous with our own spirit by an act of the imagination 'if we have once knit ourselves in hearty fellowship', seems to reiterate Coleridge's vision of the imagination's goal in 'Religious Musings', 'to know ourselves | Parts and proportions of one wondrous whole': (ll. 127–8).[28] The difference however, resides in this, that where the unity manifested in the highest forms of imaginative exercise is frequently presented by Coleridge as pre-established or absolute, for Hazlitt, it is more often elicited or constituted by the inspired mind. In his dynamic, the mind is not simply an integral part of the unity of nature, it is the very origin of that unity. The imagination 'moulds' the works of nature, 'informing them with life and sympathy', where 'sympathy' denotes the associative process through which the imagining mind achieves unity by drawing external nature into itself.

The associative tendency of the imagination, described in 'The Indian Jugglers' and in the essay 'On the Love of Country', is a recurrent theme in Hazlitt's writings. As I have already indicated, this is in no way a mitigation of his theoretical opposition to Hartley, expressed most fully in the *Remarks on the Systems of Hartley and Helvetius* (i. 50–83). By Hartley's account, the associative process of the mind is utterly dependent on the sense impressions that impinge upon it, so that all mental operations, which arise out of this process, are given an external origin, and the mind is denied innate power: 'all the intellectual Pleasures and

---

between Hazlitt and Coleridge is the difference between a secular and a religious understanding. J. C. Sallé, however, has strongly opposed Schneider's remark regarding the pantheistic implications of Hazlitt's thought, by arguing that his assumption of a complex of relations between mind and nature arises from an associationist view of the imagination.—J.-C. Sallé, 'Hazlitt the Associationist', *RES* xv (1964), 38–51. There is little to indicate that Hazlitt is actually a pantheist by belief; it is always imagination rather than deity that he is concerned with. However, we can find a link between pantheism and associationism through the analogy with the Priestleian view of deity; the chain of being posited by Priestley does suggest a resemblance to the pantheist notion of immanent deity (see above). At the same time, Sallé's categorizing Hazlitt an 'associationist' is no less mistaken than calling him a pantheist, and his view that Hazlitt's thought was pervaded by 'the doctrine of associationism' (ibid. 42) does less than justice to the critique of that doctrine that we find throughout his metaphysics.

[28] Coleridge, *Poems*, i. 113–14.

Pains are deducible ultimately from the sensible ones,' and again, 'According to the Theory here laid down, all human Actions proceed from Vibrations in the Nerves of the Muscles, and these from others, which are either evidently of a mechanical Nature, as in the automatic Motions; or else have been shewn to be so in the Account given of the voluntary Motions.'[29] Hartley, and in his footsteps, Priestley, treat the phenomenon of association as validating materialism—the notion that the process of the mind is absolutely determined by the properties of physical matter—and hence mechanism: because our ideas are externally determined, they must be perceived as mechanically determined. As Priestley observes, 'mechanism is the undoubted consequence of materialism,' and 'the pretended *self-determining power* is altogether imaginary and impossible.'[30] By denying a self-determining power of the mind and by positing further that God is the external first cause who determines the impressions made upon the senses and therefore the manner in which our ideas originate, the Unitarian philosophers evolve from the association of ideas a necessarian doctrine that is central to Unitarian belief. In Hazlitt's theory, on the other hand, it is the imagination which is the first cause in the associative process. By making the imagination, i.e. the mind itself, the source of our association of ideas, Hazlitt validates human agency.

Such a theory of association is integral to Hazlitt's model of the imaginative or empowered mind, as we find from the essays of *The Plain Speaker*, where it is a major focus. In the essay 'On Dr. Spurzheim's Theory', he writes, 'Indeed the capacity of association, possessed in a greater or less degree, seems to be the great discriminating feature between man and man' (xii. 146). The associative weight of an object transforms it into an 'expressive symbol' ('The New School of Reform'; xii. 194), attesting to the constitution of that object by the mind, and confirming that our apprehension can and does move beyond the sensory or merely mechanical. As the product rather than source of the imagination's working, association affirms the reality of the intellectual over the bodily perception. It is this intellectual or imaginative apprehension of things that gives us their just value ('On Egotism; xii. 161). Corroborating Wordsworth's famous line

---

[29] Hartley, *Observations*, i. 416–17, 503.   [30] Priestley, *Disquisitions*, 356.

from 'Tintern Abbey' ('We see into the life of things'), Hazlitt writes, 'there is an inner sense, a deeper intuition into nature that is never unfolded by merely mechanical objects, and which . . . [is] called out by a new soul being suddenly infused into an inanimate substance' ('On a Portrait of an English Lady, by Vandyke', *The Plain Speaker*; xii. 290).

The notion of an inward eye or 'new soul' which achieves the condition of unity between mind and nature recurs frequently in *The Plain Speaker* to mark the difference between imaginative intuition and mechanical observation. According to the essay 'On Novelty and Familiarity', 'the indifferent observation of the outward signs' does not 'attain to the truth of nature, without the inward sympathy to impel us forward' (xii. 297). Again, the French display a 'perverse fidelity of detail', so that 'that which is literally true, is naturally false' ('Madame Pasta and Mademoiselle Mars'; xii. 333), and similarly, 'Sir Walter's mind is full of information, but the *'o'erinforming power'* is not there' ('Sir Walter Scott, Racine and Shakespear'; xii. 340).

The 'o'erinforming power' is the basis of 'relation' which, with Hazlitt, always refers to the mind's innate formative capacity; its tendency to organize into a whole what would otherwise be diverse disconnected physical impressions left upon it:

I never could make much of the subject of real relations in nature. . . . The forms of things in nature are manifold; they only become one by being united in the same common principle of thought. The relations of the things themselves as they exist separately and by themselves must therefore be very different from their relations as perceived by the mind where they have an immediate communication with each other. (*Some Remarks on the Systems of Hartley and Helvetius*; i. 71–2)[31]

Not only the organization of objects in relation to each other, but even the organization into a coherent structure of the constituent parts of each object in itself belongs to the mind, by which alone it surmounts the 'infinite divisibility of matter' ('On Tooke's "Diversions of Purley"', *Lectures on English Philosophy*; ii. 282):

---

[31] Schneider cites this passage as 'the nearest Hazlitt ever comes to an acceptance of Berkeleyan idealism' (Schneider, *Aesthetics*, 19). But the notion that the structure of an object is dependent on the act of perception underlies the whole concept of 'relation' that is so recurrent in Hazlitt's thought. In Hazlitt's understanding of 'relation', we do indeed see the influence of Berkeley; this is especially in evidence in his view of artistic creation as the truest embodiment of imaginative 'relation'.

Without the cementing power of the mind, all our ideas would be necessarily decomposed and crumbled down into their original elements and flexional parts. . . . *The mind alone is formative*, to borrow the expression of a celebrated German writer, or it is that alone . . . that constructs the idea of the whole. Ideas are the offspring of the understanding, not of the senses. In other words, it is the understanding alone that perceives relation, but every object is made up of a bundle of relations. ('On Tooke's "Diversions of Purley"'; ii. 280)

'Relation' defined as the mind's 'cementing power' projecting itself into the diversity of natural existence so as to elicit an ordered unity from that diversity amounts after all to a kind of internalization, and although Hazlitt never goes far in the direction of pure subjectivity, the notion is fundamental to his critical judgement, that 'sympathy' with the external world is manifested not in objectively realistic descriptions or in a factual accuracy of observation, but in the individual's capacity to internalize Nature, to see it not 'with our eyes, but with our understandings and our hearts'. In the later essay on the 'Outlines of Taste', this notion informs his identification of 'genius' in the rendering of impressions internalized in this way and 'taste' as the sensibility to that rendering:

We do not see nature with our eyes, but with our understandings and our hearts. To suppose that we see the whole of any object, merely by looking at it, is a vulgar error: we fancy that we do, because we are, of course, conscious of no more than we see in it, but this circle of our knowledge enlarges with further acquaintance and study, and we then perceive that what we perhaps barely distinguished in the gross, or regarded as a dull blank, is full of beauty, meaning, and curious details. He sees most of nature who understands its language best, or connects one thing with the greatest number of other things. (*Miscellaneous Writings*; xx. 388)

As in the passage cited previously from 'The Indian Jugglers' (viii. 82–3), here too the interpretative imagination reads Nature, enabling it thereby to approximate to language, by means of an associative power that allows it unendingly to accrue meaning. We can recognize the allusion to Locke's *tabula rasa* in the phrase 'dull blank'; adroitly reversing Locke's epistemology, Hazlitt makes Nature the blank that gains meaning from the mind. The formative mind brings about a relation with Nature that is lacking in Locke's more uncompromising view of the dualism. Hazlitt offers in place of the pessimistic dichotomy a confident assertion of the value of human perception. There 'is a power in true poetry', he writes in the essay on Scott in *The Spirit of the Age*, 'that penetrates the inert, scattered, incoherent materials presented to it, and by a force and inspiration of its own, melts and moulds them into sublimity and beauty' (xi. 59).

The realization through the associative process of the imagination of a sympathetic relation between the imagining self and an objective material reality, compels some of Hazlitt's warmest admiration for writers ranging across the chronological span of the *Lectures on the English Poets*. In Chaucer, for instance, 'There is a meaning in what he sees; and it is this which catches his eye by sympathy... Inanimate objects are thus made to have a fellow-feeling in the interest of the story; and render back the sentiment of the speaker's mind' ('On Chaucer and Spenser'; v. 22–7). The associated chain of images testifies to the effectiveness of the authorial presence or imaginative power as a constructive principle, and it is precisely this effect that Hazlitt discerns in the writings also of Thomson: 'He puts his heart into his subject, writes as he feels, and humanises whatever he touches. He makes all his descriptions teem with life and vivifying soul' ('On Thomson and Cowper'; v. 87). The investing of nature with meaning by infusing it with 'life and vivifying soul' marks the highest species of composition, the poetry of nature, according to Hazlitt's account in the essay 'On Dryden and Pope':

The poet of nature is one who, from the elements of beauty, of power, and of passion in his own breast, sympathises with whatever is beautiful, and grand, and impassioned in nature, in its simple majesty, in its immediate appeal to the senses, to the thoughts and hearts of all men; so that the poet of nature, by the truth, and depth, and harmony of his mind, may be said to hold communion with the very soul of nature; to be identified with and to foreknow and to record the feelings of all men at all times and places, as they are liable to the same impressions; and to exert the same power over the minds of his readers, that nature does. He sees things in their eternal beauty, for he sees them as they are; he feels them in their universal interest, for he feels them as they affect the first principles of his and our common nature. Such was Homer, such was Shakespeare, whose works will last as long as nature, because they are a copy of the indestructible forms and everlasting impulses of nature, welling out from the bosom as from a perennial spring, or stamped upon the senses by the hand of their maker. The power of the imagination in them, is the representative power of all nature. It has its centre in the human soul, and makes the circuit of the universe. (v. 69–70)

The movement in the passage is outward from poet to nature, its ruling trope being the circle described in the last line as centred in the human soul and radiating from it to encompass the universe. The sympathetic (associative) relation enables an identity or 'communion' of the human soul and the soul of nature, where the eucharistic resonance of the term is far from irrelevant to an understanding of the process it describes. Further, by perceiving nature in terms of relation, the poet, who has the 'representative power of all nature', bestows upon it ideal form: 'things in their eternal beauty'. The very essence of nature ('things . . . as they are') is understood through the poet's perception.

Hazlitt's vision of the human soul as granting meaning to nature may be compared to the 'ensouling of observation by meditation' in Coleridge's description of imaginative process.[32] But where Hazlitt never leaves the sphere of individuality, Coleridge is always looking towards a general 'Truth' that is beyond the individual: 'Meditation, and Observation as its vehicle—chiefly used to bring enough external individualities to balance the internal *character*—and the general Truths;' 'S. shaped his characters out of the Nature within—but we cannot so safely say, out of *his own* Nature, as an *individual person*;' 'Meditation looks at every character with interest, only as it contains something generally true, and such as might be expressed in a philosophical problem.'[33]

For Hazlitt, the individual is at once the origin and the scope of imaginative truth; at the same time, 'relation' sets up a symbiotic process that precludes the condition of pure subjectivity. It describes not only the imaginative life given to nature by the artist's perception, but also and simultaneously the validation of that perception as continuous with the natural order of things. The full significance of 'relation' is perfectly encapsulated in his epigrams for Hogarth and Coleridge. Of Hogarth he writes, 'His mind had feet and hands, but not wings to fly with' ('On the Works of Hogarth: On the Grand and Familiar Style of Painting', *Lectures on the English Comic Writers*; vi. 146). The reverse is

---

[32] Coleridge, *On Literature*, i. 512.   [33] Ibid., ii. 115, 148, 480.

true of Coleridge, 'His genius has angel's wings, but neither hands nor feet' ('Mr Coleridge's Lay Sermon', *Political Essays*; vii. 117). In Coleridge, the ideal or imaginative is developed so far that it becomes dissociated from nature; in Hogarth, the natural is so exactly represented that it does not allow a passage into the mind: both sever relation, but at opposite poles.

'He is the greatest artist, not who leaves the materials of nature behind him, but who carries them with him into the world of invention' ('On the Ideal', *Art and Dramatic Criticism*; xviii. 77).[34] Hence Hazlitt's criticism of Shelley: 'Poetry, we grant, creates a world of its own; but it creates it out of existing materials. Mr. Shelley is the maker of his own poetry—out of nothing' ('Shelley's Posthumous Poems', *Contributions to the Edinburgh Review*; xvi. 265). To Hazlitt, art is the embodiment of a relation between mind and nature, so that 'each image in art should have a *tally* or corresponding prototype in some object in nature' ('On the Elgin Marbles', *Art and Dramatic Criticism*; xviii. 151). Even while he insists that the mind constitutes its own objects, i.e. that it reacts upon and remoulds every impression brought to it by the senses, he is equally emphatic in affirming that its freedom from subjugation to sense impressions does not drive it into the solipsistic trap: 'By nature, we mean actually existing nature, or some one object to be found *in rerum naturâ*, not an idea of nature existing solely in the mind' (xviii. 150). It is that 'solely' that Hazlitt denies; in the *Remarks on the Systems of Hartley and Helvetius*, he declares that it would make 'the whole structure of language' a 'continued absurdity' to suppose that 'Whatever can be made the object of our thoughts must be a part of ourselves' (i. 89). The 'idea of another person' does not become 'the idea of myself because it is I who perceive it' (i. 89). This is not to deny that the mind is the origin of ideas, but it does deny that all the ideas of the mind are reducible to a narrow selfhood.

Released from physiological manipulation by the objects of the external world, the mind nonetheless establishes meaningful relation with that which is outside it. The symbiotic tie between mind and nature is integral to Hazlitt's associationism in *The*

---

[34] As Eagleton observes, Hazlitt's ideal 'is a literature at once responsive to and transformative of its subject-matter, rooted in the very conditions it imaginatively transcends'—Terry Eagleton, 'William Hazlitt: An Empiricist Radical', *New Blackfriars Review* (1973), 111.

Plain Speaker, where sympathetic association brings about an 'affinity between the imitation and the thing imitated' ('On a Portrait of an English Lady, by Vandyke'; xii. 289). In the essay 'On Application to Study', he writes, 'The closer we examine it [nature], the more it refines upon us; it expands as we enlarge and shift our view; it 'grows with our growth, and strengthens with our strength' (xii. 60). Hazlitt captures here the circularity of the symbiotic relation, where nature grows with the growth of the mind, whose growth is generated from its involvement in nature. Thus when he says of the pictures of Rembrandt that 'the thoughts seem identical with the objects' ('Whether Genius is Conscious of its Powers?'; xii. 120), the identity asserts not only the mind's transformation into nature (thought to objects), but also nature's internalization within the mind (objects to thoughts).

From this, the term 'natural' for Hazlitt describes less an independent and external quality inhering in nature, than the inwardly produced property or feeling with which it is invested by the mind, whence the equivalence between the natural and the imaginative: 'Poetry acts by sympathy with nature, that is, with the natural impulses, customs, and imaginations of men' ('On People of Sense'; xii. 245). This equivalence must be understood to underlie observations such as 'There is neither truth nor beauty without nature' ('On Novelty and Familiarity'; xii. 298); it is implied also in Hazlitt's perpetual indictment of the French. French literature looks neither 'at home into itself' nor 'abroad into nature', where Hazlitt is clearly suggesting that the one vision 'into itself' is exchangeable with or equivalent to, the other, 'into nature'; the 'genuine English intellect', by contrast, 'constantly combine[s] truth of external observation with strength of internal meaning' ('On Old English Writers and Speakers'; xii. 312, 322–33). Hazlitt appears to be echoing here Francis Bacon's phraseology in the *Advancement of Learning*, in a passage that he quotes in the *Lectures on the Age of Elizabeth*, 'The corrupter sort of mere politiques, that . . . never look abroad into universality, do refer all things to themselves' ('Character of Lord Bacon's Works'; vi. 329). The altered sense of Hazlitt's adaptation is suggestive; where Bacon condemns the referring of 'all things to themselves' in favour of looking 'abroad into universality', Hazlitt treats the two perceptions as equivalent: looking into oneself *is* looking into 'nature' or universality. In 'Madame Pasta and Mademoiselle Mars', he observes of the French character that

> There seems no *natural* correspondence between objects and feelings, between things and words. . . . It is this theatrical or artificial nature with which we cannot and will not sympathise, because it circumscribes the truth of things and the capacities of the human mind within the petty round of vanity, indifference, and physical sensations, stunts the growth of the imagination, effaces the broad light of nature . . . (xii. 327–8)

The implications that may be drawn from the syntax of these sentences are significant: the equivalence between the 'truth of things' and 'the capacities of the human mind', the link between the 'growth of the imagination' and 'the broad light of nature'; the suggestion, furthermore, that where correspondence exists between objects and feelings, there exists also a correspondence between things and words.

> Natural objects convey given or intelligible ideas which art embodies and represents, or it represents nothing, is a mere chimera or bubble; and, farther, natural objects or events cause certain feelings, in expressing which art manifests its power, and genius its prerogative. . . . Genius is the power which equalises or identifies the imagination with the reality or with nature. ('Madame Pasta and Mademoiselle Mars'; xii. 334)

The power of art and the prerogative of genius consists in the ability to achieve the relation between mind and nature in the expression of those feelings or ideas that are stimulated by natural objects. In the essay 'On People of Sense', the charm of poetry resides in exactly the union of fancy with reality, whereby it finds 'a tally in the human breast', i.e. of the reader (xii. 246). The sympathetic link with external nature generated from the individual self is made, by extension, to include the reader, so that poet, nature, and reader are held together in a complex of relations. The unifying relation between poet and nature results in the rendering of nature in its ideal form of universal applicability, thereby making the reader susceptible to its impression; the ability to elicit the universally applicable ideal from his individual perception of nature brings the poet into sympathy with all mankind. In the *Lectures on the English Poets*, Thomson 'does not go into the *minutiae* of a landscape, but describes the vivid impression which the whole makes upon his own imagination; and thus transfers the same unbroken, unimpaired impression to the imagination of his readers' ('On Thomson and Cowper'; v. 87). Again, Collins 'had that true *vivida vis*, that genuine inspiration, which alone can give birth to the highest efforts of poetry. He leaves stings in the minds of his readers, certain traces of thought and feelings which never wear out, because nature had left them in his own mind' ('On Swift, Young, Gray, Collins, etc.'; v. 115).

'What a Proteus is the human mind!', Hazlitt exclaims in the essay 'On Personal Identity', 'All that we know, think of, or can admire, in a manner becomes ourselves' (*Uncollected Essays*; xvii. 274). The unusual application of the term 'Proteus' to the mind's metamorphosis of objects into itself, rather than to the metamorphosis of itself into external objects, is suggestive. In Hazlitt's view, the poet 'is one and the same intellectual essence, looking out from its own nature on all the different impressions it receives, and to a certain degree moulding them into itself' ('On Dr. Spurzheim's Theory', *The Plain Speaker*; xii. 151). The imagination, from this, is not a faculty which, devoid of selfhood, enters into the nature of that other to it, but rather one which, being the attribute of a strong selfhood, brings the forms of external nature within itself. It is usual to distinguish the two modes of the imagination as 'sympathetic' and 'associative' respectively.[35] But even when Hazlitt is talking of imaginative 'sympathy', the process that he describes is invariably associative, taking the form of the mind's carrying itself into, rather than losing itself in, a character external to it:

> Imagination is, more properly, the power of carrying on a given feeling into other situations, which must be done best according to the hold which the feeling itself has taken of the mind. In new and unknown combinations, the impression must act by sympathy, and not by rule; but there can be no sympathy, where there is no passion, no original interest. . . . in general the strength and consistency of the imagination

---

[35] J. D. O'Hara, for instance, makes the distinction when he distinguishes between two types of sympathetic identification in Hazlitt: with objects, by the associative operation that produces a subjective response to that object, and with human nature, by a process which, for O'Hara, may more properly be called 'sympathy': an identification with the feelings of others *from within* the other: 'The sympathetic imagination, as he understood the idea, ordinarily exercises itself only when the artist and audience turn from nature to human nature' ('Hazlitt and the Functions of the Imagination', 554). Prior to O'Hara, Schneider uses the terms 'projectivism' and 'assimilation', and makes the former the characteristic of Hazlitt's view of the imagination (Schneider, *Aesthetics*, 39–40).

will be in proportion to the strength and depth of feeling; and it is rarely that a man even of lofty genius will be able to do more than carry on his own feelings and character, or some prominent and ruling passion, into fictitious and uncommon situations. ('On Genius and Common Sense', *Table-Talk*; viii. 42)

By this account, sympathy is not so much the tendency of genius to enter into other feelings and situations, but the tendency to carry 'his own feelings and character', into other situations, hence, 'there can be no sympathy, where there is no passion.' Far from making a distinction between 'sympathy' and 'association', Hazlitt clearly describes sympathy as brought about by the associative process. We have seen that the associative imagination projects itself into the external world in order to bring about 'relation'; this relation is the origin of sympathy both with natural objects and, as in the extract above, with human character. If sympathy is always the product of the associative process of the imagination, then contrary to the usual classification, 'sympathy' and 'association' cannot be treated as two distinct categories in Hazlitt's thought; they are one.

Association and Necessity

The distinguishing characteristic of Hazlitt's associative imagination is the spontaneity of its expression:

men of the greatest genius produce their works with . . . facility (and, as it were, spontaneously) . . . It is, indeed, one characteristic mark of the highest class of excellence to appear to come naturally from the mind of the author, without consciousness or effort. The work seems like inspiration—to be the gift of some God or of the Muse. . . . It is almost as natural for those who are endowed with the highest powers of the human mind to produce the miracles of art, as for other men to breathe or move. ('On Posthumous Fame', *The Round Table*; iv. 24)

Again, 'the dialogues in Shakspeare are carried on without any consciousness of what is to follow, without any appearance of preparation or premeditation' ('On Shakspeare and Milton', *Lectures on the English Poets*; v. 50). The lack of preparation or premeditation is the test of true poetry, as the evidence of labour indicates the false. In the *Lectures on the Age of Elizabeth*, for instance, Heywood, who 'writes on carelessly, as it happens,' is praised for the 'unembarrassed facility of his style' ('On Lyly, Marlow, Heywood, etc.'; vi. 214), while the drawback of Ford's work is an 'artificial elaborateness . . . quite distinct from the exuberance and unstudied force which characterised his immediate predecessors' ('On Beaumont and Fletcher, etc.'; vi. 270). The laboriousness of Ben Jonson's writing is vividly captured in the observation that 'there is a specific gravity in the author's pen, that sinks him to the bottom of his subject' ('On Miscellaneous Poems, etc.'; vi. 304). Hazlitt reiterates here his sense of the ponderous weight (and hence imaginative lack) in Jonson's work that he has earlier remarked in the *Lectures on the English Comic Writers*: 'The sense of reality exercised a despotic sway over his mind, and equally weighed down and clogged his perception of the beautiful or the ridiculous. . . . There was nothing spontaneous, no impulse or ease about his genius: it was all forced, up-hill work' ('On Shakspeare and Ben Jonson'; vi. 41). This may be contrasted with say, his comments on Vanbrugh: 'he works out scene after scene, on the spur of the occasion, and from the immediate hold they take of his imagination at the moment, without any previous bias or ultimate purpose . . . He has more nature than art: what he does best, he does because he cannot help it' ('On Wycherly, Congreve, Vanbrugh, and Farquhar'; vi. 79).

Spontaneity, then, is a gauge of the imaginative; it appertains to the 'involuntary movement' of the imagination which, according to the essay 'On Poetry in General', distinguishes the poetic from the ordinary language constituted of 'voluntary signs' (v. 12). The spontaneous working of the imagination is not confined to poetry alone; in *The Plain Speaker*, Hazlitt expresses his approval of the spontaneity in Northcote's conversations ('On the Old Age of Artists'; xii. 91), of the 'involuntary, silent impulse' in Rembrandt and Caravaggio ('Whether Genius is Conscious of Its Powers?'; xii. 119), and of the spontaneity of Burke ('On the Difference between Writing and Speaking'; xii. 273). Its involuntary character marks the unhindered operation of the associative process, which is always taken to express a profound truth; this is the non-literal truth of the poetic imagination.

Such a truth is akin, if not identical, to the truth manifested involuntarily in dreams and the subconscious. In his account of dreaming, Hazlitt suggests the identification, familiar in Romantic thought, of dreaming with the process of the poetic imagination. In dreams, 'our imagination wanders at will,' and we are solely under its direction. 'There is, . . . a sort of profundity in sleep; and it may be usefully consulted as an oracle in this way. It may be said, that the voluntary power is suspended, and things come upon us as unexpected revelations, which we keep out of our thoughts at other times' ('On Dreams', *The Plain Speaker*; xii. 23).

Hazlitt's emphasis on the involuntariness of poetic composition bespeaks a kind of compulsion, a lack of volition that might appear to go against the grain of his doctrine of empowerment, trapping it within exactly the necessarian dogma into which the mechanical theory of association falls. The reverse, however, is the case.

In order to reconcile Hazlitt's metaphysical belief in agency with the notion of the involuntary or unarbitrary character of poetry, I will turn to Friedrich Schiller's *On the Naive and Sentimental in Literature* (1795). So far, I have focused on the anti-empirical, anti-materialist perspective in Hazlitt's view of the British philosophers with whom he was most familiar: Tooke, Burke, Hartley, Locke. The anti-empirical stance suggests, perforce, a strongly idealistic tendency in Hazlitt, highlighting his common ground with the German idealist philosophers with whom we are more accustomed to associate Coleridge. What I am suggesting by placing Hazlitt side by side with Schiller is not so much influence (as in Coleridge's relation with German thought) as parallelism, a correspondence of ideas so marked that each may usefully be brought to bear upon the other. Hazlitt's familiarity is more with Schiller's literary compositions than his theory, nevertheless, that theory; where it converges with Hazlitt's own, grants us some important insights that are independent of any claims of direct influence.

Towards the opening of the essay *On the Naive and Sentimental in Literature*, Schiller writes, 'But only . . . when the will freely follows the law of necessity and when reason enforces its rules in spite of all the flux of the imagination, then the divine or the ideal emerges. . . . the genius, with one single happy brush-stroke, gives his idea an eternally fixed, firm and yet quite free outline.'[36] Thus, 'the language [of genius] leaps from the idea as through an inner

---

[36] Schiller, *Naive and Sentimental*, 22–30.

The Secret Soul of Harmony

necessity and is so much at one with it, that even underneath the corporeal covering the spirit stands revealed.'[37] Schiller's postulate, that the combination of fixity and freedom in the language of genius is the enabling condition for the identification of word with thing, is relevant to our understanding of the importance to Hazlitt of the involuntary character of poetry. When language, which is directed by volition, by virtue of that choice appears freely to follow a law of inner necessity, then it becomes poetry, in which expression approximates to the nature of the thing expressed. The preposition in '*as* through an inner necessity' is vital: what Schiller is claiming is not a compulsion (which would imply mechanism), but a free choice that is so right as to *appear* compelled or inevitable.

Schiller's thought here is recognizably Kantian and may be compared to Kant's discussion of the moral imperative in relation to a perfectly rational being. In a perfectly rational being, the antinomy of freedom and necessity, and hence the whole concept of an imperative, vanishes. The action of such a being is necessary, but not necessitated:

A perfectly good will would thus stand quite as much under objective laws (laws of the good), but it could not on this account be conceived as *necessitated* to act in conformity with law, since of itself, in accordance with its subjective constitution, it can be determined only by the concept of the good. Hence for the *divine* will, and in general for a *holy* will, there are no imperatives: '*I ought*' is here out of place, because '*I will*' is already of itself necessarily in harmony with the law.[38]

It is exactly this notion of a 'holy will', in which the distinction between freedom and necessity is elided, that we find in Schiller's account of genius.

For Schiller, 'inner necessity' refers to 'the eternal unity within themselves' that the forms of nature possess, and towards which all human nature strives; that striving is generated from the will and marks the moral tendency of the human being.[39] In Hazlitt's case, the appearance of an inner necessity which authenticates inspired language springs from the imagination, the manifestation, in its

---

[37] Ibid. 30.
[38] Immanuel Kant, *Groundwork of the Metaphysic of Morals*, trans. H. J. Paton, 3rd edn (1956; repr. New York: Harper 38; Row, 1964), ch. ii, p. 81.
[39] Schiller, *Naive and Sentimental*, 22.

highest form, of the mind's agency and moral potential; by it also, the unity between mind and nature, or object, is realized. The Aristotelian condition for unity in tragedy, that of probable or necessary sequence, is transmuted in both so as to emphasize will in the process of poetry. The principle of unity becomes inseparable here from the celebration of human agency.

The oneness posited by Schiller, between the language of genius and the idea that it expresses, begins to raise the question of constitutiveness. To what extent does the word actually partake of the reality that it renders intelligible? In other words, to what extent does language participate in the mind's constitution of its objects? Such questions, however, are not focal to Hazlitt, who is generally much less concerned than Coleridge with the constitutive character of language as the expression of reality. Verbal constructions such as 'the music of language, answering to the music of the mind' ('On Poetry in General'; v. 12) or, 'words . . . answer . . . to the truth of things' ('Sir Walter Scott, Racine, and Shakespear', *The Plain Speaker*; xii. 337), seem to posit not an identity of word and thought, but a correspondence—language answering mind, words answering things—which solves the problem of arbitrariness without treading the depths of Coleridge's theory of symbols. In Hazlitt's claims for poetic language, sign so aptly expresses signification as to gain universal applicability, hence suggesting necessity. Words occur to the author 'only as *tallies* to certain modifications of feeling. . . . Certain words are in his mind indissolubly wedded to certain things' ('On the Difference between Writing and Speaking', *The Plain Speaker*; xii. 277–8). The appearance of necessity is the mark which indicates that such language manifests the spirit with which it is instinct.

As the language which expresses inspiration, and which is explicitly identified with it, poetry 'is the perfect coincidence of the image and the words with the feeling we have, and of which we cannot get rid in any other way, that gives an instant "satisfaction to the thought"' ('On Poetry in General'; v. 7). Hazlitt is not offering a merely abstract definition here; in his account of Shakespeare's language in the essay 'On Application to Study', he provides us with concrete examples of the match between word and feeling in poetry:

there is scarcely a word in any of his more striking passages that can be altered for the better. If any person, for instance, is trying to recollect a favourite line, and cannot hit upon some particular expression, it is in vain to think of substituting any other so good. That in the original text is not merely the best, but it seems the only right one. I will stop to illustrate this point a little. I was at a loss the other day for the line in Henry v.

> 'Nice customs curtesy to great kings.'

I could not recollect the word *nice*: I tried a number of others, such as *old*, *grave*, &c.—they would none of them do, but seemed all heavy, lumbering, or from the purpose: the word *nice*, on the contrary, appeared to drop into its place, and be ready to assist in paying the reverence required. (*The Plain Speaker*; xii. 58)

Another example is in the lines from *Love's Labour's Lost* (v. ii. 861–2): 'A jest's prosperity lies in the ear | Of him that hears it'. 'I thought, in quoting from memory, of "A jest's *success*," "A jest's *renown*," &c. I then turned to the volume, and there found the very word that of all others expressed the idea' (xii. 58).

It cannot pass without notice that such observations once again confirm Hazlitt's closeness to Coleridge, this time in practical criticism rather than theoretical formulation. In his analysis of *The Tempest*, Coleridge similarly remarks the effect of single words in Shakespeare:

The power of poetry is, by a single word perhaps, to instil that energy into the mind, which compels the imagination to produce the picture. Prospero tells Miranda,

> 'One midnight,
> Fated to the purpose, did Antonio open
> The gates of Milan; and i' the dead of darkness,
> The ministers for the purpose hurried thence
> Me, and thy crying self.'

Here, by introducing a single happy epithet, 'crying,' in the last line, a complete picture is presented to the mind, and in the production of such pictures the power of genius consists.[40]

Such instances exemplify, for Hazlitt, if not the identity, at least the perfect correspondence of word with thought or feeling in poetry, where the arbitrariness of language, arising from the

---

[40] From Collier's text in *Seven Lectures on Shakespeare and Milton* (1856) (Coleridge, *On Literature*, ii. 523).

indeterminate nature of the connection between signifier and signified, is removed:

> there is nothing either musical or natural in the ordinary construction of language. It is a thing altogether arbitrary and conventional. Neither in the sounds themselves, which are the voluntary signs of certain ideas, nor in their grammatical arrangements in common speech, is there any principle of natural imitation, or correspondence to the individual ideas, or to the tone of feeling with which they are conveyed to others. . . . But poetry makes these odds all even. It is the music of language, answering to the music of the mind, untying as it were 'the secret soul of harmony.' (v. 12)

The harmony of poetry arises from the unarbitrary fittedness of word to thought; it is brought about by the purity and intensity of the inspired mind, and is independent of 'the regular mechanism of verse', factors such as rhyme or diction: 'every one who declaims warmly, or grows intent upon a subject, rises into a sort of blank verse or measured prose' (v. 13).[41] Adapting Pope's famous aphorism in *An Essay on Criticism*, Hazlitt writes, 'It is to supply the inherent defect of harmony in the customary mechanism of language, to make the sound an echo to the sense, when the sense becomes a sort of echo to itself' ('On Poetry in General'; v. 12). In Pope's dictum, 'The *Sound* must seem an *Eccho* to the *Sense*',[42] the verb 'seem' is telling; Pope prescribes no more than the mere appearance of similitude, and so stops far short of Hazlitt's claim for poetic language, where the sound *is* an echo to the sense. Further, by asserting an actual or absolute link between sign and signification in poetry, Hazlitt is engaging, not only with Pope, but also and more combatively, with Samuel Johnson, especially in his writings on 'representative metre'.

Opposite to Hazlitt, Johnson narrows the scope of Pope's maxim for metre in his own analysis of the metrical effect of poetry. He allows the maxim only a very limited application, for

---

[41] Jeffrey Robinson asserts that 'the "passion" of Hazlitt's writing as well as of the object of his criticism stands for him in a mutually exclusive relationship to harmony, the latter being a mask for what is really the repression of the former.'—J. C. Robinson, 'Romanticism through the Mind of Hazlitt', *Review* vii (1985), 70. In fact the reverse is the case: for Hazlitt, the 'harmony' of imaginative creation, far from being excluded, is brought about by intensity of passion.

[42] Alexander Pope, *An Essay on Criticism*, l. 365, in *Pastoral Poetry and An Essay on Criticism*, ed. E. Audra and A. Williams, vol. i of *The Twickenham Edition of the Poems of Alexander Pope* (London: Methuen, 1961), 281.

instance, in the case of onomatopoeia: 'Every language has many words formed in imitation of the noises which they signify. . . . in English to *growl*, to *buzz*, to *hiss*, and to *jarr*. Words of this kind give to a verse the proper similitude of sound'.[43] Conceding such exceptions, however, Johnson generally takes the verb 'seem' in Pope's criterion for poetry even further, arguing that the correspondence of sound and sense is usually 'chimerical'.[44] In 'such resemblances', he writes in his life of Pope, 'the mind often governs the ear,' hence, 'Beauties of this kind are commonly fancied; and when real are technical and nugatory.'[45]

Johnson's analysis is typically literal; the question of representative metre is for him a question of whether similitude may reasonably be established between two entities that share no grounds of comparison: 'The fancied resemblances, I fear, arise sometimes merely from the ambiguity of words; there is supposed to be some relation between a *soft* line and a *soft* couch, or between *hard* syllables and *hard* fortune.'[46] By contrast, Hazlitt adopts Pope's prescription for poetry on imaginative rather than literal grounds. The correspondence of sound to sense is intuitive and qualitative, rather than literal or quantitative, and this does not diminish its validity, but the reverse. That the mind governs the ear attests to the subordination of the senses to the imagination; for Hazlitt, this would not be a criticism, but the highest praise accorded to poetry. His perspective is the opposite of Johnson's. Where, throughout his discussion of 'representative metre', Johnson is at some pains to emphasize that the correspondence of sound and sense in poetry is often fortuitous, 'without design', 'without much labour of the writer', rather than the result of conscious artistry, in Hazlitt's view, it is exactly this involuntary character of poetic language that vouchsafes the evidence of genius.[47] His clause, 'when the sense becomes a sort of echo to itself', refers to the combination of meaning and feeling in poetry: the sense is an echo to itself, if the meaning of language is identical with the feeling that it expresses. To Hazlitt, intensity of feeling

---

[43] Samuel Johnson, *The Rambler*, ed. W. J. Bate and A. B. Strauss, no. 94, vols iii–v of *The Yale Edition of the Works of Samuel Johnson* (New Haven: Yale University Press, 1969), iv. 138.   [44] *The Rambler*, no. 94 (ibid. 136).
[45] Samuel Johnson, *Lives of the English Poets*, ed. G. B. Hill, 3 vols (Oxford: Clarendon Press, 1905), iii. 231, 232.   [46] Ibid. 231.
[47] *The Rambler*, nos. 92, 94 (Johnson, *Works*, iv. 125, 138).

brings about a perfect accord between itself and the language in which it is expressed. Under that condition of inherent unity, the correspondence of sound and sense is realized.

Unity of Design

In Berkeley's essay on vision, the invariable character of its signs makes Nature the ideal universal language of its Author and the key to his purpose. 'Upon the whole,' he asserts, 'I think we may fairly conclude that the proper objects of vision constitute an universal language of the Author of nature' and again, 'the voice of the Author of nature, which speaks to our eyes, is not liable to that misinterpretation and ambiguity that languages of human contrivance are unavoidably subject to.'[48] For Hazlitt, poetic language, possessed of the identical quality of invariability, similarly becomes the index of *its* author. The interpretative imagination turns nature to text, so that poetic language also comprises a 'volume of nature': the author's.

I have shown that the creative power in Hazlitt's theory is, like the Unitarian deity, one and indivisible; like the Unitarian system, too, the oneness of the creator is inseparable from the unity of his design. 'The slightest want of unity of impression', Hazlitt observes in the lecture 'On Wit and Humour', 'destroys the sublime' (*Lectures on the English Comic Writers*; vi. 23–4). In Guido's Virgin, for instance, 'there is a complete unity and concentration of expression, the whole is wrought up and moulded into one intense feeling;' the perfection of Titian's faces 'consists in the entire unity and coincidence of all the parts' ('On a Portrait of an English Lady, by Vandyke', *The Plain Speaker*; xii. 283, 287). Without leaning, as Coleridge does, on the notion of a transcendent Unity, Hazlitt's theory nonetheless posits a unity of imaginative design, generated from within.

In his analysis of Coleridge's *Biographia*, Paul Hamilton writes that 'the most famous, self-professed attempt in English literature to exhibit the relation of philosophy to poetry disintegrates.'[49] In Hazlitt, ever in Coleridge's shadow, we also find such an attempt,

---

[48] Sections 147, 152 (Berkeley, *Works*, i. 231, 233).
[49] Paul Hamilton, *Coleridge's Poetics* (Oxford: Basil Blackwell, 1983), 8.

The Secret Soul of Harmony

neither famous nor self-professed, but for all that more successful—successful precisely because Hazlitt remains untouched by what Hamilton identifies as Coleridge's fundamental dilemma: the conflict between his view of the human or self-conditioned origin of poetic truth and the unconditioned absolute basis of his religious belief.[50] In contrast to Coleridge, the integrity of Hazlitt's vision, of imaginative creation generated purely from within the self, remains complete.

Hazlitt's account of the origin of the unity of imaginative creation manifests a continuity between his philosophical interests and his aesthetic criteria. It may be derived from the *Essay on the Principles of Human Action*, which is an attack upon the philosophies of Locke and Hartley for their assumption of the mechanical operation of the human mind: its susceptibility to, and therefore moulding by, sensations imposed entirely *ab extra*—from without. In place of the mechanic philosophy, Hazlitt offers a system that allows, by postulating an innate intellectual principle, for the self-impelled function— *ab intra*—of the human mind. This principle, which alone provides the impulse to voluntary action, he identifies as the imagination. In other words, the exercise of the imagination is the manifestation of a transcendental mental activity. Consequently, composition that is brought about by such exercise, necessarily participates in the transcendental character, i.e. since it is the innate and indivisible power of the imagination that produces a work of art, that power imparts to the work an inwardly produced unity of design. The 'organic form', familiar from the Shakespeare criticism of Schlegel and Coleridge, may be recognized also in the unity of imaginative design in Hazlitt's critical theory.

For Hazlitt, given the metaphysical weight attached to the whole notion of innateness, a theory of the integral or inwardly generated unity of imaginative design must be inferred from the consistent and pervasive criticism of mechanism which defines

---

[50] It is owing to this conflict that 'frequently his description of the means by which he thinks we appropriate religious and spiritual certainties is a description of an experience which escapes from and lies beyond the power of language to symbolize', 'The immediate intuition of spiritual truths through religious symbols is irreconcilable with Coleridge's poetics' (ibid. 196, 200).

his philosophical and aesthetic theory.[51] Hazlitt's every reference to mechanism has, of course, a bearing on his great attack against Bentham's Utilitarianism and its consequences in the progressive mechanization of men. At the same time, this anti-Utilitarian position is itself consistently epistemological in its origin. In *The Plain Speaker*, the denial of mechanism by affirming an imaginative or purely intellectual dimension of being is integral to such a position. 'Besides my automatic existence, I have another, a sentimental one, which must be nourished', says the sentimentalist to the rationalist in 'The New School of Reform' (xii. 192). In the essay 'On People of Sense', Hazlitt reiterates, 'Man is not a machine; nor is he to be measured by mechanical rules' ('On People of Sense'; xii. 251). Since the starting-point of each of Hazlitt's refutations of mechanism is always the vision of an empowered mind, the attack on Utilitarianism must be treated as a particular corollary of the epistemological argument and not vice versa.

'Mechanism' is a quality against which we find Hazlitt embattled in every possible area. In his metaphysics, it characterizes the passive model of the mind which, being subjugated to sensation, is directed externally rather than from within. As applied to literature, it describes the servility of composition to set rules and preconceived systems, again, extraneous rather than inwardly generated criteria. In the former area, the opposition to mechanism constitutes the whole rationale of Hazlitt's philosophical theory; in the latter, it underlies and connects particular appraisals of diverse individual writers to some of his broadest critical generalizations. There may be extracted a number of instances from Hazlitt's practical criticism that fall in with the differentiation of the 'mechanic artist' from 'true genius' in the essay 'On Imitation' (*The Round Table*; iv. 76), or of 'mechanical excellence', acquired by rules and study, from 'genius' in the essay on 'The Indian Jugglers' (*Table-Talk*; viii. 82). Citing randomly, we have his indictment of Samuel Johnson: 'he could not quit his hold of the commonplace and mechanical,' 'He was . . . without

---

[51] Roy Park finds that 'Hazlitt's sparing use of an imagery of mechanism was almost entirely confined to his criticism of Bentham and Plato' (Park, *Hazlitt*, 3.). On the contrary, Hazlitt's use of the imagery of mechanism is by no means sparing, but extensive, pervading a variety of subjects in which neither the polemical anti-Utilitarian purpose nor the anti-Platonic stance is immediately evident or operative.

any particular fineness of organic sensibility' ('Preface' to *Characters of Shakespear's Plays*; iv. 175, 176), his dismissiveness of Joanna Baillie, whose characters are 'moral puppets' with no 'real passions of their own' ('On the Living Poets', *Lectures on the English Poets*; v. 148) and of Southey's Kehama, equally puppet-like, 'a loose sprawling figure, such as we see cut out of wood or paper, and pulled or jerked with wire or thread, to make sudden and surprising motions, without meaning, grace, or nature in them' ('On the Living Poets'; v. 164); also the polarization of Shakespeare against Ben Jonson, where Jonson is distinguished by 'his understanding rather than his imagination, by rule and method, not by sympathy, or intuitive perception' ('On Shakspeare and Ben Jonson', *Lectures on the English Comic Writers*; vi. 41) and the approbation of Montaigne, 'In criticising books he did not compare them with rules and systems, . . . There is an inexpressible frankness and sincerity, as well as power, in what he writes' ('On the Periodical Essayists', *Lectures on the English Comic Writers*; vi. 93).

It will be perceived that the attack upon the mechanical procedure in every case suggests a parallel theory of dynamic or integral formation which stems directly from a concept of a single informing presence within poetic creation: 'true genius', 'organic sensibility', 'real passions', 'meaning, grace, or nature', 'sympathy, or intuitive perception', 'sincerity, as well as power'. Such a presence eliminates mechanism, giving rise to forms based not upon superficial structural criteria, but upon the singleness of an internal power which infuses and organizes the forms which express it.

Perhaps the best example of the convergence of all the various aspects that comprise Hazlitt's criterion of unity—indivisibility, association, and oneness of design—is to be found in his description of Poussin's work in *Table-Talk*. Here, 'one feeling . . . pervades the painter's canvas, and we are thrown back upon the first integrity of things' ('On a Landscape of Nicholas Poussin'; viii. 169). In Poussin, we have a 'unity of character,' a 'conscious keeping, and, as it were, *internal* design' (viii. 169, 171). Nature is produced from within the mind of the artist, who 'works out her images according to the standard of his thoughts,' yet '*His* art is a second nature; not a different one' (viii. 169, 170). Poussin is 'of all painters, the most poetical,' and his pictures epitomize the poetic (associative) effect of the imagination: 'the first conception being given, all the rest seems to grow out of, and be assimilated to it, by the unfailing process of a studious imagination' (viii. 171, 169). His work is instinct with the presence of its creator, and so achieves the relation between mind and nature that transforms the external world into a language:

> Even inanimate and dumb things speak a language of their own. His snakes, the messengers of fate, are inspired with human intellect. His trees grow and expand their leaves in the air, glad of the rain, proud of the sun, awake to the winds of heaven. In his Plague of Athens, the very buildings seem stiff with horror. (viii. 171)

The criterion of unity governs Hazlitt's theory of imaginative creation. The indivisible imaginative power manifested in artistic creation grants to that creation an inwardly generated unity of design; this unity attests to the mind's original ability to create 'relation', therefore to perceive wholes. For Hazlitt, unity is always a function of the self-projecting attribute of the mind. It is Keats, on the other hand, whose theory exemplifies the ideal of intuitive absorption—sometimes rather indiscriminately categorized as 'Romantic'—into the essence or otherhood of objects, inanimate as well as living, external to the self.[52]

In Hazlitt's view of the imagination as a single and indivisible presence and in his development from this notion of a theory of association and imaginative unity, he at once incorporates and undermines his Unitarian background and the Coleridgean influence. Another and more straightforward indication of the Unitarian connection in Hazlitt's vision of imaginative power may be found in his comparison of the dissenting with the established religion in *Political Essays*. In the essay 'On the Clerical Character', the imposition *ab extra* of the 'artificial distinctions' of dress (vii. 243) and of 'external forms and ceremonies' by the established church, has been at the cost of 'all the inward acts of worship' (vii. 246). 'The form of religion has superseded the substance,' and the priest 'thinks more of external appearances

---

[52] See Walter Jackson Bate, 'The Sympathetic Imagination in Eighteenth Century English Criticism', *ELH* xii (1945), 144–64, in which the approach to the imagination as self-annihilating is described as characteristically 'romantic'; it is one among 'the more common romantic *dicta*' (ibid. 144), and Bullitt, 'Hazlitt and the Romantic Conception of the Imagination', pp. 343 ff.

than of his internal convictions' (vii. 246, 247). By contrast, the religion of the dissenter who 'is taught to appeal to his own bosom for the truth and sincerity of his opinions,' and who relies 'on the testimony of his own heart,' is generated *ab intra*; his single standard of reference is within ('On Court-Influence'; vii. 240). The first is mechanistic, the second imaginative and spiritual, and Hazlitt is thinking of his father when he writes, 'We have known instances of both. The one we would willingly forget; the others we hope never to forget, nor can we ever' (vii. 241).

3

The Mighty Intellect

The Self as Focus in Hazlitt's Theory

LINGUISTICS, poetics, and epistemology converge at a single point of reference in Hazlitt's theory: the empowered mind. Its formative ability is embodied in the very structure of language; it is the presence inherent within artistic creation and imparting to that creation an inwardly generated unity. The construct of the empowered mind is inseparable from the delineation of an imagining self as the paradigm for all human activity. Power is fundamental to selfhood, and as we unravel the concept of power at the centre of Hazlitt's thought, a model of the self, at once the origin and the product of power, is brought sharply into focus.

Hazlitt and Butler

The nature and process of selfhood in Hazlitt's metaphysics may usefully be clarified by examining the *Essay on the Principles of Human Action* in relation to one of the most important of its precursor texts. Joseph Butler's *Fifteen Sermons Preached at the Rolls Chapel* (1726) is a work which, like Hazlitt's, resists traditional philosophical categorizations, formulating its key concept, 'conscience', as an innate or a priori principle, but at the same time, appealing to experience and empirical observation to establish the validity of its claims for human nature. The main objective of the *Sermons*, as defined in the lengthy 'Preface' to its second edition is 'to state the notion of self-love and disinterestedness, in order to shew that benevolence is not more unfriendly to self-love, than any other particular affection whatever.'[1] This argument is

---

[1] Joseph Butler, 'Preface' to the *Fifteen Sermons preached at the Rolls Chapel*, section 35, in *Butler's Fifteen Sermons preached at the Rolls Chapel and A Dissertation of the Nature of Virtue*, ed. T. A. Roberts (London: Society for Promoting Christian Knowledge, 1970), 12.

conducted through the *Sermons* as a whole; apart from the Preface, it is most directly explicated in the first, second and third Sermons, 'Upon Human Nature', and in the eleventh and twelfth Sermons, 'Upon the Love of our Neighbour'.

Hazlitt's extensive knowledge of the British philosophers, and particularly the major philosophical figures of the eighteenth century, is itself sufficient to account for his interest in Butler; he claims to have had his attention drawn specifically to Butler's *Sermons* by Coleridge on the occasion of their meeting in 1798 ('My First Acquaintance with Poets'; xvii. 113). At this point, according to his account, he had already made his metaphysical discovery. 'I told Coleridge I had written a few remarks, and was sometimes foolish enough to believe that I had made a discovery on the same subject (the *Natural Disinterestedness of the Human Mind*)' (xvii. 113–14). However, the *Essay on the Principles of Human Action* was not published till 1805, by which time, as his own note indicates (i. 50n.), Hazlitt had certainly read the *Sermons*. Regardless, then, of the date of the conceptual origins of the *Essay*, the *Sermons* can be shown to have had a considerable influence on its argument as developed in the published version.

Hazlitt conducts his *Essay* almost exactly according to the terms of Butler's discussion, with 'self-love' and 'benevolence' as the focus of a new metaphysical analysis. His object is to disprove the thesis of incompatibility between self-love and benevolence in order to establish man's *natural* potential for altruistic behaviour; in his own words, 'to shew that the human mind is naturally disinterested, or that it is naturally interested in the welfare of others in the same way, and from the same direct motives, by which we are impelled to the pursuit of our own interest' (i. 1). For all his claims to a new 'metaphysical discovery' (*A Letter to William Gifford*; ix. 51), this clearly echoes Butler in both language and content: 'there are as real and the same kind of indications in human nature, that we were made for society and to do good to our fellow-creatures; as that we were intended to take care of our own life and health and private good: . . . There is a natural principle of *benevolence* in man'.[2]

Butler maintains that the nature of man is not all constituted by self-love, whose object is internal (because exercised upon itself),

---

[2] Sermon 1, 'Upon Human Nature', sections 5 and 6 (ibid. 19).

but contains also 'a variety of particular affections, passions, and appetites to particular external objects,' in other words affections which are outwardly directed towards some definite object.[3] Thus, the pursuit of honour, say, and the seeking of injury to another, are equally particular and external.[4] It is this part of man's nature that comprehends benevolence. Benevolence belongs to the external tendency of man, and is no less 'natural' than self-love, his internal tendency. There is and can be no *necessary* incompatibility between two tendencies which, though distinct, are equally part of man's nature, any more than there exists such *necessary* incompatibility between self-love and any other particular passion, or affection, or appetite whatsoever.[5] Incompatibility arises only when any single propensity, whether general or particular, is indulged to excess, and so violates the third, and highest principle of man's nature, conscience.[6]

Hazlitt's claim is also that benevolence or 'disinterestedness' is equally natural to man as self-love. He shows that the origins of self-love are identical to those of benevolence, in order to establish that if the first is 'natural', then perforce, the second must be so also. His argument, like Butler's, effects the redemption of selfhood from selfishness, by denying that all action is reducible to a single selfish impulse. In the *Essay*, Hazlitt declares that 'The reason why a child first distinctly wills or pursues his own good, is not because it is *his*, but because it is *good*' (i. 12) and in the precursor text, similarly, it is not because we love *ourselves* that we desire an object, but because we love that *object*, because we have an affection for that object in particular.[7] 'And if, because every particular affection is a man's own,' Butler writes, 'according to this way of speaking, no creature whatever can possibly act but merely from self-love, . . . But then this is not the language of mankind'.[8] In exactly this vein, although with considerably more heat, Hazlitt observes, continuing the argument of the *Essay* in the lecture 'On Self-Love', 'To call my motives or feelings selfish, because they are felt by myself, is an abuse of all language'

---

[3] Sermon 11, 'Upon the Love of our Neighbour', section 5, Butler, *Fifteen Sermons*, 100.   [4] 'Preface', section 35 (ibid. 12–13).
[5] Sermon 11, 'Upon the Love of our Neighbour', section 12 (ibid. 104–5).
[6] Sermon 2, 'Upon Human Nature', section 13 (ibid. 33).
[7] 'Preface', section 37 (ibid. 13).
[8] Sermon 11, 'Upon the Love of our Neighbour', section 7 (ibid. 100–1).

(*Lectures on English Philosophy*; ii. 227).[9] The metaphysical exposition of both philosophers hinges upon a close analysis and consequent redefinition of selfhood; as Hazlitt puts it, 'I endeavoured to define the nature and meaning of this word, self' (*A Letter to William Gifford*; ix. 52).

If the parallels between Hazlitt's *Essay* and the precursor text foreground a close attention to selfhood, their divergences are no less significant in this regard. In Butler's analysis, the chief distinction is between the 'internal' and 'external' objects of pursuit. Each man has a general desire for his own happiness, produced from his reflection upon himself; this is self-love, which alone occupies the 'internal' category.[10] Self-love is both inwardly directed and, because general and unparticularized in its character, abstract. All other passions, appetites, and affections are particular, directed towards specific objects, hence, away from the self; these are 'external'. The inwardness of self-interest separates it from every other object of volition, including sensory gratification, and Butler places such gratification (of 'appetites') along with that of 'passions' and 'affections' in the 'external' category of objects.[11] Being external, sensory gratification, equally as benevolence, must be distinguished from the internal self-interest. The separation of the inward intellectual process from sensory response is merely a subsidiary stage in Butler's argument, leading, by extension and analogy, to establishing the position of benevolence with respect to self-love, without other theoretical or polemical significance.

In Hazlitt's *Essay*, by contrast, voluntary action springs solely from the mind, never the senses, and the separation of mind and senses itself constitutes the metaphysical and polemical end towards which the *Essay* is directed: the refutation of the mechanistic model of the human mind and the concomitant release and redemption of the human self as agent. In the appended *Remarks on the Systems of Hartley and Helvetius*, Hazlitt uses Butler's

---

[9] Butler is also an influence upon Adam Smith's *Theory of Moral Sentiments*, which argues that sympathy cannot be regarded as a selfish principle simply because it brings the case home to oneself (VII. iii. 1. 4). Adam Smith, *The Theory of Moral Sentiments*, ed. D. D. Raphael and A. L. Macfie, vol. i of *The Glasgow Edition of the Works and Correspondence of Adam Smith* (Oxford: Clarendon Press, 1976), 317.

[10] Sermon 11, 'Upon the Love of our Neighbour', section 5 (Butler, *Fifteen Sermons*, 100).   [11] 'Preface', section 35 (ibid. 12–13).

proof of the distinction between self-interest and sensory gratification, that two propensities which are so frequently and demonstrably at odds with each other cannot be treated as identical (i. 84–6; Hazlitt acknowledges Butler in 84n. and 85n.). On Butler's showing, the immediate gratification of a sensual impulse may be actually detrimental to the interest of the self, so that self-interest must consist in something other than such gratification. 'Man may act according to that principle or inclination which for the present happens to be strongest, and yet act in a way disproportionate to, and violate his real proper nature.'[12] This comment is modified by Hazlitt, in the observation that although it is the strongest inclination that produces the impulse to action, such inclination is not always bent towards 'pleasure', hence such action cannot be resolved into a single mechanical tendency of the self (i. 85). Hazlitt draws out to the full the implications of the abstract or general character of self-apprehension and its detachment from immediate sensory response as posited by Butler, in order to assert the alterity of our sense of ourselves as well as of our neighbours: as the objects of volition, self and other are alike imaginary. Where Butler's categories of internal and external separate self-interest from all other objects of volition, Hazlitt's distinction is between sensory and imaginary and draws a dividing line, not at self-interest, but at sensory response. The imaginary comprehends all objects of volition including self-interest; the sensory is excluded from volition altogether.

Hazlitt's deviation from Butler in categorizing the objects of volition extends also to the analysis of its origins. Butler maintains the distinctness of the origins of self-love and benevolence, even while establishing their compatibility, in his assertion that if each is acted upon truly and according to the dictates of reflection or conscience, it will be found to be complementary to, and corroborative of, the other, as well as subordinate to a design constituted by nature and ordained by God.[13] Where he concludes that self-love, benevolence, and the innate reflective principle ('conscience') existing in all men are mutually compatible, though

---

[12] Sermon 2, 'Upon Human Nature', section 10, Butler, *Fifteen Sermons*, 31. Cf. also Sermon 11, 'Upon the Love of our Neighbour', section 18 (ibid. 108).

[13] Sermon 3, 'Upon Human Nature', sections 8 and 9 (ibid. 38–9).

distinct, Hazlitt's conclusion is that self-love and benevolence are precisely and to the same degree manifestations of an innate principle ('imagination') common to all men.[14]

In many respects, Hazlitt's perception of the identity of self-love, benevolence, and the innate intellectual principle works to the same purpose as Butler's theory of compatibility, confirming that 'self-love is one chief security of our right behaviour towards society.'[15] The *Essay* may be read as supporting the Christian viewpoint in which Butler's argument is grounded; in Hazlitt's case, the merging of self-love and benevolence in an identical and single principle would accord, in particular, with the language of Unitarianism.

However, that Butler's 'conscience' or the voice of God may be traced in Hazlitt's 'imagination' does not in fact indicate a simple parallelism. Rather, it confirms a displacement of the spiritual by the imaginative that effects, in Hazlitt's theorizing, a magnification of the self. By distinguishing between the origins of self-love, benevolence, and the innate reflective principle, Butler limits selfhood to denote strictly that area in which the object of action is literally, the self. By merging self-love, benevolence, and the innate reflective principle into a single imaginative faculty, Hazlitt expands selfhood to encompass all possible objects of action. The expansion of the self is the focus towards which the *Essay* directs its audience in order to create a new and enlarged awareness: of a natural potential for disinterestedness in ourselves. It is in establishing this potential that Hazlitt's claim to an original intellectual 'discovery' stands vindicated.

Hazlitt's transmutation of Butler's notion of conscience also displays his secularizing impulse in the celebration and magnification of the self. Butler defines conscience as an innate capacity of reflection in man, by which he becomes, in confirmation of the biblical truth, a law unto himself. 'There is a principle of reflection in men, by which they distinguish between, approve and disapprove their own actions. We are plainly constituted such sort of creatures as to reflect upon our own nature. The mind

---

[14] Kinnaird perceives this conclusion as reductive: 'Butler and Hume were content to argue that self-love and benevolence are consistent and correlative; and [Hazlitt attempts] to go further—to reduce both motives to the same mode of "sympathy"' (Kinnaird, *William Hazlitt*, 61).

[15] Sermon I, 'Upon Human Nature', section 6 (Butler, *Fifteen Sermons*, 20).

can take a view of what passes within itself'.[16] It is precisely this idea, that the mind has an innate reflective capacity, independent of external sensation, that is Hazlitt's chief weapon against Locke:

> the human mind is a thinking principle, . . . To perceive relations, if not to choose between good and evil, to prefer a greater good to a less, a lasting to a transient enjoyment belongs only to one mind, or spirit, the mind that is in man, which is the centre in which all his thoughts meet, and the master-spring by which all his actions are governed. (i. 69–73)

However, where Hazlitt's 'thinking principle . . . belongs only to one mind, . . . the mind that is in man,' Butler's conscience, as a law of our nature, is identified with the authority of God, and originates from God. The welding of moral philosophy and Christian theology in the notion of conscience effects a kind of transcendence of the self or at least, undermines the emphasis on an inly generated principle by locating its authority in the external origin, God, 'the Author of our nature'.[17] 'Conscience', then, has a necessary moral bent; moreover, it ought, but by no means always does direct action, being evident only in action that is virtuous. Hazlitt's 'thinking principle' on the other hand, is the source of all action, whatever its moral character. The stress here is not God, but the self or inward nature of man, and since the inner principle is entirely self-generated, it is dependent solely on the nature of the individual—the constant point of reference of Hazlitt's entire metaphysics.

Hazlitt and Coleridge: The Divergent Positions

Hazlitt's secularizing of Butler and the enlargement of selfhood effected thereby, recalls the nature of his divergence from Coleridge that began to emerge in the previous chapter. If, in the Coleridgean literary theory, language, text, or artistic creation externalizes, usually imperfectly, a meaning or spirit that is always deciphered as a whole, in Hazlitt's artistic theory and criticism this 'whole' always composes a self. More specifically, Coleridge's 'whole' tends towards the transcendent, lifting the individual to

---

[16] Sermon 1, 'Upon Human Nature', section 8, Butler, *Fifteen Sermons*, 21.
[17] Sermon 3, 'Upon Human Nature', section 5 (ibid. 37).

blend with the universal, while Hazlitt's is rather transcendental, constantly bringing the universal within the compass of the individual self.[18]

A comparison of Hazlitt's key notion of benevolence with the equivalent concept in Coleridge will serve more fully to elucidate their positions in this regard. In an article 'On the Slave Trade', published in the fourth issue of *The Watchman* (25 March 1796), Coleridge defines 'benevolence' in the following terms: '"Natural Sympathy made permanent by an acquired Conviction, that the Interests of each and of all are one and the same," or in fewer words, "Natural Sympathy made permanent by enlightened Selfishness."'[19] In an earlier (1794), less obviously political context, we have,

> 'Tis the sublime of man,
> Our noontide Majesty, to know ourselves
> Parts and proportions of one wondrous whole!
> This fraternises man, this constitutes
> Our charities and bearings. But 'tis God
> Diffused through all, that doth make all one whole;
> ('Religious Musings', ll. 126–31)[20]

The conjunction of the two extracts clarifies the manner in which the Unitarian concept of a single and divine principle of life inherent in all of creation ('God | Diffused through all') provides a continuity between Coleridge's religion, politics, and literary

---

[18] In his review of Herschel Baker's book on Hazlitt, Kinnaird provides an acutely penetrating statement of Hazlitt's position in relation to Coleridge: 'Hazlitt differs from all his contemporaries—or at least from Coleridge—in seeing the human dialectic not as primarily a dynamic of transcendence and intellectual progress, but as the binding force of all individuality. Even when his subject is not himself but, as it actually is most of the time, something general or objective, it nonetheless takes the form of a self'—John Kinnaird, 'The Forgotten Self', *Partisan Review* xxx, no. 2 (1963), 305. These observations contain an insight that is central to Hazlitt criticism, yet they have remained, within the limited scope of the review and despite Kinnaird's own later book on Hazlitt, unsupported generalizations. Prior to Kinnaird, Elisabeth Schneider has made a similar point regarding Hazlitt and Coleridge: 'Most often in Coleridge there is the aim toward a mystical transcending of the self by reaching out to God' (Schneider, *Aesthetics*, 39). Unlike Kinnaird, however, Schneider sees the difference between them in Coleridge's 'reaching out to God,' rather than in the 'mystical transcending of the self', since she finds a self-transcendence in Hazlitt's theory also (ibid. 39–40).

[19] S. T. Coleridge, *The Watchman*, ed. Lewis Patton, vol. ii of *The Collected Works of Samuel Taylor Coleridge*, Bollingen series no. 75 (Princeton, NJ: Princeton University Press, 1970), 132.   [20] Coleridge, *Poems*, i. 113–14.

theory in the mid-1790s. The faculty by which we acquire the conviction that the interests of each and of all are one and the same, or know ourselves parts and proportions of one wondrous whole, is the imagination; reading one passage by the other, 'benevolence', the great Godwinian term produced, in Godwin's work, out of the address to man's reason, is taken over by Coleridge as an attribute or outcome of the imagination.[21] The imagination enables the sense of self to merge into the identity with all, and when 'all' includes 'self', benevolence is also, and necessarily, selfishness.

In the *Essay on the Principles of Human Action* (1805) Hazlitt arrives at exactly this conclusion—that self-love can be identified with benevolence—and to this extent affirms the Unitarian vision. He does this, however, not like Coleridge, by establishing that individual self-interest is unimaginative, but rather the opposite, that individual self-interest is equally as imaginative as enlightened self-interest (benevolence or 'disinterestedness'), his logic being that the means by which the mind is carried out into its own future existence is identical to that by which it can be carried out into the feelings of others. 'I could not love myself, if I were not capable of loving others. Self-love, used in this sense, is in it's fundamental principle the same with disinterested benevolence' (i. 2).

Coleridge's definition states that benevolence is enlightened selfishness, Hazlitt's that self-love is the same as benevolence. The reversal in construction corresponds to a certain reversal in emphases. The direction of Coleridge's thought is towards a submergence of the self in its participation in the universal Nature. For Hazlitt, on the other hand, the discovery of the common origin—the imagination—of the love of self and the love of other, achieves the recovery and vindication of selfhood from the mechanical status to which it had been assigned in the 'matter-of-fact' philosophy.

It may be argued, of course, that the individual self is no less a vehicle in Coleridge's account of imaginative process than in Hazlitt's; my contention is merely that the whole tendency of Coleridge's language and imagery is towards the sublimation of that self, while Hazlitt preserves it. The argument of the *Essay on*

---

[21] See William Godwin, *An Enquiry Concerning Political Justice*, 2 vols (1793; repr. Oxford: Woodstock Books, 1992), vol. i, especially pp. 341–61.

the Principles of Human Action turns on the notion of 'self' and 'identity' which is its focus; it aims primarily to demonstrate that the love of self is an act of the imagination, with the corollary that if then self-love is natural, the love of others, which is *given* to be an imaginative act, must be equally natural to the human mind. The active capacity of the mind is shown to include the apprehension of both self and other; the second is established as 'natural' only by refuting the passive or mechanistic model of the first. Rather than sublimating selfhood in the movement towards the other, Hazlitt seeks so to define it as to absorb that movement within the self's own sphere of origin.

The preservation of the self in the *Essay* highlights its emphasis on volition, power, or agency, obviated in Coleridge's transcendent vision. To Hazlitt, the recognizably Coleridgean notion of a 'perfect universal sympathy' would imply that 'I must love all others as myself, because I should then be nothing more than part of a whole, of which all others would be equally members with myself' (i. 38). It is that 'must' that he rejects. By contending that the very idea of self arises from the simultaneous awareness of a disseverance from, as well as connection with, the other, the *Essay* establishes the condition of choice (i. 37–8).

The focus on an active self marks, then, Hazlitt's shifting of ground from the transcendent Coleridge. A small but telling variation in the usage of a common image perfectly encapsulates this shift. The favourite emblem of Coleridge's holistic vision is the Aeolian harp, which signifies the unity with the infinite of the inspired mind. Such a mind, in the metaphor, seems to assume a passive, because self-effacing, attribute:

> And what if all of animated nature
> Be but organic Harps diversely fram'd,
> That tremble into thought, as o'er them sweeps
> Plastic and vast, one intellectual breeze,
> At once the Soul of each, and God of all?
> ('The Eolian Harp' ll. 44–8)[22]

By contrast, Hazlitt's stress upon the self-directed condition for imaginative activity makes the harp fail to achieve, in his view, holistic character. This is evident in one of his observations on

---

[22] Coleridge, *Poems*, i. 102.

Wordsworth: 'He cannot form a whole. He has not the constructive faculty. He can give only the fine tones of thought, drawn from his mind by accident or nature, like the sounds drawn from the Aeolian harp by the wandering gale' ('On the Living Poets', *Lectures on the English Poets*; v. 156). This is, incidentally, a sufficiently unusual view of Wordsworth, and is less than consistent with other of Hazlitt's remarks; what is most to my point here, however, is his unambiguous rejection of Coleridge's favourite emblem of the inspired self in poetic composition. The rejection pertains exactly to the suggestions of passivity and submergence that that emblem contains—the harp is also, of course, a standard empirical image—a passivity deeply and fundamentally antithetical to Hazlitt's vision of the self-affirming activity of the imagination.

The Artistic Ideal

The model of the empowered self is the basis of Hazlitt's idealism, and his critical writings may be deciphered as embodying a theory of the ideal. In the *Lectures on the English Poets*, the ideal world of the imagination is the 'better reality' of the essay 'On Poetry in General'; it reappears in the *Lectures on the English Comic Writers*, as 'another mightier world, that which exists *only in conception and in power*' ('On the Works of Hogarth'; vi. 146, my italics).

'Conception' is, of course, 'idea', and Hazlitt's approximation of 'idea'—the product of the conceptual process—to 'ideal' is shared with Coleridge, with the characteristic difference in emphases.[23] By Coleridge's account, the 'essentially ideal' being of poetry implies its independence of individual signification:

I adopt with full faith the principle of Aristotle, that poetry as poetry is essentially *ideal*, that it avoids and excludes all *accident*; that its apparent

---

[23] See Coleridge's note to ch. v of *Biographia Literaria*, on the usage of 'idea' 'in the original sense, or platonically, or in a sense nearly correspondent to our present use of the substantive, Ideal' (Coleridge, *Biographia*, i. 97). Again, in *The Friend* (1818), 'idea' is merged with the Platonic concept of 'ideal': 'A distinguishable power self-affirmed, and seen in its unity with the Eternal Essence, is, according to Plato, an IDEA'—S. T. Coleridge, *The Friend*, ed. B. E. Rooke, vol. iv of *The Collected Works of Samuel Taylor Coleridge*, Bollingen series no. 75, 2 vols (Princeton, NJ: Princeton University Press, 1969), i. 492.

individualities of rank, character, or occupation must be *representative* of a class; and that the *persons* of poetry must be clothed with *generic* attributes, with the *common* attributes of the class; . . .[24]

Even when Coleridge acknowledges, in a note to this definition, the 'individual form' of poetry, his primary emphasis is still the absolute or 'universal truth' that is 'clothed' in this form.[25] Where his view of the imagination appears always to strain beyond the individual, for Hazlitt, the individual is both origin and limit. 'In the ideal there is no fixed stint or limit but the limit of possibility: it is the infinite with respect to *human* capacities and wishes' ('On the Picturesque and Ideal', *Table-Talk*; viii. 321, my italics). In the essay on *Romeo and Juliet*, 'Its root is in the heart of *man*: it lifts its head above the stars' ('Romeo and Juliet', *Characters of Shakespear's Plays*; iv. 250, my italics). By foregrounding the self in the conceptual process, Hazlitt insists, to a far greater extent than Coleridge, that the ideal or essential and hence the highest forms of nature exist *only* in the vision of the creative artist, that they are therefore created by him. The ideal is the offspring of the imagination's transformation of reality, and the validity of the intellectual transformation at once derives from and vindicates 'the innate bias of the mind to elevate itself above every thing low, and purify itself from every thing gross' ('On the Works of Hogarth', *Lectures on the English Comic Writers*; vi. 147).

The 'elevation' of reality in imaginative composition, brought about by the power of the authorial self, is invariably a determinant of Hazlitt's critical judgement. In the *Lectures on the Age of Elizabeth*, the distinction between imaginative association and false poetry is that the second is randomly or mechanically associative, while the first elevates, 'enriching one idea by another, which has the same feeling or set of associations belonging to it in a higher or more striking degree' ('On Miscellaneous Poems, etc.'; vi. 322). In the *Lectures on the English Comic Writers* also, 'elevation' is the quality used most frequently to distinguish the productions of the imagination from those of wit. Wit, in the introductory essay, is analysed through a series of comparisons with the imagination, as tending rather

---

[24] Coleridge, *Biographia*, vol. ii, ch. xvii, pp. 45–6.   [25] Ibid. 45–6 n.

to let down than to raise up, to weaken than to strengthen, to disconnect our sympathy from passion and power, than to attach and rivet it to any object of grandeur or interest, to startle and shock our preconceptions by incongruous and equivocal combinations, than to confirm, enforce, and expand them by powerful and lasting associations of ideas, or striking and true analogies. ('On Wit and Humour; vi. 23)

'Analogy', like 'transformation', is a useful way of understanding Hazlitt's concept of the relation between nature and the text which represents it, always with the proviso that the identifying attribute of the imaginative analogy is elevation, described in the extract above as the tendency 'to confirm, enforce and expand'. By this yardstick, the metaphysical poets are not imaginative: 'The object of the poetry of imagination is to raise or adorn one idea by another more striking or more beautiful: the object of these writers was to match any one idea with any other idea, *for better for worse*' ('On Cowley, Butler, Suckling, Etherege, etc.'; vi. 50). By the same criterion, Godwin *is* imaginative, 'an imagination projecting itself into certain situations, and capable of working up its imaginary feelings to the height of reality. The author launches into the ideal world, and must sustain himself and the reader there by the mere force of imagination' ('On the English Novelists'; vi. 130).

Since the *Essay on the Principles of Human Action* contends that human activity is intrinsically imaginative, what Hazlitt views as unimaginative always signifies what is least imaginative, rather than what is not imaginative at all. False poetry mimes the mechanism of the senses, true poetry realizes to the full the imagination's power over the senses. The 'reality' represented in Godwin's novels is generated entirely from the imagining self, so that the ideal world that contains this truth or reality is sustained absolutely by the power ('force of imagination') of that self.

The power of the imagining self, manifested in its ideal and elevated vision, is exemplified by Hazlitt in a recurrent image, 'finer', as he says to Northcote, 'than any thing in Shakspeare': Jacob's dream (*Conversations of Northcote*; xi. 246). The representation of the biblical story, in a painting displayed in the Dulwich Picture Gallery, is described by him as the very type of the ideal, 'realising that loftiest vision of the soul' ('On the Picturesque and Ideal', *Table-Talk*; viii. 321). Hazlitt's statements of the genius of Rembrandt refer repeatedly to this painting, for instance, in the essay on 'The Dulwich Gallery' (*Sketches of the Principal Picture Galleries in England*; x. 21, 22), in his 'Thoughts on Taste' (*Uncollected Essays*; xvii. 62) and 'Outlines of Taste (*Miscellaneous Writings*; xx. 391), and in the article on 'Fine Arts' in the *Encyclopaedia Britannica* (xviii. 123). Like all great works of the imagination, the painting—which, ironically enough, is not conclusively attributed to Rembrandt, merely to the Rembrandt school—is ideal, but its particular emblematic value inheres in its content as much as its execution. The ladder between earth and heaven captures the reach of the imagining self, here, the visionary Jacob. In the lecture 'On Poetry in General' Hazlitt warns us against the tendency of science to circumscribe this range of the imagination: 'There can never be another Jacob's dream. Since that time, the heavens have gone farther off, and grown astronomical' ('On Poetry in General', *Lectures on the English Poets*; v. 9). Again, in what is perhaps his most moving tribute to Coleridge, he describes him in the same terms, mourning the loss of an ideal:

His mind was clothed with wings; and raised on them, he lifted philosophy to heaven. In his descriptions, you then saw the progress of human happiness and liberty in bright and never-ending succession, like the steps of Jacob's ladder, with airy shapes ascending and descending, and with the voice of God at the top of the ladder. ('On the Living Poets'; v. 167)

Jacob's ladder represents not only the range of the imaginative ideal, but also and importantly, its human origin. Hazlitt's theory is of a transcendental, as opposed to a transcendent, ideal, one that is produced from within the mind rather than one that has a reality beyond it. Such a theory highlights, once again, his closeness to German idealist thought, in particular, to Schiller's exposition of the ideal in the essay *On the Naive and Sentimental in Literature*.

In Schiller's essay, the ideal is 'nature', and the naive and sentimental poets are distinguished by their different relations to that ideal: 'The poet, as I have said, either *is* nature or he will *seek* it.'[26] The province of the naive is reality, and of the sentimental, the relationship between reality and the ideal.[27] That is to say, the ideal is realized in the first, which is therefore at one with reality, and it is perpetually striven for in the second, which is never at one with reality, but always at variance with it. In the second case,

---

[26] Schiller, *Naive and Sentimental*, 38.   [27] Ibid. 103 n.

where real experience precludes the ideal, poetic talent makes it perceptible.[28] The ideal finds expression in poetry and since poetry, by definition, 'means nothing else than *to give humanity its most complete expression possible*', the boundary of the ideal is set by the human.[29] This is Schiller's transcendental vision, of an ideal that can and must go beyond the bounds of particular experience, but never so far 'that it disputes the restrictions of all possible experience', because in the latter case, 'human nature would have to be abandoned completely.'[30]

The vision of the human as the source and boundary of the ideal brings Hazlitt into close accord with Schiller's theory, except in one important respect. Unlike Schiller's, Hazlitt's ideal is marked by its particularity: '*The* IDEAL *is only the selecting a particular form which expresses most completely the idea of a given character, or quality*' ('On the Elgin Marbles', *The London Magazine*, February 1822; xviii. 158). The stress upon self-affirmation in his critical theory prohibits, as with Schiller, the ideal from transcending possible experience; by the same token, that very stress, while retaining the criterion of universal applicability, denies the demand for transcendence of particular experience.

The ground of particularity makes Hazlitt's ideal the polar opposite of the 'shadowy middle forms' of Joshua Reynolds against which he argues so persuasively. His refutation of the artistic theory of Reynolds's *Discourses* contains the following definition, which encapsulates the manner in which the ideal— the idea of a thing—can retain the particular: 'The ideal is that which answers to the idea of something, and not to the idea of any thing, or of nothing' ('On the Ideal', *The Champion*, 8 January 1815; xviii. 78). Hence, although 'The leading characters in Don Quixote are strictly individuals,' they also 'may be said to be purely ideal' ('On the English Novelists, *Lectures on the English Comic Writers*; vi. 110.). The emphasis on the individual or particular attributes of the ideal is derived from Hazlitt's view of its origin: the self-affirming tendency of the imagination.[31]

---

[28] Schiller, *Naive and Sentimental*, 62.   [29] Ibid. 39.   [30] Ibid. 73.
[31] The emphasis on the particular in Hazlitt has led many critics to lose sight of the theory of the ideal or universal which is founded upon that emphasis. A notable exception is C. I. Patterson's account of Hazlitt's criticism of the novel: 'He saw considerable merit in works that possessed realistic and factual qualities, but he rarely placed in the highest rank a novel without an element of the ideal.'—C. I. Patterson, 'William Hazlitt as a Critic of Prose Fiction', *PMLA* lxviii, no. 5 (1953), 1006.

The Bias of Genius

The implication of locating the ideal in the poet's transformation alone rather than in a hypothetical 'reality' outside that transformation to which it might refer, indicates that for Hazlitt, the poet's 'truth' or reading of reality is usually individual and idiosyncratic, a peculiar original insight of which the authorial ego compels the general application. 'Genius in ordinary is a more obstinate and less versatile thing. It is sufficiently exclusive and self-willed, quaint and peculiar. It does some one thing by virtue of doing nothing else: it excels in some one pursuit by being blind to all excellence but its own' ('On Genius and Common Sense', *Table-Talk*; viii. 42–3). Here, Hazlitt extends to 'genius' a quality which elsewhere he perceives as a general rule of human achievement (and the standard by which Coleridge, in particular, fails): 'It is hard to concentrate all our attention and efforts on one pursuit, except from ignorance of others' ('Mr. Coleridge', *The Spirit of the Age*; xi. 30), and again: 'To do any one thing best, there should be an exclusiveness, a concentration, a bigotry, a blindness of attachment to that one object' ('Qualifications Necessary to Success', *The Plain Speaker*; xii. 197). This, together with the epithet in his phrase 'Genius *in ordinary*', confirms that the operation of genius is envisioned by him as an intensification of the ordinary tendency to self-affirmation in the empowered mind, the difference in the imaginative activity of genius being only one of degree, and not of kind. Correspondingly, the partial and exclusive aspect of genius will be found to have its roots in Hazlitt's general theory of human development, this being governed by a notion, integral to his thought, of intellectual 'bias'.

'Bias' is a favourite term in the description of character in *The Plain Speaker*. We find references to 'the internal, original bias', 'the first predisposing bias' ('On Personal Character'; xii. 230), 'natural bias', 'first bias' ('On the Difference between Writing and Speaking'; xii. 263, 275), and 'ruling bias' ('On Depth and Superficiality'; xii. 349); relatedly, the refutation of Spurzheim's theory is based upon the postulate of 'original character' ('On Dr. Spurzheim's Theory'; xii. 152). The concept of a 'bias' is fundamental to Hazlitt's rejection of mechanism because it denies circumstances as substantially influential in the shaping of character. According to the essay 'On Personal Character', manners and situation, which pertain to the outward and the accidental, are powerless to penetrate or influence the inner nature of man. Rather than admitting the *ab extra* or mechanical cause, Hazlitt claims that the development of character is largely *ab intra*, directed by an innate bias or predisposition with which we are naturally endowed: 'the mind contrives to lay hold of those circumstances and motives which suit its own bias and confirm its natural disposition' (xii. 236). Although 'contrives' suggests free choice, equally, 'natural disposition' asserts a determinism, so that both together construct a paradox of volition simultaneous with necessity. Out of inward necessity, the will 'selects the impressions by which it chooses to be governed' (xii. 236). This 'selection' marks the difference between mechanical composition and the inwardly generated work of genius; in Shakespeare, 'the combination of objects depend[s] on the pre-disposition of the mind, moulding nature to its own purposes; in Sir Walter, the mind is as wax to circumstances' ('Sir Walter Scott, Racine, and Shakespear'; xii. 343). In the essay 'On Novelty and Familiarity', Hazlitt refers again to 'The resistance of the will to outward circumstances, its determination to create its own good or evil' (xii. 309). Thus association becomes a matter of choice, confirming Hazlitt's rejection of Hartley's mechanistic necessarianism; however, that choice is inescapably directed by an innate intellectual bias, and is therefore 'a bundle of prejudices and abstractions' ('The New School of Reform'; xii. 194). While the emphasis on the will celebrates the fact of human volition, the notion that the will is itself naturally preformed or biased in a certain direction contains an element of predeterminism which Hazlitt himself acknowledges towards the close of the essay 'On Personal Character' (xii. 241).

The theory of 'bias' gives us the mind as uniquely individual, hence partial and exclusive rather than comprehensive or inclusive.[32] Moreover, since intellectual activity is defined by the bias of the mind, it partakes of its exclusive nature. Applying this to art, Hazlitt finds that the artist is constrained by the peculiar

---

[32] Bromwich draws an extensive parallel between William James's metaphor of natural selection and Hazlitt's phrase 'elective affinity' in the essay 'On Genius and Common Sense' (viii. 47), but does not touch on the theory of 'bias', a term that Hazlitt uses much more extensively and in wide-ranging contexts (Bromwich, *Hazlitt*, 88–91).

constitution of his own mind in his expression of the ideal. The artist's vision is never comprehensive, but always exclusive, since he can be perfect only 'in giving some single quality or partial aspect of nature, which happened to fall in with . . . the bias of his genius' ('On the Portrait of an English Lady, by Vandyke'; xii. 291). In other words, the authorial presence immanent within imaginative creation is not only single, but singular, and it is the 'intense sympathy with some one beauty or distinguishing characteristic in nature' that 'constitutes rare genius or produces the most exquisite models of art' ('On Genius and Common Sense; viii. 49).[33] Consequently, the 'natural' in art refers always to the particular bias of the artist's mind.

Earlier, I have shown that the term 'natural' for Hazlitt must be taken to signify less an external or independent attribute of things than the inwardly produced basis of 'relation', whence the equivalence between the natural and the imaginative. By this equivalence, Hazlitt's repeated emphasis upon truth and nature must be read as being, in fact, an insistence that the mind be true to itself. Such a reading is necessary to reconcile his demand for universality with the criterion, equally insistent, of originality, whose source is the innate or unique bias of an individual's mind. Bias brings about the 'first impulse of genius . . . to create what never existed before' ('General View of the Subject', *Lectures on the Age of Elizabeth*; vi. 187). Lacking originality, the universal degenerates into the commonplace. 'Taste limps after genius, and from copying the artificial models, we lose sight of the living principle of nature' (vi. 187). This 'living principle of nature' must be produced from the uniquely biased mind of genius. Hence, for all his stress on the universal applicability of the ideal, Hazlitt finds, in the essay 'On the Difference between Writing and Speaking', that authors are at their best in isolation rather than in society. To elicit the imaginative and universal truth, 'they look into their own minds, not in

---

[33] To support his account of genius as being singular and partial in the essay 'On Genius and Common Sense', Hazlitt cites, half-flippantly, Adam Smith's principle of the division of labour (viii. 49). Unlike Hazlitt, however, Smith himself explicitly denies the difference in innate capacity to be the origin of this principle; to a large extent, indeed, he denies innate capacity altogether. See Adam Smith, *An Inquiry into the Nature and Causes of the Wealth of Nations*, ed. R. H. Campbell and A. S. Skinner, vol. ii of *The Glasgow Edition of the Works and Correspondence of Adam Smith*, 2 vols (Oxford: Clarendon Press, 1976), vol. i, ch. ii, pp. 28–30.

the faces of a gaping multitude,' and by so doing, see farther and feel deeper than most others (*The Plain Speaker*; xii. 279).

Hazlitt's belief in a bias or 'ruling character' of the mind is the context for his characterization of genius as innate, exclusive, and uniquely individual: 'As to genius and capacity for the works of art and science, all that a man really excels in, is his own and incommunicable' ('On Personal Character', *The Plain Speaker*; xii. 239). Genius is 'that which originates in a man's self' ('On Genius and Originality', *The Champion*, 4 December 1814; xviii. 69); thus, its imaginative truth is an exclusive original insight. This truth, then, is not absolute: it is *a* truth rather than *the* truth.

The Egotistical Sublime

'[Genius] is just the reverse of the cameleon; for it does not borrow, but lend its colour to all about it' ('On Genius and Common Sense', *Table-Talk*; viii. 43). Concomitant with the exclusive nature of genius is its character of forcefulness. The essay 'Why Distant Objects Please' presents the imagination stamping the void with the 'image of itself'. The verb deliberately conveys the full force of that impression, the emphatic delivery of the mind's innate 'power'. The power of Milton's mind is 'stamped on every line' ('On Milton's Versification', *The Round Table*; iv. 37). Wordsworth 'stamps' his character 'on whatever he meets' ('On Genius and Common Sense'; viii. 44). In every display of creativity, 'it is the strong character and impulse of the mind that forces out its way and stamps itself upon outward objects;' 'Mr. Kean' 'stamped himself the first night in Shylock' ('On Novelty and Familiarity', *The Plain Speaker*; xii. 305). In Burke's writing, 'Whatever stamps the original image more distinctly on the mind, is welcome' ('On the Prose-Style of Poets', *The Plain Speaker*; xii. 10). The tendency of genius to stamp objects with an image of itself, or in the words of the essay 'On Genius and Common Sense', to 'lend its colour to all about it,' refers to Hazlitt's peculiar associative version of 'sympathy' or 'relation', which I have shown to be a manifestation of the 'power' of the inspired self; it seems frequently to denote a quality of compulsion that is inseparable from his descriptions of such power.

The correlation between power, exclusiveness, and force is

pointed out by Burke in the *Philosophical Enquiry*: 'the mind is so entirely filled with its object, that it cannot entertain any other . . . Hence arises the great power of the sublime, that . . . hurries us on by an irresistible force.'[34] In Hazlitt's critical theory, the awareness of this correlation invests the term 'power' with a quasi-political sense, so that it amounts to a kind of rule by force:

> Greatness is great power, producing great effects. It is not enough that a man has great power in himself, he must shew it to all the world in a way that cannot be hid or gainsaid. . . .To impress the idea of power on others, they must be made in some way to feel it. It must be communicated to their understandings in the shape of an increase of knowledge, or it must subdue and overawe them by subjecting their wills. ('The Indian Jugglers', *Table-Talk*; viii. 84–5)

I have shown already that the forms of the powerful imagination are substantial, owning a weight that seems actually to make itself felt. From the passage above, this weight, the product of imaginative power, is forcefully communicable. Hazlitt's choice of words—'power', 'impress', 'subdue', 'overawe'—posits a kind of tyranny, the colonization and subjection of lesser understandings by the powerful assertion of an individual ego. Ulysses' comment to Achilles in *Troilus and Cressida*, in a passage that Hazlitt quotes as one of the most striking in Shakespeare (v. 54), 'That no man is the lord of anything, | Though in and of him there be much consisting, | Till he communicate his parts to others' (III. iii. 115–17), is almost certainly at work in this definition of greatness as consisting not merely in potential, but in prowess; the presence of the precursor text in the definition adds to the sense of an almost martial operation of the inspired self. There are also echoes, again, of Burke: 'by the contagion of our passions, we catch a fire already kindled in another, which probably might never have been struck out by the object described.'[35] In much the same vein as Burke, Hazlitt affirms that 'it is in the nature of greatness to propagate an idea of itself, as wave impels wave, circle without circle' ('The Indian Jugglers'; viii. 86). In the essay 'On Envy', similarly, he calls our susceptibility to genius, a 'transfusion of mind': 'The excellence that we feel, we participate in as if it were our own—it becomes ours by transfusion of mind' (*The*

---

[34] Burke, *Philosophical Enquiry*, part II, section 1, pp. 95–6.
[35] Ibid., part v, section 7, p. 340.

Plain Speaker; xii. 101). The quality of compulsion that we can identify in Hazlitt's descriptions of the workings of genius is the corollary of its partial and exclusive character, by implication of which imaginative truth does not constitute a fixed or absolute reality, but must be brought about by the authorial self in the compelling of its self-willed originality to general application.

Such a vision of the imagination seems repeatedly to be confirmed by Hazlitt's own experience as a practical critic. If we compare the language of the extract from 'The Indian Jugglers' with that employed, for instance, in the *Round Table* essay on *The Excursion*, we will find in the second an acknowledgement of exactly the subjection described in the first: 'The poem . . . has . . . overwhelming, oppressive power. . . . We are surrounded with the constant sense and superstitious awe of the collective power of matter' ('Observations on Mr. Wordsworth's Poem The Excursion'; iv. 111–12). The rhetoric that emerges as common to both ('power', 'impress', 'subdue', and 'overawe' in the one matching 'power', 'oppressive', 'overwhelming', and 'awe' in the other) is sufficient to establish that Hazlitt has already perceived in Wordsworth a practical fulfilment of the theoretical criteria of genius that he later sets out in 'The Indian Jugglers'. The correspondence is so close as to suggest that the origins of the abstract definitions set out in the *Table-Talk* writings might be found in the perception of Wordsworth that appears in the essay on *The Excursion*.

Hazlitt is after all no less a practical critic than an abstract philosopher; that a critical theory, in his case, would be formulated descriptively from the actual works of literary genius that he undertakes to analyse is therefore only to be expected. By treating Wordsworth as the exemplar of his view of genius and the imagination, his theory of artistic composition can not only be shown to be continuous with the vital concerns of his metaphysics, confirming the focus on self towards which the whole tendency of his philosophy of action and power is directed, but also to be borne out by a wealth of practical examples. In the essay on *The Excursion* itself, the comparison is made between Wordsworth and Rembrandt, suggesting that Wordsworth is by no means an extraordinary or isolated instance of the egotistical genius. The essay 'On Genius and Common Sense' develops the comparison, describing the Rembrandt as the paradigm of genius manifested as an extraordinary function of self-will, the attribute of an ego which 'does not borrow, but lend its colour to all about it'. In the egotism of both artist and poet, Hazlitt identifies the hallmarks of their genius. The note of censure where Wordsworth is concerned is readily discernible, but it does not in any way interfere with the acknowledgement that he too, like Rembrandt, manifests 'genius':

> He is the greatest, that is, the most original poet of the present day, only because he is the greatest egotist. . . . He thrusts aside all other objects, all other interests with scorn and impatience, that he may repose on his own being, that he may dig out the treasures of thought contained in it, that he may unfold the precious stores of a mind for ever brooding over itself. His genius is the effect of his individual character. He stamps that character, that deep individual interest, on whatever he meets . . . (viii. 44)

From the above, as from the essay on *The Excursion*, it would be mistaken to interpret Hazlitt's dislike of Wordsworth as pertaining to poetic egotism, because of the paradox to which such an interpretation is inevitably led: it is surely the power of the Wordsworthian ego that compels Hazlitt's admiration in the first place.[36] Indeed this compulsion, in the teeth of the antipathy that so obviously vies against it, becomes so much the more a tribute to the egotistical genius. The simultaneous feeling of repulsion and admiration in Hazlitt's claims for Wordsworth's genius is even more intensified in his view of Byron:

> a mind preying upon itself, and disgusted with, or indifferent to all other things. . . . There is nothing more repulsive than this sort of ideal absorption of all the interests of others, of the good and ills of life, in the ruling passion and moody abstraction of a single mind, as if it would make itself the centre of the universe, . . . But still there is power; and power rivets attention and forces admiration. ('On the Living Poets', *Lectures on the English Poets*; v. 153)

That last sentence makes my case: the strong manifestation of a particular poetic self may excite Hazlitt's antipathy; nonetheless, such self-centredness is also always regarded by him as a strength.

---

[36] I am corroborating here, Kinnaird's observation on Hazlitt in the review of Baker, 'Hence he could publicly damn Wordsworth, for instance, as an insufferable egotist because he knew he was also able to praise that same self, for much the same reasons, as an original and great poet' (Kinnaird, 'The Forgotten Self', 305).

Equally, a want of 'rivetting power' represents a failing—as in the poems of Thomas Moore: 'The graceful ease with which he lends himself to every subject, the genial spirit with which he indulges in every sentiment, prevents him from giving their full force to the masses of things, from connecting them into a whole. He wants intensity, strength, and grandeur' ('On the Living Poets'; v. 151). In another context, Hazlitt makes much the same sort of criticism even of Shakespeare, denying him gusto: 'The infinite quantity of dramatic invention in Shakespeare takes from his gusto. The power he delights to show is not intense, but discursive' ('On Gusto', *The Round Table*; iv. 79).[37] Force, closely allied to Hazlitt's 'gusto', is the attribute of the powerful ego; its absence in Moore manifests the lack of the first characteristic of inspired composition: a strong unifying spirit. The holistic character of a work of art presupposes a self, and in his criticism of Moore, Hazlitt unequivocally connects poetic power and the stable sense of selfhood: 'It requires the same principle to make us thoroughly like poetry, that makes us like ourselves so well, the feeling of continued identity' ('On the Living Poets'; v. 151). The 'continued identity' of the poet connects the parts of his composition into a whole, only thereby giving it the force that compels us to identify with it.

Hazlitt's antipathy to Wordsworth and Byron, whatever its source—a sense of personal as well as political estrangement from a reneged liberal and a 'Noble Poet' ('Lord Byron', *The Spirit of the Age*; xi. 70) is surely a factor here—must not be allowed to obscure the fact that he elsewhere celebrates the very qualities by which he characterizes these two writers. I have mentioned Rembrandt and Titian as instances of this; William Godwin is another: 'the chains with which he rivets our attention are forged out of his own thoughts, link by link, blow for blow, with glowing enthusiasm: we see the genuine ore melted in the furnace of fervid feeling, and moulded into stately and *ideal* forms' ('William Godwin', *The Spirit of the Age*; xi. 25). The

---

[37] Contrary to John Mahoney's assertion, that 'Shakespeare is his favourite example of gusto' (J. L. Mahoney, 'William Hazlitt: The Essay as a Vehicle for the Romantic Critic', *CLB* lxxv (July 1991), 95), Hazlitt is explicitly commenting here on Shakespeare's want of gusto. Prior to Mahoney, Harold Bloom also mistakenly glosses this comment as 'Shakespeare's gusto is in his exuberance of invention' (Bloom, *William Hazlitt*, 3).

The Mighty Intellect

authenticity of Godwin's genius ('genuine ore') abides in its self-generation ('out of his own thoughts'); the forms of his imagination are 'ideal'. In the introductions both to the *Lectures on the English Comic Writers* and the *Lectures on the Age of Elizabeth*, the term 'rivet' describes the operation of the sympathetic imagination, confirming its associative character (vi. 23, 183). In the essay on Godwin, similarly, the 'chains with which he rivets our attention' refers to the associative chain by which the inspired author draws us into himself, the image of the furnace attesting both to the power of his imagination, and to our subjugation, as readers, to it. In writing of Byron, Hazlitt has suggested just such an image, in a fragment of common phraseology ('rivets . . . attention', see above); it recurs also in his account of Otway's *Venice Preserved* 'rivetting breathless attention' ('On Ancient and Modern Literature', *Lectures on the Age of Elizabeth*; vi. 354) and even more importantly, recalls the comments in the *Lectures on the English Poets* on Chaucer: 'The chain of his story is composed of a number of fine links, closely connected together, and rivetted by a single blow' ('On Chaucer and Spenser'; v. 21).

The furnace of intellectual energy is emblematic of Hazlitt's vision of inspiration, whose ruling trope is fire, the 'power' which forges the associative chain of the imagination. It occurs in his description of Burke—'his blows struck fire from the flint, and melted the hardest substances in the furnace of his imagination' ('Character of Mr. Burke', *Political Essays*; vii. 310)—and also of Milton, the supreme exemplar of his theory of the powerful genius. 'The power of his mind is stamped on every line. The fervour of his imagination melts down and renders malleable, as in a furnace, the most contradictory materials. In reading his works, we feel ourselves under the influence of a mighty intellect' ('On Shakspeare and Milton', *Lectures on the English Poets*; v. 58). These few lines perfectly capture Hazlitt's theory of genius. The inspired mind enacts its propensity to self-affirmation, imposing itself irresistibly on the reader; its works are the manifestation of an exclusive authorial presence, or 'mighty intellect', whose primary attributes are power and the implied concomitants: intensity ('fervour', 'furnace') and force ('stamped'; 'melts down and renders malleable').

By considering Hazlitt's model of the inspired self in poetic composition as verifying a theory of the Wordsworthian or egotistical sublime, i.e. a theory exemplified by the Wordsworthian genius, we can apply this model to numerous instances from his critical experience, making it consistent with his role as a practical critic, because furnished from the materials of his own reading. The example of the authorial ego in literary composition corroborates precisely the notion of an empowered self that is elicited from Hazlitt's metaphysics, to which an active and empowered mind is central. By treating his critical theory as a theory of the empowered self, we are able readily to provide that theory with a conceptual basis from his philosophical expositions.

On Diction

In the foregoing discussion, I have tried to show that Hazlitt's criticism of Wordsworth cannot be accounted for as pertaining simply to 'egotism', since he elsewhere celebrates exactly the mode of egotistical genius that he appears to indict in Wordsworth. I have suggested that personal as well as political antipathy, the latter pertaining to Wordsworth's reneging on the radical views of his earlier years, is a factor in this indictment. In the essay 'On Consistency of Opinion', Hazlitt explicitly connects Wordsworth's political affiliations with his literary theory, so as to express, by their being at odds with one another, his own contempt for both:

> his whole system turns upon this, that the thoughts, the feelings, the expressions of the common people in country places are the most refined of all others; at once the most pure, the most simple, and the most sublime:—yet, with one stroke of his prose-pen, he disfranchises the whole rustic population of Westmoreland and Cumberland from voting at elections, . . . (*Uncollected Essays*; xvii. 25–6).

Given Hazlitt's radical leanings, the reasons for his political divergence from Wordsworth are obvious enough. It remains to be discovered in what manner Wordsworth's literary theory is particularly inimical to Hazlitt's. I believe it can be shown that with reference to critical theory, the grounds for Hazlitt's opposition to Wordsworth are to be found in his principles of poetic diction.

Hazlitt's remarks on poetic diction frequently contain a polemical tone, indicating that they are directed towards a specific target; this target can be located in Wordsworth's 'Preface' to the *Lyrical Ballads* which contains the great revolutionary manifesto for diction: 'There will . . . be found in these volumes little of what is usually called poetic diction; I have taken as much pains to avoid it as others ordinarily take to produce it; this I have done . . . to bring my language near to the language of men.'[38]

In a review of *Biographia Literaria* (August 1817), Hazlitt undertakes to counter Coleridge's defence of the Wordsworthian theory of diction, by making the distinction between two types of poetic language, each appropriate, respectively, to two distinct kinds or moods of poetry. The first, 'a simple and familiar language, common to almost all ranks, . . . is the language of the best poetry as well as of the best prose,' and this 'common or natural style is the truly dramatic style.' At the same time, he insists that due place be given to 'another language . . . which has been called *poetic diction*,—. . . most proper to descriptive or fanciful poetry, . . . a language that, by custom and long prescription, reflects the image of a poetical mind' ('Coleridge's Literary Life', *Contributions to the Edinburgh Review*; xvi. 135).

Hazlitt's contributions to the *Edinburgh Review* were, of course, heavily edited by Jeffrey, who actually claims this review of the *Biographia* as his own. The claim is debatable (see Howe's notes, xvi. 425), but since Hazlitt goes on to give a more explicit account of his theory of diction in his later writing, the authorship of the remarks extrapolated here is not finally crucial to the examination of that theory. The introduction to the *Lectures on the English Poets* pushes the point made in the *Edinburgh Review* much further, dropping such concessions as 'There is, no doubt, a simple and familiar language . . . which is the best fitted for the direct expression of strong sense and deep passion', or 'the common or natural style is the truly dramatic style' (xvi. 135), to argue unequivocally in favour of a 'separate language' for poetry:

Poetry is in all its shapes the language of the imagination and the passions, of fancy and will. Nothing, therefore, can be more absurd than the outcry which has been sometimes raised by frigid and pedantic critics, for reducing the language of poetry to the standard of common sense and reason: . . . Let who will strip nature of the colours and the

---

[38] Wordsworth, *Prose*, i. 130.

shapes of fancy, the poet is not bound to do so; the impressions of common sense and strong imagination, that is, of passion and indifference, cannot be the same, and they must have a separate language to do justice to either. ('On Poetry in General'; v. 8)

The separate language of poetry accords with its separate world from reality as posited in the essay 'On Poetry in General', and the dualism of poetry and reality begs the question of 'nature' and its implication for poetic language. Wordsworth's *Lyrical Ballads* manifesto makes the first step towards a natural language for poetry—the 'real language of nature'—by discarding what he calls poetic diction in favour of 'simple and unelaborated expressions,' 'the very language of men'.[39] But Hazlitt's early work on grammar foregrounds, as we have seen, a distinction between 'common speech' (presumably, Wordsworth's 'the very language of men') and imaginative utterance. By virtue of this distinction, he reclaims as 'natural' to poetry the 'artificial' resources of classical allusion, rhetoric, and stylization in diction:

> it is the common cant of criticism to consider every allusion to the classics, and particularly in a mind like Milton's, as pedantry and affectation. Habit is a second nature; and, in this sense, the pedantry (if it is to be called so) of the scholastic enthusiast, who is constantly referring to images of which his mind is full, is as graceful as it is natural. It is not affectation in him to recur to ideas and modes of expression, with which he has the strongest associations, and in which he takes the greatest delight. Milton was as conversant with the world of genius before him as with the world of nature about him; the fables of the ancient mythology were as familiar to him as his dreams. ('On Milton's "Lycidas"', *The Round Table*; iv. 33)

I have already discussed Hazlitt's sense of the mind's prerogative in bestowing ideal form upon nature which, together with his concept of 'relation', authenticates the imaginative creation that is so constituted. From the above, art formed of art takes an equal place as 'second nature', to art formed of the objects of the natural or external world; 'nature' in both is organic, the attribute of the innate mental principle. Correspondingly, diction produced from a textual world of imaginary forms is also the outcome of an organic mental activity: the associative operation of the imagination. In the essay 'On the Old English Writers and Speakers',

---

[39] Wordsworth, *Prose*, 142, 124, 130.

Hazlitt uses the organic imagery of plant life to describe the luxuriant use of ornamentation by the old writers: 'It is the luxuriance of natural feeling and fancy. I should as soon think of accusing the summer-rose of vanity for unfolding its leaves to the dawn, or the hawthorn that puts forth its blossoms in the genial warmth of spring, of affecting to be fine' (*The Plain Speaker*; xii. 321). 'Fine' as a commendatory adjective for diction is also used by Keats ('I look upon fine Phrases like a Lover'); Hazlitt's theory of diction is relevant to Keats, offering as it does a potential source for Keats's use of the word 'naturally' in his famous 'axiom', 'if Poetry comes not as naturally as the Leaves to a tree it had better not come at all.'[40] On Hazlitt's authority, the 'natural' process of poetry could include the peculiarities of Keats's own poetic diction: the exuberant innovations in vocabulary and constant recourse to modes of expression not grounded in familiar usage.

To Hazlitt, the artificial forms of the imagination nevertheless achieve the truest mimesis of nature, from a perfect attunement between language and mind (harmony) that yet escapes the limitations of factual reality: 'Extremes are said to meet: and the works of imagination, as they are called, sometimes come the nearest to truth and nature' ('On the English Novelists', *Lectures on the English Comic Writers*; vi. 106–7). The abdication of the resources of poetic diction amounts to a denial of the ideal character of poetry; circumscribing imaginative activity by imposing limits on the language which expresses it, obscures the true core of that activity, and imposes extraneous criteria on that which is to be judged solely by the power of the self which directs it. Thus Hazlitt defends the rhetoric of Burke:

Burke was so far from being a gaudy or flowery writer, that he was one of the severest writers we have. His words are the most like things; his style is the most strictly suited to the subject. . . . He exults in the display of power, in shewing the extent, the force, and intensity of his ideas; he is led on by the mere impulse and vehemence of his fancy, not by the affectation of dazzling his readers by gaudy conceits or pompous images. He was completely carried away by his subject. He had no other object but to produce the strongest impression on his reader . . . ('Character of Mr. Burke', *Political Essays*; vii. 309)

---

[40] To Bailey, 14 August 1819, to Taylor, 27 February 1818 (Keats, *Letters*, ii. 139, i. 238–9).

Burke is Hazlitt's favourite example of the successful use of poetic diction, and Hazlitt is careful always to distinguish Burke's diction from the 'gaudy or glittering style' which 'consists in producing a momentary effect by fine words and images brought together, without order or connexion' (vii. 310). Hazlitt's phraseology here actually resembles Wordworth's account of poetic diction in the 'Preface' to the *Lyrical Ballads*, but Wordsworth, for Hazlitt, does not sufficiently discriminate between the true and the false poetic diction, or between the successful and unsuccessful use of ornamental language, when he rejects poetic diction altogether in favour of 'simple and unelaborated expressions'. In contrast to the 'gaudy' style, the successful use of poetic diction is a vindication of the innate capacity or active potential of a mind which produces its own reality in a shape—language—that does not conform literally to the forms of external nature; the denial that diction can be so employed would, by implication, place a restriction upon that intellectual potential. Such restriction is, for Hazlitt, 'morbid', and the limits imposed thereby upon the sphere and mode of operation of the authorial ego, make that ego manifest itself as trite and mean:

The great fault of a modern school of poetry is, that it is an experiment to reduce poetry to a mere effusion of natural sensibility; or what is worse, to divest it both of imaginary splendour and human passion, to surround the meanest objects with the morbid feelings and devouring egotism of the writers' own minds. ('On Shakspeare and Milton'; v. 53)

It is important to recognize that the issue here is strictly the misapplication of a power, which in itself is taken as given. The vehemence of Hazlitt's comments arises from their polemical basis; the implications of the 'modern' or Wordsworthian theory of diction strike at the very heart of his construction of poetry as the illustration *par excellence* of his metaphysical position. In this context, his application of the empiricist image of the Aeolian harp to Wordsworth becomes more comprehensible; Wordsworth's repudiation of poetic diction amounts to a denial of innate power that counterfeits an empiricist model of the mind.

It should be noted too that Hazlitt's development of a theory of diction directed polemically against Wordsworth, targets not so much the vocabulary, as the objects of Wordsworth's poetic discourse, not so much his practice, but his declared principles of poetry. The claim to 'the very language of men' can hardly be literally applied, even to Wordsworth's linguistic practice in the *Lyrical Ballads*, and Hazlitt must not be taken so to apply it. Rather, he treats the claim as outlining the single objective to which his entire literary judgement remains inherently opposed: the lowering of the elevated world of poetry from its ideal height: 'His homely Muse can hardly raise her wing from the ground, nor spread her hidden glories to the sun' ('Mr. Wordsworth', *The Spirit of the Age*; xi. 86).

Hazlitt, Keats, and Shakespeare

'Genius and understanding are a man's self, an integrant part of his personal identity' ('On the Aristocracy of Letters', *Table-Talk*; viii. 208). Given the powerful affirmation of selfhood in Hazlitt's theory of imaginative composition, it would seem that the Romantic doctrine of poetry that provides the most pointed counter to it is Keats's view, as set out in his letters, of the annihilation of the self in poetic composition. Extracting from the famous letter to Woodhouse of 27 October 1818, we find that the 'poetical Character' with which Keats identifies is not that 'which is a thing per se and stands alone', rather, 'it is not itself—it has no self—it is every thing and nothing—It has no character.' This poetical character, which has no character, is summed up in Keats's phrase, 'camelion Poet.'[41]

Keats's ideal is the 'camelion Poet', Hazlitt's genius, 'just the reverse of the cameleon'. The difference is not merely trivial. Although in so describing genius, Hazlitt specifically excepts Shakespeare, that exception need not be interpreted as detrimental to his rule. His description does indeed signify a limitation of sorts, but it is one that vindicates the very foundation of his philosophical vision. Hazlitt's notion of a partial and exclusive genius has its roots in a theory of abstraction and 'innate bias' which, as we have seen, is integral to the vision of an empowered and active mind, directed inwardly by the laws of its own fixed constitution. In his metaphysics, we find the celebration of the mind, not as it is acted upon, but as it acts, not as it is susceptible

[41] Keats, *Letters*, i. 386–7.

to external influences (that which is 'other' to it), but as it manifests its own innate constitution—the 'bias' that defines a powerful but determinate self. The chameleon represents to Hazlitt exactly that model of the mind that his entire metaphysic seeks to refute: 'a chameleon, colourless kind of thing, the sport of external impulses and accidental circumstances' ('On Liberty and Necessity', *Lectures on English Philosophy*; ii. 269). If the mind is to be susceptible to all impressions alike, as Keats would have the poet's be, then its direction by its own innate bias must be denied, rendering it passive and mechanistic rather than active and self-determined.[42]

The whole notion of a 'bias' that is so integral to Hazlitt, confining, as it does, the genius to the limits of its particular selfhood, would appear inimical to Keats's view where, even while describing genius in action, he invests it with passive attributes. If, for Hazlitt, power describes that quality which is the 'reverse of the cameleon', in Keats's poetic theory it is the absence of power that constitutes genius: 'Men of Genius are great as certain ethereal Chemicals operating on the Mass of neutral intellect—by [*for* but] they have not any individuality, any determined Character. I would call the top and head of those who have a proper self Men of Power.'[43] By calling those who have a proper self Men of Power, Keats clearly displays that his usage and associations in this context are close enough to Hazlitt's, from whom his theoretical deviation becomes, thereby, all the more explicit. Where Keats sets up an opposition between Men of Genius and Men of Power, Hazlitt would assume their identity.

It has been indisputably established, nonetheless, not only that Keats admired Hazlitt, but also that many of the best-known

---

[42] Thus, when Roy Park draws a parallel between Hazlitt and Keats in the following terms, his citation of Hazlitt must be perceived as taken misleadingly out of context: 'For Hazlitt, the artist must be "awake", "alive", or "open to all impressions alike". For Keats, the mind must be "a thoroughfare for all thoughts". The demand is the same in both cases' (Park, *Hazlitt*, 38). Further on in his study, however, Park acknowledges that while 'Hazlitt's notion of protean genius fulfils Keats's demand for negative capability,' his theory of genius overall 'is in effect a theory of non-protean genius' (ibid. 181, 179). Yet by continually stressing the 'limitation' of mind implied in the theory of abstraction upon which Hazlitt's formulation of genius relies, Park misses the extent to which the non-protean genius is celebrated by Hazlitt as the embodiment of imaginative power and the vindication of his metaphysics.

[43] To Bailey, 22 November 1817 (Keats, *Letters*, i. 184).

passages on poetic identity in Keats's letters are derived from his reading of Hazlitt.[44] Most notably, for instance, the passage on the poetical character in the letter to Woodhouse cited previously may be traced to the following extract from Hazlitt's essay 'On Posthumous Fame': 'He seemed scarcely to have an individual existence of his own, but to borrow that of others at will, and to pass successively through "every variety of untried being,"—to be now *Hamlet*, now *Othello*, now *Lear*, now *Falstaff*, now *Ariel*' (*The Round Table*; iv. 23). Such derivation has led to the identification of Hazlitt's principles of literary criticism with Keats's, supported by the fact of Hazlitt's antipathy to Wordsworth, whom Keats perceived as the polar opposite to his own ideal of poethood.[45] It has been also in the light of the canonical status that Keats's writing has now assumed, that the recognition that Hazlitt stands in a precursive relation to him has amounted, conversely, to a reading of Hazlitt's literary theory as proto-Keatsian, containing an emphasis on self-annihilation as the condition for poetic

---

[44] For Keats's admiration of Hazlitt, see, for instance, the letters of 10 January 1818 to Haydon and of 13–19 January 1818 to George and Tom Keats (ibid., 203, 205); also the letter of 3 March 1819 to George and Georgiana Keats (ibid. ii. 69).

The following is a brief survey of the established view of the Keats–Hazlitt relation: C. L. Finney's *The Evolution of Keats's Poetry*, which gives Hazlitt the role of philosophical mentor to Keats, is one of the earliest works to examine the influence of Hazlitt upon Keats in some detail. R. T. Davies and Kenneth Muir supply lists of specific sources in Hazlitt for some of Keats's most famous pronouncements on topics such as intensity, identity, spontaneity, and the egotistical sublime. W. J. Bate adduces particular proofs of influence to make a general case that Keats's view of the poetical character and negative capability incorporates Hazlitt's philosophy, and H. M. Sikes follows Bate in opining that Keats's values in poetry are an extension and development of Hazlitt's. R. S. White connects the attitudes to Shakespeare of Hazlitt and Keats, tracing Keats's comments on the 'poetical Character' in the letter to Woodhouse of 27 October 1818 to Hazlitt's essay 'On Posthumous Fame' in *The Round Table*. Hazlitt scholars have tended to tell the same story: Roy Park's analysis of Hazlitt finds a parallel between his ideal of 'imaginative sincerity' and Keats's 'negative capability'; more recently, David Bromwich, has maintained that 'Keats found his second self in Hazlitt.' See: C. L. Finney, *The Evolution of Keats's Poetry*, 2 vols (Cambridge, Mass.: Harvard University Press, 1936); R. T. Davies, 'Keats and Hazlitt', *KSMB* viii (1957), 1–8; Kenneth Muir, 'Keats and Hazlitt', in Muir (ed.), *John Keats: A Reassessment* (Liverpool: Liverpool University Press, 1958), 139–58; W. J. Bate, *John Keats* (London: Oxford University Press, 1967), especially pp. 239–40, 244–5, 254–9; H. M. Sikes, 'The Poetic Theory and Practice of Keats: The Record of a Debt to Hazlitt', *PQ* xxxviii (1959), 401–12; R. S. White, 'Hazlitt and Keats's Attitudes to Shakespeare' in *Keats as a Reader of Shakespeare* (London: Athlone Press, 1987), 31–55; Park, *Hazlitt*, 6; Bromwich, *Hazlitt*, 369.

[45] To Woodhouse, 27 October 1818 (Keats, *Letters*, i. 386–7).

composition.[46] I have tried to show that such a reading of Hazlitt is incompatible both with his tenets as a metaphysician as well as his experience as a critic.

The misreading of Hazlitt may be eliminated upon the consideration of two factors. First: in almost every comment on poetic identity in his letters, Keats is drawing, not generally upon Hazlitt, but upon Hazlitt on Shakespeare. Secondly: that by denying 'gusto' to Shakespeare ('On *Gusto*'; iv. 79), Hazlitt's vision of genius as a triumphant affirmation of the individual self requires us to locate Shakespeare *outside* his general theory of genius and its workings. Like Keats, he perceives Shakespeare as achieving the annihilation of selfhood in poetic creation, but this quality marks Shakespeare as the exception to, rather than the type of, the ordinary rules of genius. 'Shakespear (almost alone) seems to have been a man of genius, raised above the definition of genius. . . . He was the Proteus of human intellect. Genius in ordinary is a more obstinate and less versatile thing' ('On Genius and Common Sense'; viii. 42). The distinction between the Shakespearian and the 'ordinary' genius attests to the two types of genius in Hazlitt's critical perception. The first, the Wordsworthian or egotistical sublime, comprehends the major proportion of the experience of his reading, conforming to a model of the imagination that is closely compatible with his metaphysical construct. This is the 'ordinary' genius, and it is stamped by the epithet: the egotistical sublime is the most powerful exemplification of an active tendency or innate intellectual principle that characterizes a *general* human condition. The second category of genius that Hazlitt describes comprehends 'Shakespeare (almost alone)', who reverses nearly every condition posited by the general or 'ordinary' theory.

The conventional distinction that could be invoked here is between the 'sympathetic' and the 'associative' imagination, but I am reluctant to use this distinction in classifying the difference between the Wordsworthian genius and the Shakespearian for Hazlitt. The 'sympathetic' and 'associative' functions of the imagination are not separable in Hazlitt's theory, and his insis-

---

[46] Albrecht's view of Hazlitt's theory of the poetic imagination is typical: 'loss of self, habitually encouraged, is necessary to the poet who would write truthfully and universally.' W. P. Albrecht, 'Hazlitt's Preference for Tragedy', *PMLA* lxxi, no. 5 (1956), 1044.

tence that the associative chain may be recognized as authentic only when it realizes a sympathy between the inspired subject and the objective material reality, prohibits our making the two terms mutually exclusive. However, it is safe enough to assert that another *kind* of sympathy from that effected by the affirmative self, may be seen at work in Hazlitt's Shakespeare.

In the essay 'On Dryden and Pope' Hazlitt names Shakespeare as an example of the poet of nature standing at the centre of his circle of influence. The circle also epitomizes, more generally, his vision of the empowered self; it is the emblem of the highest manifestation of that self in the poetry of the egotistical sublime. Despite the common trope, what sets Shakespeare apart from that vision? To understand the peculiar, and in many ways, paradoxical standing of Shakespeare, it becomes necessary to consider a particular case of Hazlitt's theory of genius: the dramatic genius.

Hazlitt's dramatic theory is given in detail in the *Lectures on the Age of Elizabeth*. His 'theory of the dramatic genius of that age' ('On Beaumont and Fletcher etc.'; vi. 273) is his theory of drama in its entirety. In the 'General View of the Subject', Hazlitt affirms that 'there was more dramatic excellence in that age than in the whole of the period that has elapsed since' (vi. 181). The introductory lecture identifies drama as the spirit of the Elizabethan period, and it opens with a description of the genius of the Elizabethan writers, in what we recognize, by now, as familiar terms: 'They did not look out of themselves to see what they should be; they sought for truth and nature, and found it in themselves. . . . with all their endeavours after excellence, they did not lay aside the strong original bent and character of their minds' (vi. 175). We have here a typical account of the self-affirming and exclusive genius, with truth and nature located in the author's self, and referring, therefore, to the 'bent' or peculiar innate constitution of his mind. The truth or insight of the dramatic genius is the image of itself, irresistibly compelled to universality; it arises from 'the insatiable desire of the mind to beget its own image, and to construct out of itself, . . . that excellence of which the idea exists hitherto only in its own breast, and the impression of which it would make as universal as the eye of heaven' (vi. 186).

As elsewhere, then, the 'natural' in dramatic art signifies imaginative association, 'the impression of given circumstances on the passions and mind of man in those circumstances' ('On Ancient and Modern Literature'; vi. 347). At the same time, in the particular case of drama, the conditions of the genre demand that the representation of character tell upon the reader or audience without direct authorial interpolation. Hence we find Hazlitt asserting two seemingly contradictory criteria of dramatic genius; the first, given in the theoretical outline or 'General View of the Subject', being the writer's direction by the strong original bent and character of his mind, and the second, recurring in his criticism of particular dramatists, being the disappearance or absorption of the authorial self into its dramatic creation. It is with reference to this second criterion, applicable only to drama, that Hazlitt asserts, quoting from his own review of Schlegel's lectures on dramatic literature, that 'The true poet identifies the reader with the characters he represents; the French poet only identifies him with himself' ('On Ancient and Modern Literature'; vi. 354). Hence the severity of his treatment of Sidney. Sidney is not a playwright, but Hazlitt judges him, as he judges all the writers of this period, by the standards of the dramatic genius of his age: 'He cannot let his imagination or that of the reader dwell for a moment on the beauty or power of the real object. He thinks nothing is done, unless it is his doing. He must officiously and gratuitously interpose between you and the subject' ('On Miscellaneous Poems etc.'; vi. 321).

Sidney is the object of the harshest of Hazlitt's censure, but the difficulty of reconciling the two conditions of dramatic excellence lies behind his perception that not Sidney alone, but each of the writers chosen for discussion represents at best a partial success, praiseworthy only in particular pieces, or even only in isolated passages. Marlowe, for instance, who is 'almost first in this list of dramatic worthies' (vi. 202), is described in much the same terms as Hazlitt's Milton or Godwin; '"Marlowe's mighty line"' (vi. 208) notably recalls Milton's 'mighty intellect', but the furnace of his imaginative power corrodes rather than constructs: 'There is a lust of power in his writings, a hunger and thirst after unrighteousness, a glow of the imagination, unhallowed by any thing but its own energies. His thoughts burn within him like a furnace with bickering flames; or throwing out black smoke and mists, that hide the dawn of genius, or like a poisonous mineral, corrode the heart' ('On Lyly, Marlow, Heywood, etc.'; vi. 202). Dekker fulfils

The Mighty Intellect

the second of Hazlitt's criteria, but not the first; he has 'more truth of character, more instinctive depth of sentiment, more of the unconscious simplicity of nature; but he does not, out of his own stores, clothe his subject with the same richness of imagination' ('On Marston, Chapman, Deckar etc.'; vi. 240). By contrast, Webster, giving greater play to the imagination, does so at the expense of dramatic credibility:

> Webster gives more scope to . . . various combinations and changeable aspects, brings them into dramatic play by contrast and comparison, flings them into a state of fusion by a kindled fancy, makes them describe a wider arc of oscillation from the impulse of unbridled passion, and carries both terror and pity to a more painful and sometimes unwarrantable excess. ('On Marston, Chapman, Deckar etc.'; vi. 240)

In Beaumont and Fletcher, imaginative power is diffused rather than forceful; 'Their fault is a too ostentatious and indiscriminate display of power. Every thing seems in a state of fermentation and effervescence, and not to have settled and found its centre in their minds' ('On Beaumont and Fletcher, etc.'; vi. 249).

The paradox of drama is perfectly encapsulated in a single remark on a passage in Ben Jonson's *Fall of Sejanus* which Hazlitt praises as being 'The only part of this play in which Ben Jonson has completely forgotten himself, (or rather seems not to have done so)' ('On Beaumont and Fletcher, etc.'; vi. 265); i.e. it is in the truth of represented character, giving the impression of authorial self-forgetfulness, that the dramatic genius manifests its self-affirming power.

The culmination of the dramatic prowess that his contemporaries fail to achieve is found in Shakespeare, and this is the underlying thesis of the *Lectures on the Age of Elizabeth*. Though Hazlitt claims, in his 'Advertisement' to the *Lectures*, to say 'little' of Shakespeare in the pages that follow (vi. 173), that 'little' is in fact the unifying theme of the series, where Shakespeare is present as the very spirit of drama and the standard by which it is judged: 'Shakespear alone seemed to stand over his work, and to do what he pleased with it' ('On Lyly, Marlow, Heywood, etc.'; vi. 215); 'The tone of Shakespear's writings is manly and bracing; theirs is at once insipid and meretricious, in the comparison' ('On Beaumont and Fletcher, etc.'; vi. 250); 'there were other writers living in the time of Shakespear, who knew these subtle windings of the passions besides him—though none so well as he!' ('On Single Plays, Poems, etc.'; vi. 294). For all the affection, even reverence, sometimes, with which Hazlitt approaches the Elizabethan dramatists, they are never more than 'the scale by which we can best ascend to the true knowledge and love of him [Shakespeare]'. The best of his selection are so many Shakespeare *manqués* who, 'with their united strength, would hardly make one Shakespear' (vi. 181). They give us the outline or first beginnings of the dramatic art, never its fullness. Marlowe's Dr Faustus, for instance, 'is a rude sketch, but it is a gigantic one' ('On Lyly, Marlow, Heywood, etc.'; vi. 202). Middleton's *Women Beware Women*, 'is like the rough draught of a tragedy, with a number of fine things thrown in, and the best made use of first; but it tends to no fixed goal, and the interest decreases, instead of increasing, as we read on, for want of previous arrangement and an eye to the whole' ('On Lyly, Marlow, Heywood, etc.'; vi. 215). By contrast, both Hazlitt's criteria of drama are fulfilled in Shakespeare, who, 'with the same faculty of lending himself to the impulses of Nature and the impression of the moment, never forgot that he himself had a task to perform' ('On Lyly, Marlow, Heywood, etc.; vi. 215).

At various points in this book, I have pointed out the theoretical similarities between Hazlitt and Schiller, with reference to the essay *On the Naive and Sentimental in Literature*. Schiller's theory can be brought usefully to bear on the unravelling of Hazlitt's, simply on the grounds of extensive parallelism, without making any claims for direct influence. An example of this kind of parallelism is to be found between Hazlitt's Shakespearian theory, with its fusion of self-consciousness and protean character, and Schiller's exposition of the 'naive'.

To enter into the correspondence between Schiller's 'naive' and Hazlitt's 'Shakespearian' categories of genius, is to beg the question of whether the parallelism is more general, extending also to a correspondence between their 'sentimental' and 'ordinary' categories. In Schiller's account of the 'naive' and 'sentimental' types in literature, the relationship between reality and the ideal is the index to the status of the authorial self: when the real and the ideal are one, the self is identical with nature, hence, perfectly whole; when they are divided, the self is divided from nature and eternally strives to restore a pre-existent unity, hence it is not whole, but *whole-making*. This latter is the sentimental genius, and its attribute is agency, the tendency of the will to strive towards oneness. The resources whereby it renders the fragmentary complete are within itself.[47] Consequently, the sentimental text does not lead us out into its subject-matter, but rather through its subject-matter draws us always inward to the authorial self, 'to look first of all in the work for the author, to encounter *his* heart, to reflect on his subject-matter together *with him*, in short to look for the subject-matter in the person.'[48]

It need not be laboured that there are some significant parallels between Schiller's 'sentimental' and Hazlitt's 'ordinary' genius. In Hazlitt's view, the imagining self achieves a relation of unity with nature from within itself, by the exercise of an innate attribute. Such exercise testifies to the mind's agency, therefore its product, the text, is pervaded with a strong selfhood or authorial presence. There remains, however, one crucial aspect which precludes a one-to-one correspondence between the two categories of genius in Schiller and Hazlitt. By Schiller's assertion, while the character of reality in the vision of the naive poet imparts a specificity to his forms, the sentimental genius 'abandons reality in order to ascend to ideas'.[49] In Hazlitt's theory of genius, by contrast, the power of the inspired self *authenticates* the forms of the imagination: they are not separate from, but interpretative of, reality. In other words, all the composition of genius must possess the substantial or real attribute that Schiller accords only to the naive. By incorporating a strong sense of the validity of particular experience, derived from his key theme of self-affirmation, Hazlitt evolves a theory of ordinary genius which merges both Schiller's categories, tending more towards the 'combination' which Schiller explicates towards the end of his essay.[50]

The insistence on the 'naive' attributes of Hazlitt's ordinary genius prevents an exact correspondence between his 'ordinary' and Shakespearian categories and Schiller's 'naive' and 'sentimental' categories of genius. Nevertheless, the oneness with nature that distinguishes both Schiller's naive genius and Hazlitt's Shakespeare still gives us grounds for some illuminating comparisons. The naive poet, according to Schiller, *is* nature.[51] Since nature is also the ideal, by being nature, the naive poet offers us

[47] Schiller, *Naive and Sentimental*, 68. [48] Ibid. 36. [49] Ibid. 72.
[50] Ibid. 80. [51] Ibid. 38.

the realised ideal, that is, an ideal which is indistinguishable from reality. The identity of poet and nature enables the authorial self to vanish entirely into its subject-matter.[52] Schiller names Homer and Shakespeare as exemplifying the naive, and his view of the naive consciousness as manifesting the identity of poet and nature recalls Hazlitt's definition of the 'poet of nature', also exemplified by Homer and Shakespeare. Hazlitt's definition, as we have seen, embodies a view of the imagining self that encompasses both types of genius, the ordinary and the Shakespearian. But in the case of the ordinary genius, the empowered self at the centre of the sphere of its imagination brings nature into 'relation' with itself; in the case of the Shakespearian genius, that self is nature, so that the circle drawn by it becomes identical to the circle of nature itself. The dualism of reality and the elevated 'better reality', being merged into one, disappears. Thus Shakespearian composition achieves holistic character without manifesting an assertive self-hood, and by so doing satisfies the second condition for dramatic excellence:

He seemed scarcely to have an individual existence of his own, but to borrow that of others at will, and to pass successively through 'every variety of untried being,'—to be now *Hamlet*, now *Othello*, now *Lear*, now *Falstaff*, now *Ariel*. In the mingled interests and feelings belonging to this wide range of imaginary reality, in the tumult and rapid transitions of this waking dream, the author could not easily find time to think of himself, nor wish to embody that personal identity. . . ('On Posthumous Fame', *The Round Table*; iv. 23)

This is the passage that is usually cited as the source of Keats's remarks on the 'poetical Character' in the letter to Woodhouse of 27 October 1818. The 'waking dream' is also, of course a familiar image in Keats's letters and poems; the speculation regarding Shakespeare's indifference to fame probably influenced, too, Keats's own affectation of a similar indifference in the letter to Reynolds, 9 April 1818: 'I never wrote one single Line of Poetry with the least Shadow of public thought. . . . I hate a Mawkish Popularity.'[53] To Hazlitt, Shakepeare's 'lack of individual existence' means that he is successful only as a dramatist, and he even goes so far as to declare that 'In expressing the thoughts of

---

[52] Schiller, *Naive and Sentimental*, 35–6.   [53] Keats, *Letters*, i. 267.

others, he seemed inspired; in expressing his own, he was a mechanic' ('Poems and Sonnets', *Characters of Shakespear's Plays*; iv. 358). The dynamic quality in Shakespeare's text is achieved only under the condition of alterity, being absent when the author speaks in his own voice. Correspondingly, the inherent life of the Shakespearian creation approximates rather to nature than the individual authorial ego, so that the 'truth' of the Shakespearian text with which we are brought into sympathy is universal (*the* truth) rather than specific (*a* truth). Its

distinctness and originality is indeed the necessary consequence of truth and nature. Shakespear's genius alone appeared to possess the resources of nature.... His plays have the force of things upon the mind. What he represents is brought home to the bosom as a part of our experience, implanted in the memory as if we had known the places, persons, and things of which he treats. ('Macbeth', *Characters of Shakespear's Plays*; iv. 186)

The universality of Shakespeare makes his genius comprehensive rather than restrictive, and in this respect, the essay 'On Shakspeare and Milton' in the *Lectures on the English Poets* specifically contrasts him with Chaucer, in whom 'we perceive a fixed essence of character,' and Milton, who 'took only a few simple principles of character, and raised them to the utmost conceivable grandeur' (v. 51). Again, 'passion' in Shakespeare's case, is the reverse of this quality in the ordinary or self-willed genius; it is neither forceful nor exclusive, but universal and comprehensive. 'It is not some one habitual feeling or sentiment preying upon itself, growing out of itself, and moulding every thing to itself; it is passion modified by passion, by all the other feelings to which the individual is liable, *and to which others are liable with him*' (v. 51; my italics).

The world of Shakespeare's plays is nature's world, in which the reader sometimes discovers, not the author, but himself: 'Their reality is in the reader's mind. It is *we* who are Hamlet' ('Hamlet', *Characters of Shakespear's Plays*; iv. 232). Hazlitt's understanding of the comprehensiveness of the Shakespearian imagination aligns his account of Shakespeare with Coleridge's, who also celebrates the universality by virtue of which the Shakespearian text directs us, not towards the author, but into ourselves: 'In the plays of Shakespeare every man sees himself without knowing that he sees himself as in the phenomena of nature, in the mist of the mountain a traveller beholds his own figure but the glory round the head distinguishes it from a mere vulgar copy.'[54] The same idea recurs in Lamb, who points out how our reading of Shakespeare yields a kind of partial mirror-image of ourselves, of 'those images of virtue and of knowledge, of which every one of us recognizing a part, think we comprehend in our natures the whole; and oftentimes mistake the powers which he positively creates in us, for nothing more than indigenous faculties of our own minds.'[55] Lamb's comment on Lear—'we see not Lear, but we are Lear'—is not only incorporated by Hazlitt into his own analysis of *King Lear* (iv. 271), but is also echoed in his observation that 'It is *we* who are Hamlet'.

Hamlet is the universal self, and Hazlitt takes this so literally as to bring the experiences of his own life to bear upon his understanding of the play (iv. 232–3). Interestingly enough, his description of Hamlet 'whom we may be said almost to remember in our after-years; . . . his speeches and sayings . . . as real as our own thoughts' (iv. 232) is closely matched in content and phraseology by an observation made elsewhere as a criticism of Dr Johnson: 'His reflections present themselves like reminiscences; do not disturb the ordinary march of our thoughts' ('On the Periodical Essayists', *Lectures on the English Comic Writers*; vi. 100). Johnson is censured precisely for the quality for which Shakespeare is praised, that is, the absence of a strong authorial presence that dominates the reader. That quality which marks the Shakespearian text as containing a profound, because universal truth, in Johnson's case appears merely as a lack of originality. What is the hallmark of Shakespeare's genius is the failure of Johnson's; once more, a small but significant pointer to the independence of Hazlitt's Shakespeare from the norms of his literary criticism.

I have remarked already the evidence of Hazlitt's authority in Keats's axioms for poetry in the letter to Taylor of 27 February 1818. In this same letter, it is the description of the workings of an exceptional genius in Hazlitt's remarks on Hamlet that would appear to have influenced Keats's prescription for poetry: 'I think

---

[54] Coleridge, *On Literature*, i. 352.
[55] 'On the Tragedies of Shakespeare' (Lamb, *Works*, i. 103).

Poetry should ... strike the Reader as a wording of his own highest thoughts, and appear almost a Remembrance.'[56]

Protean character is foremost in Hazlitt's account of Shakespeare; occasionally, however, his account also incorporates some of the self-affirming traits of the ordinary genius. The essay on Coriolanus, for instance, provides the context for a critique of the imagination as an 'exaggerating and exclusive faculty' ('Coriolanus', *Characters of Shakespear's Plays*; iv. 214). Again, the essay 'Sir Walter Scott, Racine, and Shakespear' describes Shakespeare in *Othello* as asserting exactly the powerful selfhood directed by 'bias' that defines Hazlitt's theory of 'ordinary' genius; the furnace image that typifies Hazlitt's Milton is here applied to Shakespeare:

> The power displayed in it is that of intense passion and powerful intellect, ... The splendour is that of genius darting out its forked flame on whatever comes in its way, and kindling and melting it in the furnace of affection, whether it be flax or iron. The colouring, the form, the motion, the combination of objects depend on the pre-disposition of the mind, moulding nature to its own purposes; ... (*The Plain Speaker*; xii. 343)

Both examples confirm that the Shakespearian genius is unique: a powerful imagination which accommodates, without inconsistency, the self-forgetfulness that is the criterion for dramatic excellence.

The understanding of Shakespeare as occupying a unique and isolated position in relation to Hazlitt's theory of ordinary genius prevents the confusion with Keats, whose adaptation of Hazlitt is founded upon that isolated case. Moreover, Keats is a poet, and as such, his theory tends naturally towards the prescriptive: what a poet ought to be; equally, Hazlitt, as a critic, tends towards the experiential, describing what a poet, most generally, is. The theory of the imagination constructed from Hazlitt's literary criticism is inseparable from the model of the mind at the heart of his metaphysics; it is a theory of the powerful self, which cannot be exemplified by the rare, if glorious, deviation from what he perceived to be the standard pattern of artistic composition.

---

[56] Keats, *Letters*, i. 238.

4

A Long-Contested Freedom
Metaphysics and Moral Theory

I HAVE focused so far on Hazlitt's construct of the self-affirming tendency of the mind, of which the fullest and most powerful manifestation is termed 'genius'. I want now to raise the question of the moral implications of that construct. Hazlitt's concerns are insistently moral, and it is a strong moral emphasis that adds to the polemical thrust of his epistemology. In this chapter, I will return once more to Hazlitt's philosophy, this time specifically as moral philosophy. Like his epistemology and indeed, inseparable from it, Hazlitt's theory of morals is all pervasive, reaching far beyond the immediate context of the philosophical lectures and essays into the fundamentals of his literary and social criticism.

Alterity and the Moral Question

The example of the authorial presence in artistic composition confirms that 'sympathy', the mode of relation of self to other, is associative, and refers to the mind's 'stamping' of external objects with the image of itself. For Hazlitt, this stamping—the assimilation of objects by the mind—constitutes imaginative exercise: 'though the things themselves as they really exist cannot go out of themselves into other things, or compromise their natures, there is no reason why the mind which is merely representative should be confined to any one of them more than to any other' (*Remarks on the Systems of Hartley and Helvetius*; i. 73). On the other hand, although sympathy, by which the mind establishes 'relation' is self-affirming, by the argument of the *Essay on the Principles of Human Action*, it may not be reduced to self-love. So to reduce it would be to deny moral action altogether. The *Essay* insists that the concept of 'other' is meaningful in the operation of the self, only by admission of which that self can be treated as susceptible to moral judgement. Alterity validates the moral nature of man. In the *Lectures on the Age of Elizabeth*, Hazlitt describes the moral reformation effected by Christ as due to his answering the question 'who is our neighbour?' ('General View of the Subject'; vi. 184). If that which is other to the self can be shown to constitute a real motive to action, then the self owns moral agency.

However, when Hazlitt defines alterity in the *Essay*, he does so in relation to our material or current being, the 'mechanical self'. In relation to this self, not only is our 'neighbour' the 'other', but our own future, imaginary, or intellectual being is 'other' to our current being. If benevolence describes those actions of which our neighbour is the object, and selfishness those of which our own future selves are the object, then, both being the outcome of imaginative exercise (and hence, by Hazlitt's lights, 'sympathetic'), neither is reducible to self-love. The characterization of the two types of action as alike imaginative implies that the imagination, as construed by the *Essay on the Principles of Human Action*, is not definitively a moral imagination. It contains a moral possibility ('I could not love myself, if I were not capable of loving others'; i. 2), but it is not directed by a moral imperative.

Again, the comparison with Coleridge is worth noticing. In a note of 1810, Coleridge summarizes some of the main issues of Hazlitt's *Essay* to arrive, unlike Hazlitt, at a moral conclusion, made possible by his religious perspective:

Mere knowledge of the right, we find by experience, does not suffice to ensure the performance of the Right—for mankind in general. . . . Much less shall we [be] led to our Duty by calculations of pleasant or harmful consequences—to our *Duty* indeed, this is impossible, & a contradiction in terms; but even to the outward acts & conventional Symbols of Duty, i.e. Legality, Experience demonstrates what the acquaintance with the Human Soul would indeed render almost certain a priori, such selfish Promises & Threats have little effect—for the more the selfish principle is set into fermentation, the more imperious & despotic does the Present Moment become—till at length to love our future Self is almost as hard as to love our Neighbour—it is indeed only a difference of Space & Time—My Neighbour is my *other* Self, *othered* by Space—my old age is to my youth an other Self, *othered* by Time.—How then shall he act upon imperfect and enslaved man? By all together—but chiefly, by setting them in *action*—Now what is the medium between mere conviction & resolve, & suitable *action*? For such a medium is absolutely necessary, since there is no saltus in nature—This medium is found in Prayer, & religious Intercommunion between Man & his Maker—.Hence the necessity of Prayer—[1]

It is remarkable that this note, written five years after the publication of Hazlitt's *Essay* and apparently without reference to it, contains two of the main contentions of the *Essay*: that the Utilitarian principle ('calculations of pleasant or harmful consequences') is inadequate to ensure moral action, and that the alterity of our future selves is on a par with the alterity of our neighbour. Typically, Coleridge translates this understanding into a religious moral: the necessity of 'religious Intercommunion between Man & his Maker'. To Hazlitt, the moral facility provided by a religious framework is unavailable.

Like Shelley's *Defence of Poetry*, Hazlitt's *Essay* makes the imagination the great instrument of moral good. But the origin of imaginative exercise is the principle of power, 'the common love of strong excitement', and this principle is morally neutral: 'It is as natural to hate as to love, to despise as to admire, to express our hatred or contempt, as our love or admiration' ('On Poetry in General', *Lectures on the English Poets*; v. 7). Again, Coleridge also remarks the moral neutrality of power, in much the same terms, in his lecture on Lear: 'to Power in itself, without reference to any moral end, an inevitable Admiration & Complacency appertains, whether it be displayed in the conquests of a Napoleon or Tamurlane, or in the foam and thunder of a Cataract.'[2] But Hazlitt, who focuses, far more than Coleridge, on the necessary and indissoluble connection between power and imagination, further makes explicit, in a way that Coleridge does not, that the morally neutral character of power defines the imagination. Iago, he declares, 'is only an extreme instance' of the working of the power principle without moral restraint, 'that is, of diseased intellectual activity, with an almost perfect indifference to moral good or evil' ('On the Love of Country', *The Round Table*; iv. 16). The example of Iago confirms that imaginative activity is

---

[1] S. T. Coleridge, *The Notebooks of Samuel Taylor Coleridge*, ed. K. Coburn, Bollingen series, no. 50, 4 vols published (Princeton, NJ: Princeton University Press, 1973), iii, n. 4017.   [2] Coleridge, *On Literature*, ii. 328.

possessed of no innate moral character.[3] It has therefore specifically to be *directed* towards a moral end, 'by shewing to man that his nature is originally and essentially disinterested; that as a voluntary agent, he must be a disinterested one; that he could neither desire, nor will, nor pursue his own happiness but for the possession of faculties which necessarily give him an interest out of himself in the happiness of others' (i. 6–7).

Further, in spite of its didactic and moral objective, the whole of the *Essay on the Principles of Human Action* is pervaded with the acknowledgement that individual consciousness has been so rooted in the immediate self-apprehension brought about by the mechanical processes of sensation and memory, as constantly and cumulatively to be impelled towards the illusion that 'self' and 'other' constitute a divided, rather than unified, interest:

Every sensation that I feel, or that afterwards recurs vividly to my memory strengthens the sense of self, which increased strength in the mechanical feeling is transferred to the general idea, and to my remote, future, imaginary interest: whereas our sympathy with the feelings of others being always imaginary, having no sensible interest, no restless mechanical impulse to urge it on, the ties by which we are bound to others hang loose upon us, the interest we take in their welfare seems to be something foreign to our own bosoms, to be transient, arbitrary, and directly opposite to the necessary, absolute, permanent interest which we have in the pursuit of our own welfare. (i. 42)

Such an observation no more than establishes, after all, that if 'the pursuit of our own welfare' is just as much an act of the imagination as 'our sympathy with the feelings of others', imaginative exercise has nonetheless been consistently limited by the first to the exclusion of the second, thus confirming its freedom from a necessary connection to a moral end. The mechanism of the senses habitually traps the imagination within sensory limits; in such a condition, the imagination simply mimes the senses, rather than exercising its power to direct them.

---

[3] Albrecht, who contends that 'denial of self' and 'loss of self' are characteristic of Hazlitt's account of the imagination, finds also that the imagination is intuitively moral for Hazlitt.—W. P. Albrecht, *Hazlitt and the Creative Imagination*. (Lawrence, Kan.: University of Kansas Press, 1965), 121. I have shown that it is self-affirmation rather than self-annihilation that typifies imaginative activity in Hazlitt's theory. Hazlitt's recognition of the imaginative tendency to self-affirmation goes hand in hand with an understanding of the imaginative impulse as morally neutral.

The habitual limitation of the empowered self is a leading subject of the great moral essays of *The Plain Speaker*, in which Hazlitt exposes the dark other side of some of his most deeply held beliefs. The exclusive intellect which, in the case of Milton, Rembrandt, and Wordsworth, is the necessary condition for genius, is shown also, in the sphere of human intercourse, to degenerate into a petty self-centredness that constricts social relations. 'A bigoted and exclusive spirit is real blindness to all excellence but our own, . . . Mr. Wordsworth, in particular, is narrower in his tastes than other people, because he sees everything from a single and original point of view' ('On Envy'; xii. 101–2). By dwelling protractedly on the evils of pure self-reference, Hazlitt seems to call into question that very ideal of the powerful ego celebrated in his lectures on literature, and upon which rests the optimistic manifesto of the *Essay on the Principles of Human Action*. Self-love which, in the *Essay*, is potentially enlarged so as to comprehend benevolence towards all of humanity, is shown to tend more usually to a lower purpose in reality. Imprisoned within the narrow sphere of personal vanity and selfishness, its relations with the 'other' are characterized by spite, malevolence, and ill-will. In the essay 'On the Spirit of Obligations', vanity is explicitly asserted to be a prime motive to action (xii. 87). Our friends are those only who form to us 'a flattering mirror,' magnifying our virtues and softening our errors (xii. 84); the portrait painter, for just this reason, appears our best friend ('On Sitting for One's Picture'; xii. 108). Appearance takes precedence over reality in forming our judgements, since 'our self-love receives a less sensible shock from encountering the mere semblance than the solid substance of worth' ('Qualifications Necessary to Success'; xii. 204).

The Plain Speaker forcefully articulates the independence of the power principle of a necessary moral purpose. The essay 'On Depth and Superficiality' asserts the blindness of the will and the imagination (xii. 351), arising from there being 'a love of power in the mind independent of the love of good' (xii. 348). 'Ridicule', observes Northcote in the dialogue 'On Envy', '. . . is sure to prevail over truth, because the malice of mankind thrown into the scale gives the casting-weight' (xii. 106). Again, the essay 'On the Pleasure of Hating' reverses the perspective on the power principle presented in the *Essay on the Principles of Human*

Action, by describing 'a secret affinity, a *hankering* after evil in the human mind' (xii. 128). Hatred becomes here the spring of thought and action; the pleasure of hating eats into every social feeling, whether of religion, patriotism, or virtue, leading finally to the hatred of ourselves (xii. 130). As self-love is capable of direction into benevolence in the *Essay*, the hatred of others is shown, conversely, to translate at last to self-hate. The reversal between the two visions, the first contained in his early writing, the second, in some of the last essays that Hazlitt wrote, could be treated, as he himself seems occasionally to treat it, as a chronological development, a progressively dawning realization culled from the experiences of his own life ('On the Spirit of Obligations'; xii. 87, 'On the Pleasure of Hating'; xii. 135–6).

The Plain Speaker gives us morality at odds with power, and hence, apparently, with the very nature of humanity itself. The tendency of a moral being is liberal and comprehensive, that of the empowered mind, bigoted and exclusive. At different points in these essays, Hazlitt is emphatic in affirming that liberalism must not be sacrificed to power. 'A great name is an abstraction of some one excellence: but whoever fancies himself an abstraction of excellence, . . . [is] equally ignorant of excellence or defect, of himself or others' ('Whether Genius is Conscious of its Powers?'; xii. 118). Although the narrowness of capacity is requisite to excellence in any one thing, the limitation of taste to that thing only leads to bigotry and blindness. In the essay 'On Egotism', Hazlitt reiterates that while 'No one is (generally speaking) great in more than one thing—if he extends his pursuits, he dissipates his strength,' yet 'Nothing but the want of comprehension of view or generosity of spirit can make any one fix on his own particular acquirement as the limit of all excellence' (xii. 164). In fact,

> The greater a man is, the less he necessarily thinks of himself, for his knowledge enlarges with his attainments. In himself he feels that he is nothing, a point, a speck in the universe, except as his mind reflects that universe, and as he enters into the infinite variety of truth, beauty, and power contained in it. . . . Personal vanity is incompatible with the great and the *ideal*. ('On Egotism'; xii. 164, 166)

Despite such declarations, Hazlitt is keenly aware, not only in *The Plain Speaker*, but throughout his experience as critic and moralist, that power, and wisdom in which moral behaviour originates, are rarely reconcilable. The essay 'Belief, Whether Voluntary?' represents the human mind as playing 'the interested advocate much oftener than the upright and inflexible judge, in the colouring and relief it gives to the facts brought before it' (*Miscellaneous Writings*; xx. 367). It is the 'bias of the will' that directs our acceptance of a truth, not the proof of that truth itself (xx. 365). The bias of the will is in turn a matter of 'disposition to attend to this or that view of the subject' (xx. 368), and it is only by setting disposition aside that we arrive at anything like a just determination. But 'disposition' is irrevocably bound up with selfhood; hence it is, says Hazlitt, that the philosopher, who must set aside disposition in the pursuit of truth, manifests madness, the 'absence of mind' (xx. 369).

The essay on 'The Spirit of Philosophy' further articulates the tension between the self-affirming tendency of the mind and the self-effacing condition of philosophy or morals. I have shown that the self-affirming genius of Hazlitt's theory does not own an absolute insight; it offers *a* truth, but not *the* truth. 'The Spirit of Philosophy' identifies philosophical failure in the confounding of one with the other. 'A man, by great labour and sagacity, finds out one truth; but from the importunate craving of the mind to know all, he would fain persuade himself that this one truth includes all others' (*Miscellaneous Writings*; xx. 375). Here again, bigotry, the attribute of power and the condition of genius is perceived as precluding philosophical judgement. The converse is also the case, as evidenced, for instance, in the character of Bacon, described in the *Lectures on the Age of Elizabeth*,

He had great liberality from seeing the various aspects of things (there was nothing bigotted or intolerant or exclusive about him) and yet he had firmness and decision from feeling their weight and consequences. His character was then an amazing insight into the limits of human knowledge and acquaintance with the landmarks of human intellect, . . . but when he quits the ground of contemplation of what others have done or left undone to project himself into future discoveries, he becomes quaint and fantastic, instead of original. His strength was in reflection, not in production: he was the surveyor, not the builder of the fabric of science. He had not strictly the constructive faculty. ('Character of Lord Bacon's Works'; vi. 328)

I have quoted this account at some length because it so explicitly conveys the point that a 'liberality' of vision—the absence of bigotry, intolerance, and exclusiveness—seems to preclude the exercise of the 'constructive faculty', the self-affirming tendency whose attributes are precisely those of bigotry, intolerance, and exclusiveness. Bacon's perfect understanding of 'what others have done' leaves him unable effectively 'to project himself'. The passage clearly suggests that it is because his strength is reflection, he is not productive, because he is a surveyor, he cannot be a builder. At the same time, 'Lord Bacon has been called (and justly) one of the wisest of mankind' (vi. 326), his wisdom residing in exactly the liberalism, 'seeing the various aspects of things', that is here described. This paradox, emerging from Hazlitt's actual experience, threatens to expose as hollow the core of his moral philosophy.

In his discussion of Hazlitt's philosophy, John Kinnaird concludes that Hazlitt is a failure as a theoretical moralist. His summary of Hazlitt's philosophical achievement is not just dismissive, but damning. Hazlitt, he declares, 'had failed even to enlarge in theory man's capacity for benevolence.'[4]

To what extent may we accept this conclusion, setting, as it does the limits of Hazlitt's philosophical vision? Undeniably, his metaphysic is based on an assertive and exclusive self; equally, his ethics advocate a comprehensive and liberal vision that appears irreconcilable with such a formulation of the self. Given, then, the didactic purpose of the *Essay on the Principles of Human Action*, to what extent may we consider it as 'failed'? Or, how does the metaphysic which is so founded in the vision of an empowered self at the same time assert its 'natural disinterestedness', the potential of that self for wisdom and hence morality?

The Moral Ideal

The theoretical possibility for the reconciliation of wisdom and power lies in this, that the self is the instrument rather than the motive for action, the motive being, rather, good: 'The reason why a child first distinctly wills or pursues his own good is not because it

---

[4] Kinnaird, *William Hazlitt*, 61.

is *his*, but because it is *good.*' (*An Essay on the Principles of Human Action*; i. 12). Again, 'We love ourselves, not according to our deserts, but our cravings after good' ('On the Knowledge of Character', *Table-Talk*; viii. 315) and 'our love of self is . . . formed out of a general principle of love of good, strengthened and determined to a particular point' ('Outlines of Morals', *Miscellaneous Writings*; xx. 385). Good, rather than self, being the motive to action, it is also good, rather than self, that must be addressed as the basis of practical morality, so that 'the doctrine of self . . . has nothing to do with . . . morals in any sense' ('Outlines of Morals'; xx. 376). In spite of his emphasis on selfhood and power, Hazlitt is unequivocal in declaring that while the self is always the instrument of morality, it is never its end.

'Power' expresses moral capacity, 'good', moral purpose. The Bible, according to Hazlitt, was the great engine of morality in the Elizabethan period because 'Its law is good, not power. It at the same time tended to wean the mind from the grossness of sense' ('General View of the Subject', *Lectures on the Age of Elizabeth*; vi. 185). Hazlitt does not spell out here what is clearly the implication of the *Essay on the Principles of Human Action*, that it is power which makes meaningful, in the first place, good as a moral goal; power signifies the mind's potential to break free of the grosser material considerations in favour of the ideal. The biblical ideal is embodied in the person of Christ: 'His whole life and being were imbued, steeped in this word, *charity*,' 'He taught the love of good for the sake of good, without regard to personal or sinister views,' 'The very idea of abstract benevolence, . . . is hardly to be found in any other code or system' (vi. 184).[5] The 'idea of abstract benevolence' owns the ability to overcome fact; hence, 'There is something in the character of Christ . . . more likely to work a change in the mind of man, by the contemplation of its idea alone, than any to be found in history' (vi. 183). In the assertion of the greater efficacy of an idea over history, imagination over past experience, resides also the moral achievement of the *Essay*.

The main 'discovery' established theoretically in the *Essay*, and

---

[5] These comments support Kinnaird's suggestion of a possible connection between Hazlitt's ideal of 'natural disinterestedness' and the Unitarian ideal of Christ as the absolutely disinterested son of man (ibid. 18–19).

the primary truth to which it directs our attention, is that benevolence or 'disinterestedness' is natural, not foreign, to the self. The admission and recognition of this truth is itself the first step towards acting upon it. If, as Hazlitt observes, the idea of a mechanical self-impulse has been a determinant of consciousness, challenging that idea must create a new self-awareness; thus it carries, implicitly, the expectation of a change in conduct or habit conformable to that new sense of self. Hence the answer to the question, how does the *Essay on the Principles of Human Action* suggest that the imagination be directed towards a moral end, is, by the force of an idea. The *Essay* contains an idea which by its power is intended to overcome the pattern set by the experience that contradicts it. The achievement of its moral end is the validation of its pivotal theme, the exaltation of the mind over the senses. Conversely, by placing the mind above the senses, the *Essay* asserts the power of ideas over experience, and it is only by virtue of such power that it can itself claim moral standing.[6] Ideas, by its argument, constitute real motives to action (i. 23). Contrary to Kinnaird's observation, it is exactly in theory that the *Essay on the Principles of Human Action* enlarges man's capacity for benevolence. It does not stop with the analysis of existing modes of behaviour, but, by reinterpreting their source, opens up the hitherto unadmitted possibility for a new mode of behaviour. In *A Letter to William Gifford*, Hazlitt reiterates that his object in the *Essay* is to show the extent of imaginative capacity, rather than to prove the fact of imaginative achievement (ix. 51). 'Disinterestedness' is affirmed in the *Essay* not as actual, but ideal.

The commitment to an ideal we may term, according to common usage, idealism, and it is this which qualifies and indeed belies, within the collection itself, the pessimism expressed in the *Plain Speaker* essays. If the *Essay* shows that attaining the ideal is possible, *The Plain Speaker* points to the condition of human affairs that makes it imperative. The critique of human nature is the manifestation of what Hazlitt elsewhere describes as 'true misanthropy'. 'True misanthropy consists not in pointing out the faults and follies of men, but in encouraging them in the pursuit' ('Aphorisms on Man'; xx. 339). His account of Swift as

---

[6] The power of ideas constitutes Schiller's definition of the moral: 'dispositions which are receptive to ideas, . . . [are] moral ones' (Schiller, *Naive and Sentimental*, 23).

a misanthrope encapsulates his own role and purpose in *The Plain Speaker*: 'What a convincing proof of misanthropy! What presumption and what *malice prepense*, to shew men what they are, and to teach them what they ought to be!' ('On Swift, Young, Gray, Collins, etc.', *Lectures on the English Poets*; v. 111). The misanthropic idealism that Hazlitt ascribes to Swift may also be claimed as his own; Hunt acknowledges just this idealistic impulse in Hazlitt's misanthropy in a *Tatler* article of 28 September 1830, written shortly after Hazlitt's death: 'Mr. Hazlitt was "at feud with the world" out of his infinite sympathy with them, and because he was angry that they were not in as great haste as himself to see justice done them.'[7]

In the context of Hazlitt's idealism, the two views of human nature contained, respectively, in the *Essay on the Principles of Human Action* and in *The Plain Speaker* are not contradictory, but complementary, affirming a single moral ideal: disinterestedness. Moreover, by virtue of the ideal standing of disinterestedness, the adjective 'natural' in Hazlitt's phrase 'natural disinterestedness' must not be taken to signify that the mind is actually or necessarily disinterested. 'Natural disinterestedness' claims only the possibility of disinterestedness, as being no less natural to man than self-love. The subtitle of the *Essay* is directed specifically against philosophies which exclude that possibility through the premiss that self-love alone may be recognized as natural or real to man. By understanding disinterestedness as a possibility rather than a fact in Hazlitt's theory, the discrepancy that Kinnaird finds, between Hazlitt's ideal of disinterestedness and his notion of power, which Kinnaird calls the knowledge of the bias or 'original sin' in all human character,[8] is removed. For Hazlitt, 'bias' signifies primarily the independence of the mind from external or circumstantial manipulation, and it is exactly this independence that allows it to surpass the empirical or material considerations of interest to achieve 'disinterested' behaviour. Like Schiller's ideal of 'nature' in the essay *On the Naive and Sentimental in Literature*, the idea of 'natural disinterestedness' in Hazlitt's *Essay* represents both a loss, brought about by the strength of the physical self and perpetuated by the mechanistic philosophies, as well as a goal—

---

[7] Leigh Hunt, *Leigh Hunt's Literary Criticism*, ed. L. H. and C. W. Houtchens (New York: Columbia University Press, 1956), 276.   [8] Kinnaird, *William Hazlitt*, 88.

ideal—towards which we must strive despite experience; thus, it highlights human agency.

Viewed in this light, the didactic purpose of the *Essay* does not contradict, but rather resides in the imagination's freedom from a necessary connection to a moral end. The condition of choice liberates the will which, when it chooses freely, if it chooses also rightly, fulfils man's highest nature as a moral agent.

Particular and Universal

Hazlitt's separation of power and good foregrounds agency as the central concern of his moral philosophy. The ideal, good, or more specifically, disinterestedness, is enabled by power. While its source is morally neutral, the ideal itself may be recognized as moral when it is also universal. The relation between power and good is a relation between particular and general, between the individual and determinate self and a universal and abstract ideal. The self is the origin of the relation. In the previous chapter, I discussed the artistic ideal, produced from the original and particular vision of the creative artist, and simultaneously compelled to universal applicability, and so validated, by the power of that biased and particular self. 'Sympathy' refers to this compulsion.[9] In the area of moral philosophy also, Hazlitt's commitment to a uniquely biased self, together with his demand for the universality of its

---

[9] In at least one place, Hazlitt appears to distinguish between the compulsive mode of sympathy and another, which is less so. In the essay 'On People of Sense', he makes the distinction between the sympathy of wisdom and the sympathy of power. 'But whoever becomes wise, becomes wise by sympathy; whoever is powerful, becomes so by making others sympathize with him. To think justly, we must understand what others mean: to know the value of our thoughts, we must try their effect on other minds' (*The Plain Speaker*; xii. 250). Despite the distinction, however (which incidentally confirms the tension between wisdom and power in Hazlitt's thought), it will be perceived that both types of sympathy are actually dependent on the self-affirming or compulsive attribute. The sympathy of wisdom is validated by the sympathy of power, since the rightness of judgement, 'the value of our thoughts', is established only by its self-affirming or colonizing effect, 'their effect on other minds'. Furthermore, the criterion for right judgement—that it must be inly determined, and never by that which is external or other to the self—also confirms its self-affirming character. The essay 'On the Difference between Writing and Speaking', for instance, warns us against the tendency of men in society to 'judge not by their own convictions, but by sympathy with others' (*The Plain Speaker*; xii. 267).

vision, forges a simultaneous or symbiotic relation between the particular and the universal; this relation, manifested as 'sympathy', typifies his idealism, in which the ideal or abstract is organically produced from the particular or concrete. The relation between particular and universal is definitive of Hazlitt's theory of morals; it is exemplified, for instance, in the essay 'On Reason and Imagination' in *The Plain Speaker*.

'On Reason and Imagination' is a celebration of particularity and individualism; selfhood, according to its argument, is the only means to truth and morality. 'The interest we take in our own lives, in our successes or disappointments, and the *home* feelings that arise out of these, . . . are the clearest and truest mirror in which we can see the image of human nature' (xii. 54). By stipulating that 'the sympathy of the individual with the consequences of his own act is to be attended to (no less than the consequences themselves) in every sound system of morality' (xii. 50), Hazlitt characterizes morality as an integral development, not to be achieved by the application of an objective or external standard but of one that is subjective and inly directed. He calls this development the 'cultivation of a *moral sense*' (xii. 49); its mode is imaginative and self-affirming, proceeding from the knowledge of the individual self to universal knowledge (xii. 55). Truth is rooted in individual experience from which alone it gathers force; relatedly, morality must be founded in individual feeling. The various individual experiences are validated not by some externally imposed rule or condition, but by the force of feeling or passion which they communicate, this being 'the essence, the chief ingredient in moral truth' (xii. 46), which alone brings us into sympathy with it.

Our feeling of general humanity is at once an aggregate of a thousand different truths, and it is also the same truth a thousand times told. As is our perception of this original truth, the root of our imagination, so will the force and richness of the general impression proceeding from it be. The boundary of our sympathy is a circle which enlarges itself according to its propulsion from the centre—the heart . . . (xii. 55)

The self is the seat of sympathy, the centre of the circle which may be enlarged to compass the universe. We recall Shelley's essay on the Colosseum, 'The internal nature of each being is surrounded by a circle,' and the description of poetry in the *Defence*: 'It is at once the center and circumference of knowledge.'[10] In Hazlitt's writings, the circle recurs as the 'circle of our knowledge' in the essay on the 'Outlines of Taste' (*Miscellaneous Writings*; xx. 388) and as the circle of influence of the poet of nature in the essay 'On Dryden and Pope'; here, too, it is a powerful self that brings about a sympathy and hence a wholeness of which it is the centre and origin: 'It has its centre in the human soul, and makes the circuit of the universe' (*Lectures on the English Poets*; v. 70).

The instrumentality of the self in determining imaginative truth has a profound implication for that truth: plurality. 'Truth is not one, but many; and an observation may be true in itself that contradicts another equally true, according to the point of view from which we contemplate the subject' (*Characteristics* CCCCXXXI; ix. 228).[11] In the essay 'On Reason and Imagination', truth considered as a whole is the effect of aggregation, so to speak, rather than distillation. It does not consist in the discarding of individual details and differences in order to arrive at a generalization, but represents that generalization which comprehends each of those details and differences. 'The sum total is indeed different from the particulars; but it is not easy to guess at any general result, without some previous induction of particulars and appeal to experience' (xii. 51).

The terms 'sum total' and 'aggregate' are crucial to understanding how Hazlitt retains, within a profoundly individualistic approach, a meaningful concept of universal truth. 'Aggregate' signifies a universal or general reality, each of whose components is individual and particular. The aggregate model of truth is the model of every ideal or universal in Hazlitt's theory, and reveals a reflexive and symbiotic relation at the basis of his epistemology: the relation between the individual or concrete and abstract or general. For the epistemological effort to be meaningful, we must garner the abstract from a number of individual instances, so as to confer a holistic character on the otherwise diffuse collation; the weight of abstract principle arises from its being indissolubly wedded to the particular, supported solely by the extensive range

---

[10] Shelley, *Prose*, 227, 293.
[11] Unlike Schneider, who perceives Hazlitt's pluralism as the outcome of a self-annihilatory emphasis—which she calls 'projectivism'—in his philosophy (Schneider, *Aesthetics*, 40–2), I myself find his pluralistic approach to be extremely compatible with the opposite emphasis, on self-affirmation.

of individual instances that it encompasses, since 'Facts, concrete existences, are stubborn things, and not so soon tampered with or turned about to any point we please, as *mere* names and abstractions' ('On Reason and Imagination'; xii. 52; my italics).

The symbiotic relation between abstract and concrete is exemplified by Hazlitt's corpus itself, of whose holistic character this relation is the basis. The abstract principle of his metaphysics is repeatedly confirmed in the numerous particular contexts supplied by the literary lectures and occasional prose; equally, the weight of the literary disquisitions in, say, the *Lectures on the English Poets*, or of the analysis of moral and social relations in *The Plain Speaker*, arises from their constant reference to the general metaphysical principle, with respect to which these essays and lectures transcend their disjointed or fragmentary character so as to compose a unified whole. Hazlitt's comment in the essay 'On Depth and Superficiality' sums up his own practice as a writer: 'the abstract naturally merges in the concrete' (*The Plain Speaker*; xii. 355).

The merging of abstract and concrete describes and is described by *The Plain Speaker*. In the essay 'On Personal Character', Hazlitt remarks the acuter comprehension of 'those who trace things to their source, and proceed from individuals to generals' (xii. 234). This procedure is elaborated in the essay 'On Depth and Superficiality', where the distinction between the partial or restricted view and the comprehensive is that the first makes the general, particular, while the second, conversely, combines 'a vast number of particulars in some one view' (xii. 358, 359). '*Depth* consists then in tracing any number of particular effects to a general principle, . . . It is in fact resolving the concrete into the abstract' (xii. 355). Abstraction deepens the perception which would otherwise be trapped within the merely local, so that 'the mind, instead of being led away by the last or first object or detached view of the subject that occurs, connects all these into a whole from the top to the bottom, and by its intimate sympathy with the most obscure and random impressions that tend to the same result, evolves a principle of abstract truth' (xii. 356). The process of combination that makes an abstract principle is the process that produces unity from multeity, and is thus recognizable as the synthetic process of the imagination. In other words, Hazlitt's account of abstraction, as the general culled from a combination of individual circumstances, describes imaginative exercise.[12]

Being the manifestation of the imagination's working, the union of abstract and concrete embodies the ideal, synonymous in *The Plain Speaker*, as elsewhere in Hazlitt, with 'truth' or the 'universal'. In the essay 'On the Difference between Writing and Speaking', the 'contemplation of a pure idea' enables the author to see farther and feel deeper than others; he 'takes an interest in things in the abstract more than by common consent' (xii. 279). The abstract character of imaginative truth prevents it from falling into the commonplace. Devoid of abstract character, the 'personal' degenerates into the purely material self that is the foundation of the Utilitarian system which, so founded, precludes idealism. 'The petty and the personal, that which appeals to our senses and our appetites, passes away with the occasion that gives it birth. The grand and the ideal, that which appeals to the imagination, can only perish with it, and remains with us, unimpaired in its lofty abstraction' ('On Antiquity'; xii. 257). When the personal is detached from the universal, the demarcation between personal and abstract coincides with that between the senses and the imagination. To the imagining mind, according to the essay 'On Jealousy and Spleen of Party', 'The personal is, as much as may be, lost in the universal' for the author (xii. 370). But that the 'universal' of imaginative truth is also produced from the personal or individual, is more clearly explicated in the essay, 'On People of Sense', in order to mark the strength of poetry over abstract philosophy, specifically, Utilitarianism. The poet's description is vivid and individual; his general result is 'the aggregate of well-founded particulars' (xii. 246). Such an aggregate owns an authentic or imaginative character, while the abstract theory which has no reference to concrete or 'actual nature' (xii. 246) is mechanistic and detrimental to moral development. When the 'abstract' signifies the representation of an

---

[12] Roy Park finds that in Hazlitt's theory of abstraction, intellectual progress consists in the linear movement from abstract to concrete: 'Intellectual progress is not towards abstraction, ... but away from it towards individuation'; 'Hazlitt's view of abstraction' is 'a process from generalization to individuation' (Park, *Hazlitt*, 99, 99 n.). On the other hand, from the *Plain Speaker* essays, we may cite Hazlitt himself to show that the progress is in the opposite direction. In view, however, of the interdependent or symbiotic character of the relation between abstract and concrete in Hazlitt's theory, I myself prefer not to discuss it in terms of linear progression at all; abstract and concrete *simultaneously* constitute Hazlitt's ideal.

object in which all particular attributes are elided, then it becomes the subject of some of Hazlitt's strongest criticism; in this sense, 'abstract' is distinguished from 'aggregate', a general view of the object that comprehends its particular characteristics. In his critique of Reynolds's *Discourses* in the essay 'On the Imitation of Nature', for instance, Hazlitt distinguishes between 'abstract' and 'aggregate' in this way (*The Champion*, 25 December 1814; xviii. 76). In the best sense of his usage of 'abstract', however, the aggregate is a product of abstraction, the process by which a number of particulars are combined into a comprehensive whole.

Epistemological Background: Hazlitt's Theory of Abstraction

Hazlitt's emphasis is not on a necessarian moral framework, but on agency; the moral thrust of his epistemology is in its statement of agency. Disinterestedness is enabled, but not necessitated by power. The relation between power and disinterestedness is a relation between particular and universal, made possible by the abstracting tendency of the mind, that tendency to unify or perceive relation which is the origin of imaginative exercise. The process of abstraction in Hazlitt's epistemology is fundamental, then, to his moral philosophy, and the value attached to the process is confirmed by his defence of abstraction in the *Lectures on English Philosophy*.

In the lecture 'On Abstract Ideas', Hazlitt begins with establishing the core of inconsistency in Locke's account of abstraction, contained in the contradiction between two statements made in the *Essay concerning Human Understanding*: first, that 'general natures or notions are . . . *abstract and partial ideas of more complex ones taken at first from particular existences*,' and second, that 'general and universal belong not to the real existence of things, but are the inventions and creatures of the understanding, made by it, for its own use, and concern only signs, whether words or ideas' (ii. 194, 195). The logical inconsistency between these statements is elicited by Hazlitt as follows: in the supposition that we do have ideas to answer to general terms, Locke implies that there actually exist some common qualities of things, which, by leaving out particular circumstances, may be taken to represent the general. But this is flatly contradicted in his assertion, made subsequently, that general notions are mere signs, answering to no actual properties of things (ii. 195). Hazlitt rejects alike the notion of the abstract as absolutely separated from the particular, and of the general as having no reference to the actual properties of things. In another context, he makes it his criticism of Hartley that 'he always reasons from the concrete object, not from the abstract or essential properties of things' (*Some Remarks on the Systems of Hartley and Helvetius*; i. 60n.). That is to say, the abstract properties *are* the essential properties of things, so that the concrete object, considered without reference to abstract properties, is inadequate for the understanding of the real nature of things.

Hazlitt not only disproves Locke's thesis of the abstract as merely notional in the lecture 'On Abstract Ideas', he also refutes Berkeley's argument, derived from Hobbes, for denying abstraction altogether. According to Berkeley, all objects are composed of essential and particular attributes, and we cannot frame the idea of an object independently of these attributes. Hence, all our ideas can only be particular and there is no such thing as an abstract idea (ii. 199–204). To counter this conclusion, Hazlitt sets out to establish the necessity of granting a power of abstraction to the mind: 'as these writers affirm that all abstract ideas are particular images, so I shall try to prove that all particular images are abstract ideas' (ii. 205). His proof rests on the premiss of the infinite divisibility of matter. Upon this premiss, all objects consist of an infinite number of particular parts, so that if it were to be a condition of our having an idea of an object that we should grasp every particular of which that object is composed, then we would be required to compass every infinitesimal division of an object, before we could grasp that object at all. From the *reductio ad absurdum*, Hazlitt argues that all our ideas in fact entail the passing over of particulars, and in the comprehension of even an apparently simple or singular object, what we have is merely a general unparticularized notion of that object, i.e. an abstract idea.[13] While matter is

---

[13] When Hazlitt writes in the *Essay on the Principles of Human Action* that 'by the word *idea* is not meant a merely abstract idea' (i. 19n.) or when he remarks the 'perverse restriction of the use of the word *idea* to abstract ideas' (i. 23), the apparent contradiction between these statements and his contention that all our ideas are abstract may be removed by the consideration that in the former he is adopting the Lockian signification of 'abstract' as that which does not belong to the real existence of things (i. 23).

infinitely divisible, the mind's tendency is unification, by which alone we are enabled to arrive at the knowledge of any object at all. The oneness of the mind surmounts the manifold nature of external reality. Objects are complex, but ideas, which embody 'relation', are unified. The mind is the origin of the unity of ideas, without which the advancement of knowledge would be impossible.[14] The entire order of nature, an infinitely divisible whole comprised of infinitely divisible wholes, is to be perceived only by means of the mind's power of abstraction, lacking which 'the fair form of nature would present nothing but a number of discordant atoms' (ii. 213).

Hazlitt's theory of abstraction contains the postulate that knowledge is impossible without abstraction. Simultaneously, abstraction marks, too, the limitation of our knowledge, which can never comprehend the infinity of particular detail. Hence Hazlitt's approbation of that generalization which is supported by a weight of particular instances and his contempt for abstract theories that are altogether devoid of the particular. His admiration of Bacon, for instance, expressed both in the *Prospectus of a History of English Philosophy* and in the introduction to the *Lectures on English Philosophy*, is precisely for the 'incorporating the abstract with the concrete, and general notions with individual objects', that was consequent upon Bacon's emphasis on experience (ii. 115).

Hazlitt's doctrine of abstraction as 'limitation' tallies also with his theory of innate 'bias', since the mind's perception of unity— its choice of particulars—is determined (limited) by its 'bias'. The inherent bias of the mind marks all perception as partial and exclusive, but it is also the condition that makes possible the

---

[14] Schneider finds a 'confusion' in Hazlitt's theory, between 'his assumption that to have an idea of a complex or manifold object (and all objects, as he says, are complex) is the same thing as to have a complex or manifold idea,' and 'his reiterated conviction that "the mind is *one*"' (Schneider, *Aesthetics*, 26–7). Far from giving rise to confusion, however, it is precisely the conviction that the mind is one that allows Hazlitt to assert its ability to surmount the complex or manifold nature of objects, so as to make knowledge possible. The same assumption of 'confusion' where none exists makes Schneider conclude that Hazlitt 'fails to perceive that, even by the terms of his own definition, by the fact that abstraction does help to supply our defect [of comprehension], it is a means of advancing human knowledge beyond what would be possible without it' (ibid. 26). On the contrary, Hazlitt is so clearly, and so ingeniously, vindicating the significance of abstraction in the epistemological process in his essay 'On Abstract Ideas', that Schneider's conclusion is entirely belied.

original vision of genius. On more than one count, indeed, it can be shown that the insistence that abstraction 'is a consequence of the *limitation* of the comprehensive faculty' (ii. 191; my italics) is somewhat specious, given the true significance of Hazlitt's doctrine of abstract ideas. This is indicated at the opening of his lecture 'On Abstract Ideas': 'I shall in this Lecture state Mr. Locke's account of generalization, abstraction, and reasoning, as contrasted with the modern one, *and then endeavour to defend the existence of these faculties, or acts of the mind from the objections urged against them* by Hume, Berkeley, Condillac, and others' (ii. 191; my italics). The connection between abstraction and the defence of the intellectual faculties denied by the philosophers listed here, may be inferred from the order of two propositions, placed consecutively, that Hazlitt lists towards the close of his lecture 'On the Writings of Hobbes'. The list is of the 'leading principles' of the school of philosophy that he sets himself 'to oppose to the utmost of my ability' (*Lectures on English Philosophy*; ii. 144, 145). The fourth of the principles that Hazlitt seeks to refute, 'That we have no general or abstract ideas,' follows immediately from the third, 'That thoughts are single, or that we can think of only one object at a time. In other words, that there is no comprehensive power or faculty of understanding in the mind' (ii. 144). The sequence of the two propositions, both vehemently opposed by Hazlitt, enables us to perceive the second as following from the first. The denial of abstraction implies the denial of a comprehensive intellectual faculty, taking philosophy on the road back to the mechanistic model of the mind. The connection between mechanism and the denial of abstraction may be perceived also in Hobbes's corollary to the doctrine of 'no abstract ideas' in his theory of language, cited at some length by Hazlitt in the lecture 'On the Writings of Hobbes'.

According to Hobbes, since all actual things are particular, there is nothing universal but the names, *man, horse, tree* etc., which signify several particular things by a single appellation. All universals are names only, corresponding to no things in nature (ii. 138). By this assertion, a person without the use of language may not formulate universal laws, and is hence precluded from taking any steps in any science or other form of universal knowledge whatsoever (ii. 138–9). It is language that defines truth, 'For True and False are attributes of speech, not of things. And where speech is not, there is neither truth nor falsehood' (ii. 140). The origin of knowledge resides in the structure of language; hence, Hobbes observes, 'The Greeks have but one word, λογος for both speech and reason, not that they thought there was no speech without reason, but no reason without speech' (ii. 141). By implication, then, we arrive at another of the 'leading principles' of the school of philosophy that Hazlitt opposes so passionately: 'That reason and understanding depend entirely on the mechanism of language' (ii. 144).

The word 'mechanism' is our indicator. To Hazlitt, reason and understanding refer to the mind's innate power or constructive ability; by positing that speech pre-exists reason, Hobbes precludes the thesis, fundamental to Hazlitt's *Grammar,* of an independent activity of the mind as the condition for language. Hobbes finds that universals are mere names, because he judges language by its correspondence to an external material reality, rather than as the expression of an innate formative ability of the mind; the universal becomes a mere name when it is shorn of reference to the mind's power. In Hazlitt's empowered model, by contrast, universals, in which knowledge resides, manifest the mind's formative ability; they are elicited from particular things by the generalizing or unifying tendency of the mind: its perception of relation. Speech is produced from the innate intellectual faculty of reason or understanding, whereby both mind and language are granted vitality.[15]

For Hazlitt to deny the validity of abstraction would be contrary to the entire thrust of his metaphysics. His doctrine of abstraction, by vindicating 'relation' or unity, offers a compromise between the unparticularized generalizations of Locke and the ungeneralized particulars of Berkeley, to which both his epistemology and his moral theory must be perceived as inescapably committed. The moral value of abstraction is spelled out in *The Plain Speaker,* where the mind's tendency to unify, 'which arranges and combines

---

[15] In the essay 'On Tooke's "Diversions of Purley"', Hazlitt aligns Hume with Berkeley and Hobbes in holding 'that abstraction is not an operation of the mind, but of language' (ii. 280–1). In the lecture 'On Abstract Ideas' also, he undertakes to refute Hume, 'who has taken up Berkeley's arguments on this subject, and affirms that the doctrine of abstract ideas implies the flattest of all contradictions' (ii. 204). Given that the theory of abstraction is central to Hazlitt's epistemology, his divergence from Hume on this key issue must, despite his admiration for Hume as a thinker, prevent us from perceiving Hazlitt, as Bromwich does, as a 'disciple of Hume' (Bromwich, *Hazlitt,* 18).

the multifarious impressions of nature into one whole,' is exactly that 'which balances the various motives of action, and renders man what he is—a rational and moral agent' ('On Dr. Spurzheim's Theory'; xii. 150–1).

Hazlitt's 'Romantic' Morality

By locating unity as a governing characteristic of Hazlitt's moral vision, we may situate that vision within the 'romantic' or 'modern' consciousness theorized in the writings, especially, of his German counterparts. In Schiller's *On the Naive and Sentimental in Literature*, the unity between mind and nature brought about by the imagining self marks the moral goal of humanity. The moral effort is embodied in art, which strains towards that unity.

Schiller's categories of 'naive' and 'sentimental' are comparable to Schlegel's distinction between classical and romantic, where the first represents an achieved but limited perfection, while the second, straining towards the perpetually unattainable, is always an approximation merely, but to a higher and infinite perfection.[16] In Schlegel's theory, the romantic perception is governed by the postlapsarian consciousness of discord or fractured unity, 'a chaos which is concealed beneath the regulated creation even in its very bosom'.[17] It is this fracture that the romantic mind strives perpetually to heal. Out of the effort arises the separation of art from literal reality; a separation unknown, according to Schlegel, to the classical mind. The romantic consciousness is dualistic; its constant endeavour is the reconciliation of two worlds, external and internal. Thus 'all contrarieties: nature and art, poetry and prose, seriousness and mirth, recollection and anticipation, spirituality and sensuality, terrestrial and celestial, life and death, are blended together . . . in the most intimate combination.'[18] Unity is the goal of romantic art and achievable only through art; hence, it is

---

[16] The theoretical congruity does not, however, extend to practical illustration. Where Schlegel exemplifies classicism by the Greek tragedians and romanticism by Shakespeare, Schiller illustrates the naive category with Homer and Shakespeare, and the sentimental with the writers of his own age.

[17] Lecture XII in Augustus William Schlegel, *A Course of Lectures on Dramatic Art and Literature*, trans. John Black, 2 vols (London: Baldwin, Cradock, and Joy, 1815), ii. 99. [18] Lecture XII (ibid. 98–9).

produced from the mind of man. If, instead of arising out of the inner intellectual compulsion, art takes its source from the external literal reality, then it is fragmented and discordant, like that reality itself. Truth inheres in unity and not in the separation of objects that characterizes factual reality; therefore we arrive at truth in feeling, which 'perceives all in all', rather than in mere conception.[19] The models of natural science, which are based on the factual separation of objects, being brought to the judgement of art are found inadequate and indeed irrelevant to it, and by implication, to truth itself.[20]

Hazlitt read and reviewed Schlegel; he also cites him at some length in the 'Preface' to the *Characters of Shakespear's Plays* (iv. 172–4). Crabb Robinson notes, in a diary entry of 12 May 1816, that the review brings out the affinity between Hazlitt and Schlegel: 'Hazlitt's review of Schlegel's lectures on the drama is a capital article, and Hazlitt's own share of the excellent matter is by no means small. He has entered into the sense of the author and evinces a kindred spirit.'[21] The evidence of intellectual kinship is affected hardly at all by the criticism of Schlegel in the review: chiefly, that Schlegel's 'grand systematic conclusion' precludes qualification or exception ('Schlegel on the Drama', *Contributions to the Edinburgh Review*; xvi. 58). In Hazlitt's own 'Opinions on Books, Men and Things', we see that rigidity undone and that system individualized. *The Plain Speaker*, with its indictment of the state of human relations in modern society, its rejection of the Utilitarian formula for life, and its advocacy of truth of feeling, enlivens every aspect of the Schlegelian theory.

'Nature seems (the more we look into it) made up of antipathies' ('On the Pleasure of Hating'; xii. 128). Underlying this awareness, we hear exactly the romantic consciousness described by Schlegel, of dichotomy—appearance and reality, body and soul, mind and nature—simultaneous with the yearning for oneness. Thus, a keen sense of antithesis, balance and imbalance is characteristic of the construction and style of Hazlitt's writing. His pairings of opposite characters and qualities are too numerous and by now, too familiar to need to be laboured.

---

[19] Lecture XII, Schlegel, *Lectures*, 99).   [20] Lecture XII (ibid. 126).
[21] Robinson, *Books and their Writers*, i. 182.

To pick instances at random, we have 'On Shakespeare and Milton' and 'On Chaucer and Spenser' in the *Lectures on the English Poets*, and 'On Thought and Action' in *Table-Talk*; antitheses are constructed also by setting Godwin against Coleridge and Byron against Scott in *The Spirit of the Age*. The famous antithesis of Ariel and Caliban, representing air and earth, or soul and body, in the *Characters of Shakespear's Plays*, is parodied in the pairing of 'Londoners and Country People' in *The Plain Speaker*.

Antithesis is a product of the fragmentation or discord that loosens mind from nature, self from world or other. Such fragmentation is indicted by Hazlitt with reference to a variety of subjects, but especially intellectual and creative activity. As his lectures on literature celebrate the achievement of poetry in eliciting the ideal from the ordinary, the *Plain Speaker* treats its pitfalls: the ideal world of poetry may, and does often break from reality, exposing the rift between beauty and truth, power and pleasure. Poets are 'winged animals' but 'when they light upon the ground of prose and matter-of-fact, they seem not to have the same use of their feet' ('On the Prose-style of Poets'; xii. 5). Scholars generally 'underrate the force of nature, and make too much of art' ('On the Conversation of Authors'; xii. 28). The bookworm 'lives all his life in a dream of learning, and has never once had his sleep broken by a real sense of things' ('On the Conversation of Authors; xii. 43). The apparently facile resolution to the problem offered by Hazlitt in one essay, that scholars and authors mingle with society ('On the Conversation of Authors; xii. 32), springs, in fact, from a deep conviction of the necessity of meaningful relation between the ideal and the ordinary that is vital to his literary and moral theory.

The origin of the breach in the relation between the ideal and the ordinary is identified in the opening essay of *The Plain Speaker*. Here, Hazlitt observes that while in treating a poetic subject, the associative link may be beauty alone, in treating a common subject, it must be truth ('On the Prose-style of Poets'; xii. 9). The author's sacrifice of truth to beauty sets the pleasure principle above the power principle and splits, instead of merging, the ideal and the real worlds. In the case of Burke, Hazlitt's paradigm for prose writing, 'The principle which guides his pen is truth, not beauty—not pleasure, but power' (xii. 10).[22] Burke's own categorical distinction in the *Philosophical Enquiry* between the 'beautiful', which is founded on pleasure, and the more powerful 'sublime', founded on pain or terror, is at work in this distinction between beauty and truth, pleasure and power. Burke himself exemplifies imaginative balance: 'The most rigid fidelity and the most fanciful extravagance meet, and are reconciled in his pages' (xii. 12).

Hazlitt's standards for art and life may be linked by means of the concept of 'significant exterior' that defines Schlegel's theory of form. According to Schlegel, the organic form is uninfluenced by accidents or external circumstances, being always the significant exterior which gives true evidence of the essence hidden within it; the form, therefore, is the true manifestation of that essence.[23] In Hazlitt's literary and art criticism, we have already seen the demand for an inwardly generated unity, by which imaginative creation may be recognized as the true manifestation of the authorial being inhering within it. In his criteria for social behaviour in *The Plain Speaker*, a similar demand is made, for continuity between exterior and interior, so that behaviour may be recognizable as the index of the personality of which it is the outward manifestation. Hence Hazlitt's watchword 'sincerity', denoting the condition under which exteriors are significant, and the forms of behaviour, the natural manifestation of the human being secreted within them. Without 'sincerity there can be no true enjoyment of society, nor unfettered exertion of intellectual activity' ('On the Conversation of Authors'; xii. 30).

The governing notion of a significant exterior, evinced in Hazlitt's sharp sense of potential or actual discrepancy between outside and inside, or appearance and reality, informs the treatment of virtually every topic in *The Plain Speaker*. Thus Hazlitt warns against the judging of genius by reputation ('On the Conversation of Authors'; xii. 29), opposes the manners of

---

[22] In his review of *The Plain Speaker* of 12 March 1828, Leigh Hunt takes a different view from Hazlitt's identification of power and truth in Burke. Hunt distinguishes between power and truth, and finds that it is one of Burke's failings that he 'substitutes the love of power for that of truth'. Of Hazlitt himself, he writes, 'But we suspect even Mr. Hazlitt's love of power to be more on a par with his love of truth than he may chuse to discover' (Hunt, *Literary Criticism*, 244).

[23] Lecture XII (Schlegel, *Lectures*, ii. 95).

polished life to the downright and the straightforward ('On the Look of a Gentleman'; xii. 219), exalts writing, which is 'thinking aloud' and hence directed from within, over speaking or 'being heard', which is a mere matter of semblance or outward projection ('On the Difference between Writing and Speaking'; xii. 274), and rejects the French art in which the 'varnish and glitter of sentiment . . . must forever intercept the true feeling and genuine rendering of nature' ('Madame Pasta and Mademoiselle Mars'; xii. 332). From the same position, he assigns praise or blame to particular persons, drawing attention to Tooke's sophistry ('On the Conversation of Authors'; xii. 41) and Spurzheim's deliberate mystification in style ('On Dreams'; xii. 18–19, 'On Dr. Spurzheim's Theory'; xii. 138–40); equally, also, to Northcote's lack of affectation ('On the Old Age of Artists'; xii. 91–2).

Under the condition of sincerity, whose test is feeling, the discrepancy between appearance and reality vanishes. Sincerity precludes fragmentation. From its lack, the French remain mechanistic in their behaviour, hence fractured in their identity and in their art:

> By yielding to every impulse at once, nothing produces a powerful or permanent impression; nothing produces an aggregate impression, for every part tells separately. Every idea turns off to something else, or back upon itself; there is no progress made, no blind impulse, no accumulation of imagination with circumstances, no absorption of all other feelings in one overwhelming one, that is, no keeping, no *momentum*, no integrity, no totality, no inflexible sincerity of purpose, . . . ('Madame Pasta and Mademoiselle Mars'; xii. 327–8)

The ideal of unity is clearly spelled out in the reiterated synonymity of 'aggregate', 'one overwhelming one', 'integrity', 'totality', 'sincerity'.

Finally, it is not incidental that Hazlitt presents his moral ideal in terms of a type of discourse: plainspeaking. If the imagination is the only possible instrument of truth, then language is chiefly its index. 'Words are a measure of truth' ('On People of Sense'; xii. 250). Language, not as a dead mechanism, but as the product of the mind's innate capacity is our primary gauge of morality. In the essay 'On Sir Walter Scott, Racine and Shakespear', Hazlitt writes, 'Words are the signs which point out and define the objects of the highest import to the human mind; and speech is the habitual, and as it were most *intimate* mode of expressing those signs, the one with which our practical and serious associations are most in unison' (xii. 336). By virtue of their associative weight, words take us beyond the matter-of-fact into the non-literal. 'Causes march before them and consequences follow after them' (xii. 337), hence words convey a 'moral and intellectual perspective' (xii. 336). Language is intimately involved with our moral and intellectual identity and is the chief element of self-analysis. Words are 'links in the chain of the universe' (xii. 337); elsewhere, they are also 'links in the chain of our conscious being' ('On Reading Old Books'; xii. 221) and 'links in the chain of thought' ('On the Difference between Writing and Speaking'; xii. 278). Taken in tandem, the three definitions connect 'thought', 'our conscious being', and the 'universe'. As the 'grappling-irons that bind us' to the universe (xii. 337), words affirm the relation between mind and nature: the moral goal, unity.

Liberty and Necessity

Hazlitt's theory of morals, with its commitment to unity and inner development, displays an alignment with a certain philosophical schema or convention, in which right action brings man into harmony with the order of the universe, and so fulfils his highest potential. Such a schema is integral, as we have seen, to the theory of the German idealist philosophers. The theoretical expositions of Schiller and Schlegel are grounded in Kantian thought, and the parallels that can be drawn with reference to Hazlitt also begin to indicate Hazlitt's closeness to Kant in the area of moral philosophy. In particular, the notion of a natural order with which the moral action of the human being brings him into accord, recalls Kant's assertion in the *Groundwork of the Metaphysic of Morals*, of an analogy between the universal law of morality and the universal law of nature.[24] Hazlitt's participation in this way of thinking does not negate, nor must it be obscured by, his unequivocal rejection of the mechanistic analogy of mind and matter that is the foundation of 'natural philosophy': 'to say . . . that we can only infer the laws which regulate the phaenomena of the

---

[24] Kant, *Groundwork*, ch. ii, p. 104.

mind from those which regulate the phaenomena of matter, is to confound two things essentially distinct' (*Prospectus of a History of English Philosophy*; ii. 114).

Hazlitt refutes the methods and ideology of natural philosophy, but maintains an affinity with what we might term the philosophy of nature. His theory, in which truth must be both inwardly generated as well as universal, constructs not just analogy, but relation, inwardly produced between the mind and the natural order of things. The grounds for comparison with Kant are substantial, and in the course of this chapter I will offer a fuller discussion of some of those grounds. At this point, however, I want to bring out Hazlitt's relationship with another version of the philosophy of nature, Abraham Tucker's *The Light of Nature Pursued* (1778).

The jump from Kant to Tucker as a subject of comparison is not without some justification. In the first place, Hazlitt believes that a common commitment to 'nature' is shared with Kant by Tucker and implicitly, himself: 'the German philosophy, or the system of professor Kant, . . . takes for granted the common notions prevalent among mankind, and then endeavours to explain them; or *to shew their foundation in nature, and the universal relations of things* ('Preface to an Abridgement of the Light of Nature Pursued'; i. 128–9, my italics). Secondly, in making the comparison between Hazlitt and the German idealists, we have necessarily to limit our claims to intellectual coincidence or kinship, without asserting direct influence or even knowledge on Hazlitt's part. The issue is quite otherwise with his compatriots. Hazlitt's primary theoretical concern is not with the Germans, but with the British philosophers, major and minor, with whom he is most familiar. Here, he is directly and immediately engaged, refuting, modifying, and transforming, frequently undermining the empiricist theories with which he is grappling, by highlighting those of their aspects that reinforce his own idealistic emphases. Nowhere is this process of subversion, even colonization, more manifest than in his treatment of Abraham Tucker.

Despite Tucker's obscurity to the modern reader, and indeed, to the readers of his own time, his importance to Hazlitt is considerable. Hazlitt produced a one-volume *Abridgement* (1807) of the original seven volumes of *The Light of Nature Pursued*, identifying himself, in the preface to this *Abridgement*, as 'The Author of An

Essay on the Principles of Human Action'. By so doing, he associates his own metaphysics and Tucker's, not only through the shared and undeserved neglect suffered by both, but also theoretically. The preface makes clear that while Tucker 'professes himself indeed, and seems anxious to be thought, a disciple of Locke' (i. 127), his editor's interest in him is as 'an arrant truant' from Locke's school (i. 130). Besides noting a general affinity between Tucker and Kant, Hazlitt calls our attention to two specific features, antagonistic to Locke, of Tucker's philosophy: the independent existence of the mind and the unity of consciousness (i. 130). Tucker, he writes, 'believed with professor Kant, in the unity of consciousness' (i. 130).[25] The value attached by Hazlitt to Tucker's epistemology is indicated not only in his particular recommendation of Tucker's chapter on consciousness in the preface to the *Abridgement*, but also elsewhere, when he cites Tucker on the independent existence of the mind in support of his own refutation of Locke in the *Lectures on English Philosophy* ('On Locke's "Essay on the Human Understanding"'; ii. 157) and in the *Morning Chronicle* review of Madame de Staël ('Madame de Staël's Account of German Philosophy and Literature'; xx. 27–8 n.).

Tucker's philosophy assumes the distinction of mind and matter, and posits, upon the basis of this distinction, 'that there is some one principle or substance, absolutely simple in its nature, and distinct from every composition of matter, which is the seat of thought, the soul of man, and the bond of our existence.'[26] This asserts not only that the mind exists independently of matter, but also that consciousness is single and indivisible: 'absolutely simple in its nature.' Moreover, prior to this declaration of the unity of consciousness, Tucker argues that 'the idea of person must precede that of consciousness.'[27] If personhood is the prerequisite of consciousness, then consciousness cannot transcend the individual self but must be contained with it. In other words, by encapsulating consciousness within personal identity, Tucker precludes

---

[25] Wellek notes that although it is Tucker rather than Kant who is Hazlitt's source, 'This "unity of thought and consciousness" is the centre of Hazlitt's doctrine and the chief point of contact with Kant.'—René Wellek, *Immanuel Kant in England 1793–1838* (Princeton, NJ: Princeton University Press, 1931), 168.

[26] Abraham Tucker, 'Independent Existence of Mind', in *An Abridgement of the Light of Nature Pursued*, ed. W. Hazlitt (London: J. Johnson, 1807), Bk III, ch. i, section 10, p. 167.   [27] Ibid., Bk III, ch. i, section 9, p. 167.

transcendent being. Since consciousness is both self-contained and 'distinct from every composition of matter', we may infer the autonomy of the individual self.

The affirmation of the self and its autonomy must be registered especially in relation to two aspects of Tucker's thought with which it appears in contradiction. One is the deterministic notion of Providence that constitutes the religious framework of his book; the other, the concept of 'mundane soul', implying transcendent being, fancifully explicated in the chapter, particularly admired by Hazlitt (i. 134), entitled 'The Vision'. Tucker's visionary account of the ideal of moral and natural philosophy may usefully be quoted at length:

> the material universe was my body, the several systems my limbs, the subtle fluids my circulating juices, and the face of nature my sensory. In that sensory I discerned all science and wisdom to direct me in the application of my powers, which were vast and mighty; extending to every member and fibre of my vast composition. I had no external object to look on, nor external subject to act upon; yet found an inexhaustible variety to employ my thoughts and unwearied activity within myself. . . . all my knowledge was brought me by communication, and my operations performed by the joint concurrence of innumerable hosts of substances of the same nature with myself. For there being a general participation of ideas through the whole community, we had all the same apprehension, the same discernment of things, the same aims and purposes: so there was no variation of sentiment nor discordance of desire among us. The thoughts of all were the thoughts of every one, and the actions of the whole, the acts of each in particular; for each was consenting to whatever was done by the others, and no sooner wished to have a thing done, than he saw it instantly performed. As we had but one mind and one will, every thing happened according to that will: . . .[28]

The phrases 'powers, which were vast and mighty' and 'unwearied activity within myself', appear to construct an active and empowered self endowed, in contradistinction to the Lockian model, with innate faculties: 'no external object to look on, nor external subject to act upon'. Independent of external influence, that self is nonetheless directed, in the application of its powers, by the 'face of nature', thus implying the existence of an order of

---

[28] Ibid., Bk III, ch. xii, section 37, pp. 296–7.

nature of which it forms a part. The thoughts, actions, and will of the individual self participate in a universal 'one mind and one will.' Tucker's emphasis on autonomy and independent agency is too strong to allow a purely transcendent interpretation of his 'vision'. Instead, consistency may be preserved if we treat it as correlating 'the thoughts of every one' and 'the thoughts of all', the 'acts of each in particular' and 'the actions of the whole'. It is just such a correlation that we find in Hazlitt's ideal of the social community, for instance, in the essay 'What is the People'; the resemblance here to Tucker's 'vision' is striking: 'The people is the hand, heart, and head of the whole community acting to one purpose, and with a mutual and thorough consent. . . . The will of the people necessarily tends to the general good as its end' (*Political Essays*; vii. 267). The correlation between the autonomous self and the whole order of things is at the core of Hazlitt's theory of morals. Its epistemological foundation is the symbiosis of particular and universal. In action, it is manifested in the union of volition and necessity.

We have already had occasion to observe the reconciliation of necessity with choice, or fixity with freedom, in Hazlitt's description of poetic language. In that context, I discussed the relevance to Hazlitt of Schiller's account of the operation of genius: 'the will freely follows the law of necessity'. For Schiller, the freely chosen and self-imposed subjugation to a 'law' of 'inner necessity' marks the moral striving of the human being.[29] In Hazlitt's case also, the correlation of liberty and necessity is fundamental to his moral vision.

In the lecture 'On Liberty and Necessity', Hazlitt makes his case for the moral nature of man. He treats necessity, as Hobbes does, not as 'blind, physical, unreasoning, unresisting necessity,' but according to 'the true, original, philosophical meaning of the term, in which it implies no more than the connexion between cause and effect' (*Lectures on English Philosophy*; ii. 256). If necessity is understood to signify no more than the connection between cause and effect, then the doctrine of necessity amounts merely to the assertion that the will does not function acausally. With such a concept of necessity, the idea of choice is in no way

---

[29] Schiller, *Naive and Sentimental*, 22–3.

incompatible, choice or freedom of the will referring, in this case, to the choice of motives.

In establishing that the will acts always from motives or causes, Hazlitt remains in perfect agreement with Hobbes. 'The doctrine of necessity', he writes, 'is stated by this author with great force and precision as a general question of cause and effect, and with scarcely any particular reference to his mechanical theory of the mind. From this naked simple view of the matter, I cannot consistently with truth withhold my full and entire assent' (*Lectures on English Philosophy*; ii. 245). He differs from Hobbes only, and crucially, on the origin of causes: 'All in which I differ from Hobbes is, that I think there is a real freedom of choice and will, as well as of action' (ii. 254). Real freedom resides in the thesis that motives originate, not from sensory response to external impressions, but from the innate constitution of the mind. Hazlitt rejects the signification of 'free' as 'unmotivated': 'by free-will I do not mean the power or liberty to act without motives, but with motives' (ii. 267). It is necessary that the will be impelled by a cause, and the necessary cause that so impels it is susceptible to moral judgement. In other words, moral agency refers not to causality itself, but to the distinction between causes: 'It is the . . . inability to distinguish between one cause and another which creates the vulgar prejudice against necessity' (ii. 262).

The distinction between motives (and hence events) marks Hazlitt's treatment of Locke's question, 'whether a man be free to will?' (ii. 258). Since choice is confined either to the performance or the non-performance of an action, both being the outcome of the will, all outcomes are willed; hence, according to Locke, we cannot avoid willing. It is not so much Locke's conclusion as his emphasis, with which we find Hazlitt in dispute: 'If by liberty be meant the uncertainty of the event, then liberty is a non-entity: but if it be supposed to relate to the concurrence of certain powers of an agent in the production of that event, then it is as true and as real a thing as the necessity to which it is thus opposed' (ii. 258–9). By focusing on the agent's role in determining the event, i.e. by distinguishing between events, rather than by accepting the undistinguished certainty of event of one kind or another, Hazlitt validates agency. At the same time, it is not willing itself, but the outcome willed that determines moral judgement, an agent being 'entitled to praise or blame, reward or punishment, not because he is a self-willed, but a voluntary agent' (ii. 267), not because he wills, but because he directs that will towards a particular purpose. We recall Hazlitt's insistence on the independence of the imagination from a necessary connection to a moral end.

The power to act from motives marks the freedom of the will since, in the choice of motives it remains inwardly rather than externally directed. 'Or in other words, motives do not impel the will immediately, absolutely, and irresistibly, but by means of the understanding which determines the choice of the object' (*Prospectus of a History of English Philosophy*; ii. 118). Choice is an act of the understanding, although the notion that the understanding itself displays 'something peculiar and essential to his [the agent's] disposition and character' ('On Liberty and Necessity'; ii. 267) contains an element of predeterminism in common with that very necessarian doctrine that Hazlitt is at considerable labour to deny.

For the validation of the empowered model of the mind, it must be understood as directed by its own innate tendency.

> In this consists its long-contested freedom. It is *free*, in as far as it is not the slave of external impressions, physical impulses, or blind senseless motives. It is free, as the body is free, when it is not subject to a power out of itself, though its operations still depend on certain powers and principles within itself. (*Prospectus of a History of English Philosophy*; ii. 118)

Liberty, within this determinate limit, describes the freedom of the mind from external manipulation, not from its own nature or constitution; it pertains to that which is within, not beyond, our power. Here too, Hazlitt draws upon Hobbes's definition, which he cites verbatim: 'liberty is the absence of all the impediments to action that are not contained in the nature and intrinsical quality of the agent' ('On Liberty and Necessity'; ii. 247). For Hobbes, however, 'the ordinary definition of a free agent, namely, that a free agent, is that, which, when all things are present which are needful to produce the effect, can nevertheless not produce it, implies a contradiction, and is nonsense' (ii. 248). Hazlitt's notion of a free agent, on the other hand, 'is not that represented by Mr. Hobbes, namely, one that when all things necessary to produce the effect are present can nevertheless not produce it; but I believe a free agent of whatever kind, is one which where all things necessary to produce the effect are present, can produce it; its own operation not being hindered by any thing else' (ii. 255). Although the content of both definitions appears congruent, Hazlitt's revision of Hobbes is not merely semantic, but carries, again, a vital shift in emphasis, from the passive to the active character of the mind. By Hobbes's definition, 'when all things are present that are needful', the effect or action *must* follow. In Hazlitt's formulation, 'where all things necessary to produce the effect are present', that effect *can* follow. In the first case, action is compelled by the concurrence of all conditions necessary to that action; in the second, action may be chosen, given the concurrence of all conditions necessary to it. Hobbes's definition renders the concept of a free agent meaningless, Hazlitt's invests it with meaning.

Hazlitt's demonstration of the compatibility of necessity with liberty in the *Lectures on English Philosophy* is strikingly akin to Kant's in the *Groundwork of the Metaphysic of Morals*, since it is from the existence of innate power that Hazlitt derives the freedom of the will. The will is free because it is subjugated to no laws that are imposed upon it from without. Similarly, Kant argues from the existence within us of a pure activity apart from sense, that we can presuppose freedom.[30] The incompatibility between the idea of a free will and that of a moral law to which the will is bound, is removed when we consider that that law arises from our own natures as intelligences and is not externally imposed.[31]

At the conclusion of his analysis, when Hazlitt sums up the relation between liberty and necessity, we find him occupying his favourite position in the middle ground between the two extremes of antithesis: 'The mind, according to the advocates for free-will, is a perfectly detached, unconnected, independent cause: according to the necessarians, it is no cause at all: neither branch of the antithesis is true' (ii. 270). This middle ground is not merely formulaic, but the metaphysically valid reconciliation between a model of a mind whose reigning principle is the amoral one of power, and a profound belief in the reality of a moral goal for humanity.

[30] Kant, *Groundwork*, ch. ii, pp. 119–20.   [31] Ibid., ch. iii, p. 125.

Hazlitt and Kant

So far, the discussion of Hazlitt's moral philosophy has been a discussion of his idealism and in so being has foregrounded his engagement with empirical British philosophy, as well as his intellectual affinity with the German idealist philosophers, Schiller and Schlegel. Such an affinity must extend, inevitably, to Kant, in whose philosophy the expositions of both Schiller and Schlegel are rooted. I have already touched briefly on the grounds for a comparison with Kant in treating Hazlitt's doctrine of liberty and necessity. I shall now endeavour to show that Hazlitt's entire theory of morals, based upon a vision of moral truth as constituting a universal reality common to all, and validating individual experience as referring to this universal truth, displays a close resemblance in its cardinal points to Kant's ethical position.

In the *Groundwork of the Metaphysic of Morals*, Kant argues from the nature of a rational being, that the conformity of actions to a universal law must alone serve the will as a principle. Hence his 'categorical imperative', given in the dictum, 'I ought never to act except in such a way *that I can also will that my maxim should become a universal law.*'[32]

I have based my discussion of Kant upon the *Groundwork*, as offering the most concise and explicit articulation of his moral theory which, like Hazlitt's, is inseparable from his epistemology and his theory of art. In the words of Madame de Staël, 'it is the same soul which he examines, and which shows itself in the sciences, in morality, and in the fine arts.'[33] Hazlitt does not himself refer to the *Groundwork*, but in drawing the comparison between Hazlitt and Kant, it is my intention to work out certain analogies, rather than to enter into the question of the extent to which Hazlitt actually knew or absorbed Kant's writings. Although it is easy enough to make the case that he had at least a limited familiarity with Kantian philosophy, the evidence of direct influence is minimal in comparison to the extent of intellectual coincidence that it is possible to establish.

The concept of a categorical imperative is relevant to Hazlitt as

---

[32] Kant, *Groundwork*, ch. i, p. 70.
[33] Staël-Holstein, Germaine de, *Germany*, 3 vols (London: John Murray, 1813), iii. 89.

imparting to every individual action a universal significance. Further, the categorical imperative carries with it the postulate of a formal principle, called duty by Kant, which exists as a motive to action independent of self-interest. In affirming this principle, Kant refutes the empirical conditions for morality; such refutation represents also Hazlitt's ethical and metaphysical objective. Since morality must have an absolute and unconditional basis, any attempt to accommodate it within empirical considerations of 'interest' must deny the very possibility of a categorical imperative and hence of morality itself. 'The principle of *personal happiness* is, . . . the most objectionable, . . . because it bases morality on sensuous motives which rather undermine it and totally destroy its sublimity, inasmuch as the motives of virtue are put in the same class as those of vice and we are instructed only to become better at calculation.'[34] The admission of the categorical imperative, on the other hand, enables us to affirm that the 'feeling' in which our commitment to moral law must be rooted may be separated from interest. Recalling Hazlitt's thesis of 'natural disinterestedness', and hence thinking of his moral theory in Kantian terms, we find that we may elicit here also, the notion of a fixed principle of duty or morality, implied in a variety of contexts and explicitly articulated in at least one place:

moral obligation is not, as it has been strangely defined to be, the strongest motive, which would justify any action whatever. It always, I conceive, expresses the hold or power (be it stronger or weaker) which certain given motives have over the mind, or the ties by which men are bound to their duty. It has its foundation in the moral and rational nature of man, or in that principle—call it reason, conscience, moral sense, what you will—which, without any reference to our own interests, passions, and pursuits, approves of certain actions and sentiments as right, and condemns others as wrong. To act right is to act in conformity to this standard. (*Prospectus of a History of English Philosophy*; ii. 118)

From this, although moral capacity—the ability to determine between causes—attests to the self-affirming principle of 'power', the positing of a 'given' indicates that moral value itself refers to a distinct 'principle' of right and wrong, that is independent of reference to the self. The 'ties by which men are bound to their duty' expresses exactly Kant's sense of our obligation to moral

---

[34] Kant, *Groundwork*, ch. ii, pp. 109–10.

law. According to Kant, this obligation, and hence the validity of moral law, arises because that law springs ultimately from our own natures as intelligences.[35] I have already established from the essay 'On Reason and Imagination' that 'moral sense' for Hazlitt refers to the application to our actions of an inwardly directed standard, dissociated from the calculation of material advantage. Our conformity to this standard is the 'principle' to which the *Prospectus* refers; apart from 'moral sense', it is here termed also 'conscience' or 'reason', this last term possibly alluding to Kant.

Hazlitt's usage of the phrase 'moral sense' should not be confused with the doctrine which propounds, as in the writing of Francis Hutcheson, a separate 'sense' or faculty, analogous to the external or physical senses, the gratification of which is supposedly the origin of our tendency to virtue.[36] This doctrine is rejected by Kant as being fundamentally empiricist, appealing as it does to a kind of 'sensibility', which must place it in alignment with those systems of morality that are determined by the pleasure principle.[37] We may reasonably suppose that the positing of another kind of 'sensory' gratification as the ground of morality could not be entertained by Hazlitt, for whom any intellectual faculty is definitively distinct from 'sense', its characteristic being exercise or activity, rather than the passivity implied in the theory of gratification. His occasional allusions to a 'moral sense' refer rather to the cultivation of a certain imaginative awareness or 'feeling', manifested in the habitual deference to a 'principle' or 'standard' of morality. Hazlitt's usage of the phrase, by supposing the binding of the will to a formal and independent principle, reveals itself as supporting Kant's ethical theory. Both 'sense' and 'feeling' do not signify his accommodation of the physical analogy, but attest to the actuality which the moral standard and our commitment to it possess for him.

In affirming the 'standard' or 'principle' of duty, Hazlitt recognizes, like Kant, that it must be both objective, or independent at least, of narrow self-interest and unconditionally binding. I have stated that while the self is a moral agent, it is not the end of

---

[35] Kant, *Groundwork*, ch. iii, p. 129.

[36] Francis Hutcheson, *An Essay on the Nature and Conduct of the Passions and Affections with Illustrations on the Moral Sense*, 3rd edn (1742; repr. Gainsville, Fla: Scholars' Facsimiles 38; Reprints, 1969), especially pp. 229–43.

[37] Kant, *Groundwork*, ch. ii, pp. 110–11.

action or morality for Hazlitt. By denying that the self is the end of action, he denies the Utilitarian thesis that 'interest' is the natural motive to action and therefore the natural basis of practical morality. According to the *Essay on the Principles of Human Action*, the motive of action and the end of morality, is not 'self', but 'good', whence 'natural disinterestedness'. In the *Lectures on the Age of Elizabeth*, Christ is 'the first true teacher of morality; for he alone conceived the idea of a pure humanity. . . . He taught the love of good for the sake of good, without regard to personal or sinister views' ('General View of the Subject'; vi. 184). This 'good', like the 'idea of a pure humanity,' is represented as independent of interest ('personal and sinister views'), and to that extent, as deontological. Since it is the basis of Hazlitt's moral principle, that principle recognizably partakes of the deontological nature of Kant's categorical imperative.

With the acknowledgement of a categorical imperative or an 'I ought' for Hazlitt, if we return to the question of the moral end achieved by the *Essay on the Principles of Human Action*, we recognize that the *Essay* sets out to address precisely that question Kant seeks to determine in the third chapter of the *Groundwork*, How is a categorical imperative possible? This is also the question, How may we establish that a non-empirical—or *disinterested*—basis for action is possible? The nature of a categorical imperative requires that it be grasped 'completely *a priori*' or prior to experience.[38] From the *Prospectus of a History of English Philosophy* and the lecture 'On the Writings of Hobbes', we know that experience signifies for Hazlitt not only sense impressions, the 'knowledge of things without us,' but also innate activity, 'all knowledge, relating to objects either within or out of the mind' (ii. 114, 124); by this signification, nothing may be admitted as separate from experience. Allowing for the variation in usage, however, the whole of Hazlitt's metaphysic argues the validity of exactly the concept of a priori knowledge, or knowledge that is not immediately dependent on sensory response. The conception of ourselves as intelligences, or as having an aspect independent of the passive receptivity to sensation, arises from the discovery in ourselves of a pure activity distinct from sense, which Kant calls 'reason'.[39] Hazlitt in turn argues from the premiss that we find in ourselves an innate

[38] Ibid. 79.   [39] Ibid., ch. iii, p. 119.

intellectual activity apart from mere sensation, that there is no such thing as a pure passivity, since the mind, being active, reacts upon and remoulds every original impulse or sense impression. In addressing the question of a non-empirical basis for action, he maintains that the basis of all action which does not arise as immediate sensory response, i.e. all voluntary action, is non-empirical or 'disinterested', originating not in the senses, but in the imagination.

Admitting the extent of compatibility between Hazlitt's moral theory and the Kantian ethics, it none the less remains to elucidate the reservations expressed by Hazlitt towards Kant. It becomes necessary, therefore, to turn to those sections of his corpus in which he engages with Kant directly. Extended reference is made to Kant's system in two contexts in Hazlitt's writings: first, the letters of February 1814 to the *Morning Chronicle* on 'Madame de Staël's Account of German Philosophy and Literature', which set out 'to shew in what that system is well founded, and where it fails' (*Miscellaneous Writings*; xx. 12); second, a review of *Biographia Literaria* of August 1817, which makes the following observation: 'As for the great German oracle Kant, we must take the liberty to say, that his system appears to us the most wilful and monstrous absurdity that ever was invented' ('Coleridge's Literary Life', *Contributions to the Edinburgh Review*; xvi. 123). The specific criticism of Kant in this second context comprises four key points: that his system is too mechanical and his assertions dogmatical; that he argues paradoxically for the existence of the material world from its appearance, while denying, at the same time, that we can have any actual knowledge of external objects at all; that he asserts that necessity is incompatible with morality and then insists that a free will is necessary to account for moral sense; that his 'invention' of the faculty of practical reason is metaphysically indefensible (xvi. 123–4).

Hazlitt's contributions to the *Edinburgh Review* are heavily edited by Jeffrey, and this particular review of the *Biographia* is actually claimed by Jeffrey as his own (see Howe's note, xvi. 425). Bearing in mind the possibility of substantial editorial revision at the very least, although it may be safe enough to assume from the review some strong reservations on Hazlitt's part with respect to Kant, and some indication of the nature of those reservations, it would seem advisable, in order to conduct a more detailed exam-

A Long-Contested Freedom

ination, to limit ourselves to the *Morning Chronicle* letters, whose authorship is more conclusively established.[40]

It is clear from Hazlitt's summary of Kant's philosophy in the *Morning Chronicle* that he perceives Kant as supporting the fundamental principle of his own metaphysics: 'The founder of the *transcendental* philosophy very properly insists on the distinction between the sensitive and the intellectual faculties, and makes this division the ground-work of his entire system' (xx. 20). This core of consensus must be recognized as present behind even the most stringent of Hazlitt's criticisms of Kant, which stem largely from certain key differences relating to epistemology. In this context, we will find the variation in their usage of the term 'experience' has a profounder implication than might at first appear.

In a note to the second letter on 'Madame de Stael's Account of German Philosophy and Literature', Hazlitt disputes Kant's postulate of a priori notions which, he writes, 'seem little better than the innate ideas of the schools, or the Platonic ideas or forms, which are to me the forms of *nothing*.' Instead, to refute the mechanical model of the mind, it must be established that there are 'certain intellectual faculties distinct from the senses, which exist before any ideas can be formed' (xx. 18n.). In this assertion, Hazlitt is much closer to Kant than he acknowledges: his 'intellectual faculties' are not in fact so markedly distinguishable from Kant's understanding of the a priori. This becomes especially evident when we turn to the definition of innate faculties in Hazlitt's account of Locke's *Essay* in the *Lectures on English Philosophy*:

I do not know that Mr. Locke has sufficiently distinguished between two things which I cannot very well express otherwise than by a turn of words, namely, an innate knowledge of principles, and innate principles of knowledge. His arguments seem to me conclusive against the one, but not against the other, for I think that there are certain general principles or forms of thinking, something like the moulds in which any thing is cast, according to which our ideas follow one another in a certain order, though the knowledge, *i.e.* perception of what these principles are, and

---

[40] Wellek's indignation about Hazlitt's view of Kant arises in large measure from his treating the review of the *Biographia* as exclusively Hazlitt's; otherwise, he concedes that 'Hazlitt, in the earlier articles, saw through all the mist of ignorance and prejudice one or two essential points which united him to Kant in a common opposition to the Lockean tradition in English philosophy' (Wellek, *Kant in England*, 171).

the forming them into distinct propositions is the result of experience. ('On Locke's "Essay on the Human Understanding"'; ii. 165)

Hazlitt's comments on Locke can be taken almost as a gloss of Kant's famous premiss, 'suppose that objects must conform to our knowledge,'[41] and in fact correspond closely to the repudiation of 'innate faculties' in the English translation of de Staël:

Far from rejecting experience, Kant considers the business of life as nothing but the action of our innate faculties upon the several sorts of knowledge which come to us from without. He believed that experience would be nothing but a chaos without the laws of the understanding; but that the laws of the understanding have no other object than the elements of thought afforded it by experience.[42]

Given the obvious parallel between Hazlitt's epistemology in the essay on Locke and this account in de Staël, which deliberately affirms 'innate faculties' rather than 'innate ideas', it can be argued that Hazlitt's objection to Kant's 'notions a priori' (xx. 18) is a misreading stemming chiefly from the Platonic emphasis in Willich's translation.[43] De Staël herself explicitly refutes the Platonist reading of Kant:

Some expressions in the doctrine of Kant having been ill interpreted, it has been pretended that he believed in that doctrine of innate ideas, which describes them as engraved upon the soul before we have discovered them. Other German philosophers, more allied to the system of Plato, have, in effect, thought that the type of the world was in the human understanding, and that man could not conceive the universe if he had not in himself the innate image of it; but this doctrine is not touched upon by Kant: . . .[44]

De Staël's rejection of the Platonist interpretation of Kant is unambiguous and strongly expressed, and Hazlitt's deliberate preference for Willich's text as 'the most tangible, authentic, and

---

[41] Kant, *Critique of Pure Reason*, 22.   [42] De Staël, *Germany*, iii. 81–2.
[43] Schneider points out that prior to his reading of Willich's *Elements of the Critical Philosophy*, which overemphasizes the Platonic elements in Kant, Hazlitt's few references to Kant are usually favourable. She also suggests that Hazlitt's tendency to identify Kant with Coleridge accounts for much of the violence of his invective against 'the great German oracle', which, like Wellek, she treats as Hazlitt's rather than Jeffrey's (Schneider, *Aesthetics*, 29). While acknowledging the partial truth of both these observations, I would argue nonetheless that it is still fruitful to examine the theoretical grounds upon which Hazlitt believes himself to diverge from Kant.
[44] De Staël, *Germany*, iii. 80.

satisfactory' (xx. 18) is certainly unfortunate. His citation of Kant on a priori ideas in the review of de Staël does not even refer to the main text of the translation, but solely to a short passage from Willich's introduction, a passage which Willich himself calls an 'imperfect account'.[45] The limitations of a poor translation, then, must at least partly account for his Hazlitt's unease with the concept of a priori in the Kantian philosophy.

At the same time, the shortcomings of Willich's translation do not entirely explain away Hazlitt's dissatisfaction with the a priori construct, and his insistence upon a difference in epistemologies repays closer attention. Kant's definition of a priori ideas is inseparable from his other definition, of 'ideas of sensation'; in other words, by allowing two kinds of ideas, one belonging to the senses and the other to the intellect, he appears to Hazlitt to represent the mind as bearing a passive as well as an active aspect. '"Whence do all the ideas and operations of the mind proceed?" *From experience*, is the answer given by the modern philosophy— *From experience and from the understanding*, is the answer given by Kant' (xx. 21). For Hazlitt, on the other hand, logic requires that the 'intellectual' philosophy be the polar opposite of empiricism. In the terms of his metaphysic, to answer 'From experience and from the understanding', to the question of the origin of ideas is to concede one half of the question to the empiricists. The answer, according to his way of thinking, ought simply to be 'From the understanding'. As it is the office of the senses to receive impressions, so it is the office of our intellectual faculty to perceive the relation between these impressions, which perception alone may properly be termed an 'idea' (xx. 21). Immediate sensible impressions cannot produce any ideas, since the mind, perceiving relation, remoulds every original impression. The mind is definitively and characteristically active and owns no passive attributes, just as the senses are definitively and characteristically passive. Thus, in a manner of speaking, all our ideas are innate, and there is no such classification as 'ideas of sensation'. This is why we find Hazlitt rejecting, in another note, Kant's classification of time and space as 'primary forms of the sensitive faculty,' since, for instance, 'Time is obviously an idea of succession or memory,

---

[45] A. F. M. Willich, *Elements of the Critical Philosophy* (London, 1798), 18.

and cannot be the result of an immediate sensible impression' (xx. 20, 20n.).[46]

The difference in epistemologies allows us to extrapolate a corresponding difference in the otherwise compatible ethical positions. The admission into Kant's theory of 'ideas of sensation' leads to the thesis of a 'sensible' and an 'intelligible' world, the second being conceptual only, and unknowable in reality.[47] The sensible world defines the limit of knowledge; however, the 'Idea of a purely intelligible world . . . remains always a serviceable and permitted Idea for the purposes of rational belief', i.e. the conception of the intelligible world may function as an ideal.[48] For Hazlitt, on the other hand, since 'experience' comprehends both sense and intellect, the ideal is never demarcated from the knowable or experiential. The abstract ideal, being the product of innate intellectual power, also belongs to experience. Thus, for instance, our obedience to the moral law may be devoid of self-interest, but never of selfhood itself, i.e. the basis of that obedience cannot be entirely deontological.

The notion, therefore, of a purely deontological principle for moral behaviour, 'duty for the sake of duty', could never constitute Hazlitt's whole case for morality. 'Duty for the sake of duty' appeals to the non-experiential alone, which Hazlitt terms 'abstract reason', in itself an insufficient basis for moral behaviour. As the object of moral action, 'good' is deontological to the extent that it is independent of empirical considerations of interest, but it is never wholly so, since it is also experienced as good.[49] Thus it

---

[46] Wellek writes, 'One wonders what is actually Hazlitt's final position if he grants to empiricism that its teaching on experience as the only source of our ideas has the advantage of simplicity, while Kant's answer that ideas arise from experience and the understanding is considered as wanting in logical proof. Personally he does not seem to require this logical proof, but proceeds on the assumption that it succeeded' (Wellek, *Kant in England*, 168). Wellek's 'wonder' arises, ironically, from a misunderstanding of Hazlitt, whom he so often accuses of misunderstanding Kant; he fails to register that Hazlitt is implying that the understanding is the only source of ideas. However, although he is generally dismissive of Hazlitt's view of Kant as a 'maze of misunderstandings' (ibid., 167), he concedes, albeit somewhat patronizingly, that his criticism of Kant's classifications of time and space 'is good philosophy and shows speculative abilities in Hazlitt which are little known' (ibid. 168).
[47] Kant, *Groundwork*, ch. iii, p. 119.   [48] Ibid. 130.
[49] This twofold aspect of morality may be understood through Soame Jenyns's observations on virtue, cited by Dr Johnson in his review of *A Free Inquiry into the Nature and Origin of Evil* (1757): 'But though the production of happiness is the essence of virtue, it is by no means the end: the great end is the probation of mankind,

can be made the object of both reason and passion. Indeed, 'Passion speaks truer than reason' ('Preface', *Political Essays*; vii. 12); passion is the great self-affirming and experiential quality which 'should itself govern and lend its impulse and direction to abstract reason' in order that the good be attained ('Character of Lord Chatham', *Political Essays*; vii. 300).

Experience and verifiability are attributes that possess a value for Hazlitt that cannot be minimizsed. As the essay 'On Reason and Imagination' indicates, it is only upon the experiential basis of morality that individual feeling is validated, so that every moral action is self-affirming in the manner essential to his doctrine of empowerment. According to Hazlitt, all abstraction or universals must be inducted from particulars, and systems which either claim or manifest independence from the particular, are mechanical or *mere* systems. His rejection of Kant as the proponent of such a system is expressed primarily as a condemnation of Kant's method. Thus he complains,

> this author's account of the intellect, after all, appears to be rather dogmatical than demonstrative. . . . His reasoning is seldom any thing more than a detailed, paraphrased explanation of his original statement, instead of being (what it ought to be) an appeal to known facts, or a deduction from acknowledged principles, or a detection of the inconsistencies of other writers . . . (xx. 19–20)

The complaint is, quite simply, of a lack of concreteness, but its implication is serious. Kant's method of assertion without the appeal to experience unfits his philosophy effectively to counteract that other system, comprising the physical theories of the mind, against which, by virtue of its fundamental principle, it must be placed in logical opposition (xx. 20–1). What Hazlitt is expressing here is a keen sense of the detriment to his own metaphysical 'truth', arising from the system which would appear to assert it, yet offers nothing more than one empty abstraction in place of the other.

. . . And thus indeed it answers two most important purposes; those are the conservation of our happiness, and the test of our obedience.'—Samuel Johnson, 'Review of [Soame Jenyns], *A Free Inquiry into the Nature and Origin of Evil* (1757)' in *The Oxford Authors: Samuel Johnson*, ed. Donald Greene (Oxford: Oxford University Press, 1984), 537–8. By this account, although 'the production of happiness' is not the motive or 'end' of virtue, that end is nonetheless achieved by it. As the 'test of our obedience', virtue is deontological; as it is conducive to 'the conservation of our happiness', it is experiential.

Such a view of Kant's method is likely to have gained conviction from Madame de Staël's account.[50] Although de Staël constantly refers to Kant's reconciliation of the experiential and the ideal,[51] she tends also to emphasize an attention to the purely abstract in her account of his method: 'all the fine affections of the soul defended with the strictness of the most abstract reasonings', 'setting all that is fine in the heart, on the basis of a theory', 'singularly abstract and logical mode of reasoning.'[52] Hazlitt's objection to Kant's reasoning, that it does not 'appeal to known facts', echoes de Staël's complaint that 'what is known never serves as a step to what is unknown'.[53] In spite of her otherwise largely unqualified admiration for Kant, de Staël also criticizes his language and phraseology in the *Critique of Pure Reason*: 'He has made use of a phraseology very difficult to understand, and of the most tiresome new creation of words'; 'the attention of the reader is exhausted in efforts to understand the language, before he arrives at the ideas.'[54]

Ultimately, Kant fails, by Hazlitt's lights, both on account of the method of his argument and on account of the metaphysical premises upon which that argument is based, effectively to affirm the empowered mind. It is important to grasp this conclusion, but it must not detract from our understanding of the relevance of the Kantian philosophy to Hazlitt's metaphysics, nor from the insights into his moral theory granted by such understanding.

In conclusion, I would like to bring Kant to the issue with which I opened this chapter, regarding the moral standing of the *Essay on the Principles of Human Action*. I have said that the *Essay* affirms an idea and not a fact, but by Hazlitt's own stipulation, 'if a theory does not answer in practice, it is proof positive that the theory is good for nothing' ('Capital Punishments', *Political Criticism*; xix. 220). The argument of the *Essay* is theoretical and its character, ideal; at the same time, it also fulfils the function of a 'practical philosophy' as outlined by Kant at the close of the first chapter of the *Groundwork*:

---

[50] Another possibility, suggested by Wellek, is that this view of Kant's method actually arises from Willich's method of 'enumerating definitions and results' (Wellek, *Kant in England*, 167). [51] De Staël, *Germany*, iii. 81–2, 93.
[52] Ibid. 93, 94, 95. [53] Ibid. 97. [54] Ibid. 96, 97.

In this way the *common reason of mankind* is impelled, not by any need for speculation (which never assails it so long as it is content to be mere sound reason), but on practical grounds themselves, to leave its own sphere and take a step into the field of *practical philosophy*. It there seeks to acquire information and precise instruction about the source of its own principle, and about the correct function of this principle in comparison with maxims based on need and inclination, in order that it may escape from the embarrassment of antagonistic claims and may avoid the risk of losing all genuine moral principles because of the ambiguity into which it easily falls.[55]

If we accept this definition of a 'practical philosophy' and its objective, the subordination of our nature as sensory beings to our nature as rational beings, then, only substituting 'imaginative' for 'rational' to signify non-empirical nature, we must acknowledge that the *Essay on the Principles of Human Action* both fits this definition and is governed by this objective, i.e. we must acknowledge the 'practical grounds' of the *Essay*'s metaphysic. Upon the conviction carried by its argument rests the removal of certain obstacles to moral development. In Hazlitt's own words,

The object of that Essay... is to leave free play to the social affections, and to the cultivation of the more disinterested and generous principles of our nature, by removing a stumbling-block which has been thrown in their way, and which turns the very idea of virtue or humanity into a fable, viz. the metaphysical doctrine of the innate and necessary selfishness of the human mind. (*A Letter to William Gifford*; ix. 51)

The theoretical enlargement of man's capacity for benevolence may then be recognized as inseparable from the practical enlargement of this capacity, once again undermining, not only on a theoretical, but also on a practical basis, Kinnaird's conclusion regarding the 'failure' of the *Essay* as moral philosophy.

[55] Kant, *Groundwork*, ch. i, p. 73.

5
Essays Political and Familiar
Two Aspects of Hazlitt's Ideal

THE bias of the mind is at once its most enabling and limiting characteristic; its outcome is abstraction, the fundamental epistemological process that both enables and limits knowledge. Hazlitt's theory of abstraction, itself based upon the self-affirming and individual tendency of the mind, at the same time gives us an insight into a concept of the ideal that is at the heart of his moral philosophy. The ideal embodies the symbiosis of experiential and abstract, particular and general. By that symbiosis, the universal is brought within the compass of the individual self. Hazlitt's concept of the ideal makes possible his reconciliation of freedom and necessity in moral action; it is the ground of unity between his moral and aesthetic philosophies.

This book has reconstructed from the wealth of his writings, Hazlitt the metaphysician, inseparable, as I have tried to show, from that other and better-known Hazlitt, long acknowledged as a master of the 'familiar style', and more recently, for the fierceness and intensity of his political prose. This final chapter returns to that well-known and well-loved essayist. Hazlitt's idealism is no less practical than it is theoretical; it shapes both his political beliefs and his practice as a writer. In his political writings, the ideal is expressed in the merging of passion and abstraction in the innate power of the individual, pitted against the arbitrary power of tyranny. In his method as a conversational essayist, we may decipher his own attempt to translate the ideal into practice.

Abstracting Passion: The Ideal of Power

Any discussion of Hazlitt's idealism can hardly be complete without some reference to the conceptual basis of his political writings. Hazlitt's political essays and criticism are generated by a wide range of contemporary figures and events; often, they represent his strong and immediate responses to the political climate of his time. It is not my purpose to undertake a detailed analysis of that climate and Hazlitt's position in relation to it. My concern is with the conceptual relation between imaginative and political power for Hazlitt.

Hazlitt's writings as a whole are distinguished by his close attention to the structures of power, political power not excepted. 'For power', he writes in a *Morning Post* article of March 1800, 'is the sole object of philosophical attention in man, as in inanimate nature; and in the one equally as in the other, we understand it more intimately, the more diverse the circumstances are with which we have observed it to exist' ('Pitt and Buonaparte', *Political Essays*; vii. 326).

'Power' in Hazlitt's metaphysic refers to the mind's innate faculty, its freedom from subjugation to external influences. His philosophy also connects power with liberty: the mind is free since it is subject only to the laws of its own innate constitution. By affirming innate 'power', Hazlitt refutes the empirical account of epistemology in which the mind, moulded from without, remains passive or subjected. He asserts in its stead that the process of knowledge is *ab intra*, directed by the mind from within. From the *Essay on the Principles of Human Action*, 'power' may be identified as the attribute of the imagination. The creative genius celebrated in Hazlitt's literary and artistic criticism exemplifies imaginative power in its highest degree, and so vindicates the core principle of his metaphysics.

The exercise of Hazlitt's metaphysical power is frequently described in a quasi-political language. The creative genius, for instance, is perceived as effecting a kind of rule by force, so that 'The language of poetry naturally falls in with the language of power' ('Coriolanus', *Characters of Shakespear's Plays*; iv. 214). In Hazlitt's philosophical writings, the doctrine of intellectual empowerment may be said to free the mind from the subject status to which it is assigned by empirical thought. In turn, when we locate Hazlitt's political essays in the context of his entire corpus, an interplay emerges between imaginative and political, innate and assumed, involuntary and arbitrary power. Such interplay frequently highlights the diametric opposition between the two forms of power. This is especially the case in Hazlitt's polemic against political absolutism, specifically monarchy, which contains the main tenet of his ideological position. 'A king (as such) is not a great man. He has great power, but it is not his own' ('The Indian Jugglers', *Table-Talk*; viii. 84). The power invested in an individual by the doctrine of divine right is acquired *ab extra* and is hence arbitrary; it is inherently opposed to innate power, which is inwardly generated and involuntary. By virtue of our innate power, Hazlitt, like Rousseau, perceives men to be born free. The 'freeborn spirit of man' inevitably works against the fundamental assumption of monarchy that mankind is its property ('Whether Genius is Conscious of its Powers', *The Plain Speaker*; xii. 122). Thus the mutual alliance of liberty and power in his metaphysic becomes, in the political context, a polarity: 'A King cannot attain absolute power, while the people remain perfectly free' ('What is the People?', *Political Essays*; vii. 264).[1]

For Hazlitt, the placing of our intellectual constitution under the control of external circumstances turns men into machines, because it denies the *ab intra* or innate process of the mind. Thus, just as he indicts the philosophical systems of Locke and Hartley, as well as Bentham's Utilitarianism, for their role in the progressive mechanization of men, he shows the political system of monarchy as working to much the same effect. Since it is by virtue of our innate power that we are free, the curbing of our freedom amounts to a denial of that power. Political enslavement goes against the grain of intellectual empowerment; it allows only a condition of servility in which men are turned into machines. The language of automation in which Hazlitt describes the lackeys of political power closely resembles the mechanistic imagery of his literary criticism; both refer to an absence of innate power. The essay 'On the Character of Fox' describes 'the wire-moved puppets, the stuffed figures, the flexible machinery, the "deaf and dumb things" of a court' (*Political Essays*; vii. 317). Southey, as poet laureate, is a 'stuffed figure,' a 'wretched phantom' and not 'the living man' ('The Courier and "The Wat Tyler"', *Political*

---

[1] When Kinnaird observes that Hazlitt 'remains instinctively a Romanticist in that he continues to oppose individual power, as the source of value, to "power" in the world' (Kinnaird, *William Hazlitt*, 271), he implies that Hazlitt is unthinkingly ('instinctively') participating in a certain general ('Romanticist') consciousness, and thus fails to register the distinctive and philosophical validity of that opposition for Hazlitt.

Essays; vii. 185), while a *Morning Chronicle* article of December 1813, titled 'The Political Automaton: A Modern Character', refers to the government stooge as *'the thing'* and 'puppet' (*Political Criticism*; xix. 117). Arbitrary power renders mechanistic and impotent even the figure in which it is embodied; it is not only his subject, but the king himself who, lacking the innate faculty, is 'a puppet to dress up, a lay-figure to paint from' ('On the Spirit of Monarchy', *Political Criticism*; xix. 256).

Their servility to arbitrary power makes men mechanical; Hazlitt's repeated association of servility with the support of the political establishment may be contrasted with his account of the egotistical genius, exemplifying the dominion or mastery granted to the empowered mind by its capacity for self-determination. If its originality—the tendency to remould and regenerate its object—marks the active character of the powerful imagination, equally, political absolutism creates a passivity, displayed in a mechanical resistance to innovation of all kind. 'Let a thing be new (though ever so true or good), the Tory cannot make up his mind to it,—he abhors it' ('Illustrations of Toryism—From the Writings of Sir Walter Scott', *Political Criticism*; xix. 288).

As regards power, Hazlitt's ideal in literary criticism is in every respect the reverse of his standards in political criticism. Where he celebrates the power of genius as bigoted, exclusive, and overwhelming, he condemns the power of monarchs as owning exactly those qualities. For instance, the verbal similarities between the description of tyranny in the 'Preface' to the *Political Essays*, and of 'greatness' in *Table-Talk* may readily be highlighted: 'Greatness is great power, producing great effects. . . . To impress the idea of power on others, they must be made in some way to feel it. It must be communicated to their understandings . . . or it must subdue and overawe them by subjecting their wills' ('The Indian Jugglers'; viii. 84–5). This is close enough to 'that sort of tyranny that has lasted for ever, . . . that has struck its roots into the human heart, and clung round the human understanding like a nightshade; that overawes the imagination, and disarms the will to resist it' (vii. 12). The first passage describes the domination of the creative genius, the second, that of the despot. Both subjugate our understandings and our wills. In this case, the language of literary theory carries a quite different import from the language of political criticism. Tyranny, 'linked in endless succession to the principle by which life is transmitted to the generations of tyrants' (vii. 12), produces a hideous travesty of the associative chain generated by the powerful imagination. A similar comparison, of the 'diverse circumstances' of power, can be made between Hazlitt's account of majesty, 'blind and insensible to all that lies beyond that narrow sphere' ('On the Regal Character', *Political Essays*; vii. 282) and of genius, 'blind to all excellence but its own' ('On Genius and Common Sense', *Table-Talk*; viii. 43). There is, of course, no contradiction here; Hazlitt perceives innate or imaginative power as the great counter-force, equal and opposite, to political absolutism. The arbitrary power invested in a single individual is by nature inimical to the innate power with which we are all endowed; yet there also exists between them a common character.

The paradox arises, however, with the mutual affinity, 'the connexion between toad-eaters and tyrants', that is brought about by that common character: 'The admiration of power in others is as common to man as the love of it in himself: the one makes him a tyrant, the other a slave' ('The Times Newspaper', *Political Essays*; vii. 145, 148). The absolute power embodied in the monarchy typically finds a response, by a kind of transference, in the sense of power in each individual: 'Each individual would (were it in his power) be a king, a God: but as he cannot, the next best thing is to see this reflex image of his self-love, the darling passion of his breast, realized, embodied out of himself' ('On the Spirit of Monarchy', *Political Criticism*; xix. 255).

In the first part of his essay on the political content of Hazlitt's literary criticism and epistemology, Terry Eagleton makes three categorical observations that rightly draw our attention to the close connection between Hazlitt's literary, philosophical, and political thought. The first is that 'Poetry itself is for him . . . an epistemological mode . . . [which] stands as a permanent phenomenological critique of that abstracting rationalism which Hazlitt rightly identifies as one powerful form of contemporary bourgeois ideology.'[2] Second, 'What Hazlitt demonstrates, in fact, is a quite remarkable intuitive grasp of the internal relations between literary style, theories of knowledge, ideological con-

---

[2] Eagleton, 'An Empiricist Radical', 109.

Essays Political and Familiar

sciousness and political practice'.[3] Finally, 'Hazlitt's language refuses a distinction between the literary and the political'.[4]

None of these observations can be denied, yet I would argue that Eagleton's account of the internal relations between the different aspects of Hazlitt's thought—poetry, politics, and epistemology—is somewhat oversimplified. By describing poetry as a 'permanent . . . critique' of political conservatism, he bypasses the philosophical dilemma which Hazlitt is constantly addressing: the facility of alliance between poetry and established power. The 'epistemological mode' embodied in poetry runs counter to the dictates of the prevalent ideology, but it is also successfully harnessed to that very ideological purpose. In this context, as much as Hazlitt's language 'refuses' a distinction between the literary and the political, it also highlights, witness the comparison of majesty and genius, that distinction.

'But the best things, in their abuse, often become the worst; and so it is with poetry when it is diverted from its proper end' ('Illustrations of "The Times" Newspaper', *Political Essays*; vii. 142). The ambiguous status of poetry in Hazlitt's political vision arises from its moral neutrality. 'The spirit of poetry is in itself favourable to humanity and liberty' (vii. 142), but not necessarily so. The poetic imagination, whose truth is entirely self-constituted, by its very independence of an external or objective material reality, lends itself to speciousness and deceit. The power by which poets 'pour out the pure treasures of thought to the world' enables them also to 'pass off the gewgaws of corruption and love-tokens of self-interest, as the gifts of the Muse' (vii. 143). Potentially the most powerful instrument in the cause of liberty, the imaginative genius is equally effective on the opposite side. Burke, for instance,

had power to 'make the worse appear the better reason'—the devil's boast! The madness of genius was necessary to second the madness of a court; his flaming imagination was the torch that kindled the smouldering fire in the inmost sanctuary of pride and power, and spread havoc, dismay, and desolation through the world. The light of his imagination, sportive, dazzling, beauteous as it seemed, was followed by the stroke of death. ('Arguing in a Circle', *Political Criticism*; xix. 271)

[3] Ibid. 109.   [4] Ibid. 110.

Hazlitt's hyperbole, deliberately evocative of Milton's Satan, is a tribute to Burke's genius. The perversion of power, the descent from life into death, and the destruction left in its wake, represents a fall that appears as monumental as Lucifer's: 'Politics became poetry in his hands' (xix. 272).[5]

While no other writer has quite the standing of Burke in Hazlitt's eyes, the moral neutrality of the imagination, manifested in a want of principle in poets and writers, is the target of some of the sharpest of his criticism in the political essays. Hence his recurrent attacks upon the Lake School. The subversion of the cause of liberty by the defection of the poets represents to Hazlitt the defeat of genius, or the subsuming of innate by assumed power; it is, indeed, self-defeating, that self being the basis of his whole intellectual vision: Southey 'mangles his own breast to stifle every natural sentiment left there' ('The Courier and "The Wat Tyler"', *Political Essays*; vii. 185).

The conversion of poetry into a mere or empty fiction by the sacrifice of its innate power is part of the general perversion of language for political ends: 'an inconceivably large portion of human knowledge and human power is involved in the science and management of words' ('Pitt and Buonaparte', *Political Essays*; vii. 327). A recurrent theme in Hazlitt's political writings is the manner in which the power of language is put to use in the construction of a language of power. Words, which 'alone answer . . . to the truth of things' ('On Sir Walter Scott, Racine and Shakespear', *The Plain Speaker*; xii. 337) also alone distort reality. Truth is elided in the mechanical associations of language. Hence the efficacy of nicknames. 'The history of modern politics is the history of nicknames. The use of this figure of speech is that it excites a strong idea without requiring any proof' ('The Duke d'Enghien II', *Political Criticism*; xix. 134). In a nickname, the extremity of the language substitutes for the truth of its allegation; it is 'the *ne plus ultra* of Tory logic. Why? Because it implies a strong degree of mechanical hatred and contempt, without assigning any reason for it' ('Illustrations of Toryism—From the Writings of Sir Walter Scott', *Political Criticism*; xix. 288).

The same reduction of truth to verbal mechanism marks the

---

[5] For an analysis of the tension between the literary and the political in Hazlitt's account of Burke, see Whale, 'Hazlitt on Burke'.

speeches of Pitt, who 'seemed not to have believed that the truth of his statements depended on the reality of the facts, but that the things depended on the order in which he arranged them in words' ('Character of Mr. Pitt', *Political Essays*; vii. 323–4). Pitt's skill in language, to which Hazlitt attributes his political prowess, is opposite to the 'effect of nature and genius'; instead of the imaginative association of feelings and ideas, he gives us 'Words on words finely arranged, and so dexterously consequent' that we may trace 'in the effects of his eloquence the power of words and phrases, and that peculiar constitution of human affairs in their present state, which so eminently favours this power' ('Pitt and Buonaparte', *Political Essays*; vii. 331).

Given the abuse to which all language is subject, it is a process of thought, not poetry, but abstraction, that embodies for Hazlitt the radical epistemological mode that is inherently and invariably opposed to political injustice.[6] To the claims of arbitrary power, he consistently opposes an abstract notion: 'the abstract right of the human race to be free,' 'truth and abstract justice' ('Preface', *Political Essays*; vi. 12, 14), 'abstract reason' ('The Times Newspaper', *Political Essays*; vii. 152). In *The Plain Speaker*, he claims to have 'made an abstract, metaphysical principle' of the question of whether mankind is the property of monarchs ('Whether Genius is Conscious of Its Powers?'; xii. 122), and in *A Letter to William Gifford*, he writes, 'I suspect that the conviction of an abstract principle is alone a match for the prejudices of absolute power' (ix. 50).

That abstract principle is, of course, the 'discovery' of the *Essay on the Principles of Human Action*, by which every individual is endowed with an innate power of self-determination. Abstraction itself is the culmination of that power, marking the deepening of perception beyond the merely local, and separating the ideal from that which is petty and personal. The abstract ideal is universal, where political absolutism secures the élitist interest, so that Hazlitt frequently links absolutism with an incapacity for abstraction:

---

[6] At the other extreme from Eagleton, critics such as Whale have argued that a negative view of the imagination is necessarily entailed upon Hazlitt by his position as a radical. Whale finds that for Hazlitt, 'the problem with imagination arises when it moves beyond its limits: it has no proper place in questions of a political kind,' 'the imagination's dangerous affinity with abstraction . . . [is] another means of diverting attention from political reality' (ibid. 476, 478). I would argue, on the contrary, that it is precisely the tendency of the imagination towards abstraction that makes it Hazlitt's instrument and emblem of political justice.

The common regal character is then the reverse of what it ought to be. It is the purely *personal*, occupied with its own petty feelings, prejudices, and pursuits; whereas it ought to be the purely philosophical, exempt from all personal considerations, and contemplating itself only in its general and paramount relation to the State. This is the reason why there have been so few great Kings. They want the power of abstraction . . . ('On the Regal Character', *Political Essays*; vii. 284)

Elsewhere, he observes that 'A Tory may be a poet, but no Tory can be a philosopher; for he has not even the capacity of conceiving an abstract proposition' ('Illustrations of Toryism—From the Writings of Sir Walter Scott', *Political Criticism*; xix. 288).

For Hazlitt, the process of abstraction, brought about by the fundamental and innate tendency (the powerful imagination) of the human being, attests to the authenticity of human ideals. We recall his refutation of Locke's theory of abstraction and also of Tooke, by whose etymology the abstract concepts of right, wrong, just, true, etc. are denied actual existence. Hazlitt's abstract ideal is not deontological or 'objective' in the conventional sense, but a universal that must be elicited from particular experience, and it is therefore to that experience that he refers as the gauge of truth: 'We appeal . . . to the innate love of liberty in the human breast' ('What is the People?', *Political Essays*; vii. 270).

However, although the abstract ideal is enabled, it is not guaranteed by the imagination, which is morally neutral. Disinterestedness and self-interest are produced alike from the imagination, yet the habitual mechanism of consciousness most frequently directs imaginative exercise towards the lesser end.[7] By the same token, when the two manifestations of innate power—abstraction, which leads us to the universal good, and prejudice,

---

[7] It should be noted that although the intellectual self is the instrument of 'good', the material self is the basis of 'right', and self-interest, its guiding principle ('Project for a New Theory of Civil and Criminal Legislation', *Political Criticism*; xix. 303). Hazlitt defines the 'right' of an individual as pertaining to his physical being: 'each person has a particular body and senses belonging to him, so that he feels a peculiar and natural interest in whatever affects these more than another can, . . . imply[ing] a direct and unavoidable right in maintaining this circle of individuality inviolate' (xix. 310). By defining 'right' as sense-based, Hazlitt is placing intellectual expression outside the domain of legislation: 'As to matters of contempt and the expression of opinion, I think these do not fall under the head of force, and are not, on that ground, subjects of coercion and law' (xix. 314). By the same token, since morality belongs to intellect, there can be no law for the enforcement of morals (xix. 315). 'Morals . . . ought never to appeal to force in any case whatever' (xix. 304).

which works against it—are pitted against each other, the second almost invariably prevails. The ideal, moving out towards the universal, is usually weaker than prejudice, which limits us to ourselves and which, in so doing, is corroborated by the mechanical process of sensation that constitutes the material self.

'The love of liberty is the love of others; the love of power is the love of ourselves. The one is real; the other often but an empty dream' ('The Times Newspaper', *Political Essays*; vii. 152). The moral neutrality of the imagination and the habitual limitation of the empowered self brings about the great polarity of Hazlitt's political criticism, that of liberty and power:

> In general it may be said that the love of liberty makes but a faint impression on the mind of a great Statesman: the love of power sinks deeper into it, discolours every object, taints the source of every feeling, and penetrates, moves, and rouses into violent and dangerous action the whole inert mass. ('The Treatment of State Prisoners', *Political Criticism*; xix. 200)

Again, the closeness of the passage above to Hazlitt's account of the egotistical genius is unmistakable. By the terms of his own theory of bias, liberty, encompassing the universal, is too often diffused and dissipated where power, perpetually and solely focused on the individual ego, acquires a concentrated and proportionately irresistible force: 'The principle of tyranny is in fact identified with a man's pride and the servility of others in the highest degree; the principle of liberty abstracts him from himself, and has to contend in its feeble course with all his own passions, prejudices, interests, and those of the world ('Preface', *Political Essays*; vii. 19).

In Hazlitt's account of the 'true Jacobin', therefore, 'The love of truth is a passion in his mind, as the love of power is a passion in the minds of others. Abstract reason, unassisted by passion, is no match for power and prejudice, armed with force and cunning' ('The Times Newspaper', *Political Essays*; vii. 152). The partisan, as opposed to 'the bigot, or the mercenary or cowardly tool of a party,' 'is a character that requires very opposite and almost incompatible qualities—reason and prejudice, a passionate attachment founded on an abstract idea' ('On the Spirit of Partisanship', *Uncollected Essays*; xvii. 34). In other words, Hazlitt's political criticism makes explicit that the abstract ideal or 'good' which is the object of moral action can never be, for all its closeness to Kant's 'duty', entirely deontological. The good must not only be acknowledged, it must be idolized. Passion concurs with abstraction, the individual with the universal, in the idolization of the good.[8] If the denial of liberty is 'moral atheism', by implication, liberty is *theos*. Napoleon Bonaparte, as its representative, becomes 'the God of my idolatry' ('Preface', *Political Essays*; vii. 10). Hazlitt's tendency to idolize is reflected in the fervour of his polemic, where the passionate idolization of the abstract ideal refutes the servile idolization of arbitrary power, described at length in the essay 'On the Spirit of Monarchy' (*Political Criticism*; xix. 256 ff).[9]

Eagleton's observation, that 'In harnessing passion and generality, Hazlitt undercuts both rationalist and empiricist forms of conservative ideology,' perfectly summarizes the link between Hazlitt's philosophical and political thought, except in the implied subordination of his epistemology to a political purpose.[10] While Hazlitt's epistemology and political radicalism are mutually corroborative, the metaphysic is the first premiss rather than a corollary. The harnessing of passion and generality is not a political solution that can be validated philosophically, it is the *only* political solution admitted by the metaphysical construct to which Hazlitt is bound. The nature of power—imaginative and political—is self-affirming, yet it can and indeed must be directed towards a universal end. 'All power is but an unabated nuisance, a

---

[8] When poetry manifests the union of abstraction and passion, at once embodying a universal truth and an individual vision, then it is the poetry of genius, which indeed represents Hazlitt's radical epistemology. Thus Bloom's generalization about Hazlitt's thought, that 'Poetical justice is antithetical to societal justice' is much too sweeping (Bloom, *William Hazlitt*, 8). Emphatically, it is its abstract character that marks the distinction between the poetry of genius and what Hazlitt calls 'mere' poetry ('Character of Mr. Burke', *Political Essays*; vii. 229).

[9] In his outline of the 'anatomy' or satirical critique of idolatry in Hazlitt's writings, especially *Liber Amoris*, James Mulvihill does not recognize the extent to which Hazlitt perceives his own kind of political idolatry as a corrective to the general phenomenon of idolatry, described by Mulvihill as 'a species of self-aggrandizement by which a subject willfully establishes its own preconceived ideal in an object.'—James Mulvihill, 'The Anatomy of Idolatry: Hazlitt's *Liber Amoris*', *CLB* lxx (April 1990), 197. By Mulvihill's own definition, 'Idolatry is at once a desire to worship otherness and a projection of self' (ibid. 198), and this self-projecting tendency, underlying the impulse towards the other, is the chief tenet of Hazlitt's moral and metaphysical position. [10] Eagleton, 'An Empiricist Radical', 116.

barbarous assumption, an aggravated injustice, that is not directed to the common good' ('On the Spirit of Monarchy'; xix. 265).

In the socio-political context, the 'common good' is usually identified with 'the people', not a quantifiable majority or 'greatest number', but a grouping of individuals, simultaneously the instrument and the end of Hazlitt's radical purpose. Public opinion is the aggregate of individual judgements; it 'expresses not only the collective sense of the whole people, but of all ages and nations', but the '*vox populi* is the *vox Dei* only when its springs from the individual, unbiassed feelings' ('What is the People?', *Political Essays*; vii. 269, 272). In basing his standard for political justice on the collective force of individual feelings, Hazlitt appears in little doubt of their unanimity. 'The people is the hand, heart, and head of the whole community acting to one purpose, and with a mutual and thorough consent . . . The will of the people necessarily tends to the general good as its end' ('What is the People?'; vii. 267). We recognize an ideal in this account, the more so when we compare it to the account of public opinion given in *Table-Talk*:

So far then is public opinion from resting on a broad and solid basis, as the aggregate of thought and feeling in a community, that it is slight and shallow and variable to the last degree—the bubble of the moment—so that we may safely say the public is the dupe of public opinion, not its parent. The public is pusillanimous and cowardly, because it is weak. It knows itself to be a great dunce, and that it has no opinions but upon suggestion. Yet it is unwilling to appear in leading-strings, and would have it thought that its decisions are as wise as they are weighty. It is hasty in taking up its favourites, more hasty in laying them aside, lest it should be supposed deficient in sagacity in either case. It is generally divided into two strong parties, each of which will allow neither common sense nor common honesty to the other side. ('On Living to One's-Self'; viii. 98)

Like the ideal of 'natural disinterestedness' from the *Essay on the Principles of Human Action*, Hazlitt's 'the people' asserts not so much a fact about humanity, but a goal. Like 'truth' in the essay 'On Reason and Imagination', 'the people' is an 'aggregate' (vii. 268) which represents the ideal symbiosis of particular and general, at once embodying Hazlitt's strong sense of collectivism and his extreme individualism. In terms of practical social measures, the collectivist approach informs his arguments for the equitable distribution of resources (reiterated in various contexts, including in the discussion of war and taxation and the critique of Malthus), the rights of unionization of labour, and the necessity of welfare provisions (for instance, in the 'Project for a New Theory of Civil and Criminal Legislation', *Political Criticism*; xix. 309, 319). At the same time, in Hazlitt's advocacy of complete religious tolerance, including the emancipation of the Jews (*Political Criticism*; xix. 320–4), or in his denial of the concept of consensual crimes, such as drink or suicide ('Project for a New Theory of Civil and Criminal Legislation'; xix. 316), we see also a profound belief in the individual's responsibility for his own destiny.

As a metaphysician first and then only a political moralist, Hazlitt's critique is not only of the effects of social and political practices, but also of their implicit meaning. The mind or self becomes the locus of the struggle between the innate power of the individual and the arbitrary power exercised by the political machine; it is the site where a certain ability with which we are all endowed is linked with and pitted against the large-scale ramifications of social and political inequality. Hazlitt's reference to the 'principle of independent inquiry and unbiassed conviction' ('On Court-Influence', *Political Essays*; vii. 240) or to 'the greatest power of understanding in the community, unbiassed by any sinister motive' ('What is the People?'; vii. 268) in denouncing the abuses of power, may at first appear to assert exactly that detached intellectual stance, the universal prophetic voice, that we are warned against by the modern philosopher of power, Michel Foucault.[11] But his theory of bias, the recognition of the alliance between power and poetry, and of a continuity between the principle of power in the individual and the abuse of power in the political community, attest rather to the consciousness, not of detachment, but participation, in the very structures of power that are the subject of his critique. Hazlitt's account of power is 'from within', his analysis ringing true precisely because he is situated inside it. In this sense, he answers Foucault's demand, for 'one who, in the inertias and constraints of the present time, locates and marks the weak points, the openings, the lines of force.'[12]

By rigorous philosophical standards, as Eagleton suggests, Hazlitt's appeal to the inner man as the instrument of social

---

[11] Michel Foucault, 'Power and Sex: An Interview with Michel Foucault', *Telos* xxxii (1977), 161.   [12] Ibid. 161.

justice provides a foundation for his political theory that is far from adequate theoretically.[13] The political writings are most persuasive, however, as the practical illustrations of Hazlitt's theory, themselves representing a passionate commitment to the 'common good' that rarely, if ever, leads him astray in determining the rights and wrongs of specific social and political issues.

His Own Interpreter: The Essayist as Artist

The most strenuous efforts to identify Hazlitt's principles in literary criticism with the Keatsian ideal of negative capability have found it impossible to explain away the manifestation of a strong and often deeply opinionated persona in Hazlitt's writings.[14] The bias of the essayist resists even the attempt to describe it: 'Now I hate my style to be known; as I hate all *idiosyncrasy*' ('On the Disadvantages of Intellectual Superiority', *Table-Talk*; viii. 285). Hazlitt's hatreds are frequently the signals of his own idiosyncrasy, and in the transition from the literary critic of *The Round Table* to the moralist of *The Plain Speaker*, the voice of the essayist becomes increasingly personal and idiosyncratic. In *Table-Talk*, published five years prior to *The Plain Speaker*, Hazlitt is already consciously making this transition, to which he calls our attention in his advertisement to the Paris edition: 'It . . . occurred to me as possible to combine the advantages of these two styles, the *literary* and *conversational*' (viii. 333).[15] What he is referring to is the shift from the descriptive or expository procedure of the early essays to the method of narrative, and therefore to a foregrounding of the essayist as narrator. This gives to Hazlitt's conversational prose the character

---

[13] Eagleton, 'An Empiricist Radical', 116–17.
[14] Albrecht observes that 'Although Hazlitt never achieved a high degree of negative capability, much less the dramatic form that marks its culmination, he made an approach to both. In the essays after 1820, Hazlitt is less aggressive in asserting his convictions; his tone is less strident, more tolerant, more aphoristic' (Albrecht, *Hazlitt*, 149). On the contrary, the personality of the post-1820 essayist is especially too pronounced to sustain Albrecht's apology.
[15] This is a late (1825) edition of *Table-Talk*, and includes some essays from *The Plain Speaker*, which was published as a separate collection only a year later; however, the advertisement describes the transition in style as having already taken place in the original publication.

of autobiography; Lamb finds *Table-Talk* to be both 'uniformly conversational' and 'a piece of Autobiography.'[16] In the development from the short, almost fragmentary essays of *The Round Table* to the extended disquisitions of *The Plain Speaker*, we are made increasingly aware, not so much of any significant variations in thought or opinion, but of the personality of the essayist.[17]

Literature, or more generally, art, is the primary focus of *The Round Table*. We have essays on specific works ('On Hogarth's Marriage a-la-mode', 'On Milton's Lycidas', 'On the Midsummer Night's Dream', 'On the Beggar's Opera', 'Observations on Mr. Wordsworth's Poem The Excursion'), on the study and criticism of the arts ('On Classical Education', 'On Pedantry', 'On Commonplace Critics'), on the artistic character ('On Posthumous Fame', 'On Different Sorts of Fame', 'On the Literary Character', 'On Poetical Versatility', 'On Actors and Acting'), and on the character of art itself ('On Imitation', 'On *Gusto*', 'On the Catalogue Raisonné of the British Institution', 'Why the Arts are not Progressive: A Fragment'). Even in treating more general topics, Hazlitt's illustrations in *The Round Table* are typically literary. The love of life is exemplified in Milton's Satan ('On the Love of Life'; iv. 3), while 'Miss Harris, in Fielding's *Amelia*' and 'Molière's *Tartuffe*' are adduced as instances of religious hypocrisy ('On Religious Hypocrisy'; iv. 130).

The impersonal collective 'we' of *The Round Table* gives way to a distinctly assertive 'I' in *The Plain Speaker*: 'I hate the sight of the Duke of W********* for his foolish face, as much as for any thing else' ('On Envy'; xii. 99); 'I would not give two-pence for the whole Gallery at Fonthill' ('On a Portrait of an English Lady, by Vandyke'; xii. 292). Contemporary political topics and figures, the author's circle of acquaintance, and the events of his own life are repeatedly brought into the discussion. The failure of *Liber*

---

[16] Charles Lamb, *Lamb as Critic*, ed. R. Park (London and Henley: Routledge & Kegan Paul, 1980), 302, 303.

[17] It is this personality that leads Herschel Baker, at the other extreme from Albrecht, to conclude that Hazlitt is an 'incorrigible egotist', Herschel Baker, *William Hazlitt* (Cambridge, Mass: Harvard University Press, 1962), 4. More sympathetically, Harold Bloom also finds personality to be paramount in Hazlitt's method as an essayist, but his emphasis on the personality of the critic is at the expense of the philosophical Hazlitt: 'Hazlitt, like Johnson, refuses to carry philosophical aesthetics into the pragmatic realms of criticism' (Bloom, *William Hazlitt*, 9). My own argument is that Hazlitt's philosophical aesthetics are inseparable from his pragmatic criticism.

Amoris and the variable response to Hazlitt's public lectures find their way into an essay 'On the Spirit of Obligations' (xii. 79); the essay 'On the Pleasure of Hating' concludes on the author's own experience of duplicity and betrayed hope (xii. 136).

A comparison of two passages, one taken from each, gives some indication of the development from the earlier to the later collection of essays. The first occurs in the essay 'On the Literary Character' in *The Round Table*; it expresses the typically Romantic preoccupation with the problem of solipsism:

Indeed, after all, compared with the genuine feelings of nature, 'clad in flesh and blood,' with real passions and affections, conversant about real objects, the life of a mere man of letters and sentiment appears to be at best but a living death; a dim twilight existence: a sort of wandering about in an Elysian fields of our own making; a refined, spiritual, disembodied state, like that of the ghosts of Homer's heroes, who, we are told, would gladly have exchanged situations with the meanest peasant upon earth! (iv. 135)

To this last sentence, Hazlitt appends the note,

Plato's cave, in which he supposes a man to be shut up all his life with his back to the light, and to see nothing of the figures of men, or other objects that pass by, but their shadows on the opposite wall of his cell, so that when he is let out and sees the real figures, he is only dazzled and confounded by them, seems an ingenious satire on the life of a bookworm. (iv. 135n.)

The second passage is taken from the close of the essay 'On the Conversation of Authors' in *The Plain Speaker*, topically similar to the first essay, and describing the same character—the bookworm—that is the subject of the previous extract.

He browzes on the husk and leaves of books, as the young fawn browzes on the bark and leaves of trees. Such a one lives all his life in a dream of learning, and has never once had his sleep broken by a real sense of things. He believes implicitly in genius, truth, virtue, liberty, because he finds the names of these things in books. He thinks that love and friendship are the finest things imaginable, both in practice and theory. The legend of good women is to him no fiction. When he steals from the twilight of his cell, the scene breaks upon him like an illuminated missal, and all the people he sees are but so many figures in a *camera obscura*. (xii. 43)

Thematically, both passages are almost identical. Their subject is a familiar Romantic subject, the solipsism brought about by intellectual pursuit. Both describe the border or twilight existence of the solipsist; both contain a critique, recurrent in Hazlitt, of the ideal when it is divorced from the ordinary, or of the severing of the relation between internal and external, mind and nature.

In the *Round Table* extract, the tone is self-consciously literary, with its three classical references to the Elysian fields, Homer, and Plato. The comparisons drawn with the ghosts in Homer and with Plato's cave are both somewhat predictable; the language of the first especially, with its hyperbolic contrast between 'Homer's heroes' and 'the meanest peasant upon earth', is very much the language of literary cliché.

In the second passage, the subject shifts from the generic 'man of letters and sentiment' to a specific 'he', a person actually known to the author, as he tells us a few lines previously, and who is identified in the Howe edition as George Dyer (xii. 390 n.). The fake pastoral or substitute nature in which the scholar abides, evoked, in the former extract in the phrase 'Elysian fields', here appears in the simile 'He browzes on the husk and leaves of books, as the young fawn browzes on the bark and leaves of trees.' Nature is collapsed into art by the pun in 'leaves'; moreover, a parodic or satirical effect is achieved in the disparity of the two things compared (the young fawn and the scholarly recluse), that works towards the critique of solipsism contained in the passage. Similarly, the comparison of the monk's response to the illuminated missal with his response to the world, is sharper and more memorable than the familiar trope of Plato's cave. Most distinctive, however, is the cameo autobiography contained within the narrative chain of the second extract. What is brought before us by the narrative is not only its immediate subject—George Dyer, the bookworm—but also, in the undertext, the narrator himself: a figure who becomes familiar to us in these essays as disillusioned, doubting the ideals of his youth ('genius, virtue, truth, liberty'), disappointed both as to love and friendship, and proving, from the events of his own life, the legend of good women a fiction.

A comparison of two isolated passages cannot be treated as definitive, but it does give us some insight into the changing character of the essayist. The development of the authorial persona in Hazlitt's essays goes hand in hand with the development of the associative mode of these essays. As the essays grow in length, they encompass a long chain of generalization, anecdote, and autobiographical musing, largely precluded in the shorter, more narrowly focused *Round Table* articles. The associative process of the later essays exemplifies Hazlitt's own view of the active association of imagination; imaginative creation is not the product of a mechanical associationism, but it is the imagining self or authorial presence that generates the associative chain. In the essay 'On Reading Old Books', for instance, the diversity of the topics through which the essay moves—the author's aversion to the works of his contemporaries, the unthinking security of his childhood, the genius of Rousseau, the superficiality of social opinion, the influence of Richardson, Milton, and Burke, with a glance at the political associations of the two latter, the pretensions of the Lake School, and finally, despite all previous declarations, the anticipation of future pleasure in reading—is sustained throughout by the strong personality of the essayist. The unity of the essay stands solely upon the authorial self which from the outset is typically biased and assertive: 'I hate to read new books' (*The Plain Speaker*; xii. 220). In defence of his own biases as an essayist, Hazlitt writes,

All abstract reasoning is in extremes, or only takes up one view of a question, or what is called the principle of the thing; and if you want to give this popularity and effect, you are in danger of running into extravagance and hyperbole. . . . To a want of general reading, I plead guilty, and am sorry for it; but perhaps if I had read more, I might have thought less. ('On the Causes of Popular Opinion', *Uncollected Essays*; xvii. 312–13)

Hazlitt's narrative procedure enacts a version of the creative and self-affirming genius that is the focus of his own literary and moral theory. The essayist, at once artist and moralist, may relinquish neither his pronounced individualism nor the universality of his vision. The symbiosis of particular and universal is characteristic simultaneously of Hazlitt's vision for art and his theory of morals. That the insistence on the universal applicability of the artist's ideal is also a criterion for his own kind of essay-writing is clearly spelled out in the essay 'On Familiar Style'.

Like the essay 'On Poetry in General', 'On Familiar Style'

belongs to a mode of literary 'defence'. It prescribes for, as well as vindicates the genre which, of all others, is now recognized as characteristically Hazlitt's own. With its attention to diction, or the choice of words, 'On Familiar Style' is recognizably allusive to the 'Preface' to the *Lyrical Ballads*. The great contemporary manifesto for poetic diction, which Hazlitt unequivocally rejects for poetry, is here adapted to enforce his criteria for conversational prose. Wordsworth's 'the very language of men'[18] becomes his prescription 'to write as any one would speak in common conversation' (*Table-Talk*; viii. 242); the rejection of 'mere shewy, unsubstantial ornaments' (viii. 244), the combination of reflection and spontaneity in the author's choice of words, and the importance attached to the associative chain of his memory (viii. 245), are all prefigured in the 'Preface'.

The attention to diction underscores Hazlitt's predominant emphasis for the familiar style, its universality: 'A truly natural or familiar style ... is of universal force and applicability' (viii. 243). The universal achieves the relation between general and particular, nature and mind. It can be elicited, for instance, in the numerous passages interspersed throughout the essays, on the author's associations with the outdoors. The linking of the narrator's feelings to various natural objects simultaneously particularizes those objects and generalizes his feelings. When Hazlitt is writing about writing essays in 'A Farewell to Essay-Writing', he begins and concludes with this type of association, which represents for him the whole larger exercise of essay-writing itself (*Uncollected Essays*; xvii. 313–15, 319–20).

Lamb, in whose unpublished review of the first volume of *Table-Talk* we have what is arguably the best account to date of Hazlitt as an essayist, repeatedly calls attention to the coming together of the particular and the universal in these essays. Towards the conclusion of the review he writes, 'To an extraordinary power of original observation he adds an equal power of familiar and striking expression. . . . In fact, he all along acts as his own interpreter, and is continually translating his thoughts out of their original metaphysical obscurity into the language of the senses and of common observation.'[19]

Essay writing may be perceived as the effort to translate into

[18] Wordsworth, *Prose*, i. 130. [19] Lamb, *Lamb as Critic*, 306–7.

practice Hazlitt's own theory of genius and creativity. The narrator, especially of the late essays, exemplifies the associative mode of that genius and a vision which, from the symbiosis of particular and general, is both original and universal. Hazlitt's universal is an 'aggregate' of particulars, so that 'truth' in his vision is manifold and composite. Such a notion of truth can be shown to be directly relevant to his artistic project of essay writing. Considered as a whole, the pattern of development that emerges from Hazlitt's conversational essays is not based, primarily, on the chronological growth and development of ideas over time. Rather, it is a pattern that manifests development in the other sense of the word, the amplification or detailed unfolding of an idea or theme, by returning to it in its different aspects. We can group together, in this manner, 'On Pedantry' in *The Round Table*, a two-part essay very much in the style of the later prose, and the essay 'On the Aristocracy of Letters' in *Table-Talk*; also, the essay 'On Classical Education' in *The Round Table* and 'On the Ignorance of the Learned' in *Table-Talk*. Similarly, the essay 'On the Disadvantages of Intellectual Superiority' in *Table-Talk* can be paired with 'The Shyness of Scholars' in the *Uncollected Essays*, and the essay 'On Reading Old Books' in *The Plain Speaker* with 'On Reading New Books' in the *Uncollected Essays*. The essays 'On the Knowledge of Character' in *Table-Talk*, 'On Personal Character' in *The Plain Speaker*, and 'On Personal Identity' in *Uncollected Essays*, form yet another grouping.

Typically, when Hazlitt returns to a particular topic or leading theme, he presents it in a new light, sometimes contradicting, frequently corroborating and amplifying his first treatment. The development from the essay 'On Classical Education', where 'The study of the Classics is less to be regarded as an exercise of the intellect, than as "a discipline of humanity"' (iv. 4) to the essay 'On the Ignorance of the Learned', which states that 'Any one who has passed through the regular gradations of a classical education, and is not made a fool by it, may consider himself as having had a very narrow escape' (viii. 71), is not merely a passing from one extreme view to another, nor a merely wilful unsaying of what has been said before. The second essay actually qualifies and refines the generalizations of the first. The essayist now makes the distinction between 'knowledge' and mere 'learning', and the most provocative of his observations about learning no more than reiterate the familiar plea for the symbiosis of the experiential and the abstract (viii. 73). Considered together, the two essays form a structural whole, a fuller statement of the essayist's position than either of the two taken individually.

Similarly, it is almost impossible not to bring together 'On Reading Old Books' in *The Plain Speaker* and 'On Reading New Books' in the *Uncollected Essays*. 'On Reading Old Books' describes the writer's dislike of new books, 'On Reading New Books' contains his plea for reading old books. The first brings out the author's favourite reading from the perspective of the youthful associations with which it is linked, and depicts the manner in which books become intimately involved with the whole evolution of our personal identity from youth to maturity. Its counterpart, written about four years later, pursues the topic in an altogether different aspect. The perspective of this second essay is more explicitly social and moral: the susceptibility to the latest fads in reading prevents the establishment of a standard of taste, and 'Where there is no established scale nor rooted faith in excellence, all superiority—our own as well as that of others—soon comes to the ground' (xvii. 210). When each essay in this pair is read in the context of the other, the process of personal development described in the first may be recognized as participating in the formation of taste described in the second, and the influence of reading on personal identity is displayed in its relation to the cultural identity of the age.

The topic of identity and otherness binds together the three essays 'On the Knowledge of Character', 'On Personal Character', and 'On Personal Identity'. The first of these begins with describing the facial features as the most accurate indicators of character: 'Professions pass for nothing, and actions may be counterfeited: but a man cannot help his looks' (viii. 303). Here, identity is treated from the point of view of human relations, our inability to understand otherness. Where distance or the lack of common ground in the judgement of character creates the barrier between classes (viii. 307–10) and sexes (viii. 310–11), equally, closeness and intimacy prevents us from forming a just estimate of our friends and near relations (viii. 311–12) and most of all, of ourselves (viii. 315–16). In the second essay, 'On Personal Character', the emphasis on physiognomy is heightened into what amounts almost to the genetic determinism of the present day: 'No one ever changes his character from the time he is two years old; nay, I might say, from the time he is two hours old' (xii. 230). The essayist has moved on from the discussion of social and personal relations, to a concern with character as essence or inner self. Families, the sexes, nations, and races, are all marked with an essential character, and the essayist warns us always to reject accidents in favour of this essence. In the final essay of the triad, 'On Personal Identity', the relation between essence and accidents is brought to bear on the relation between self and other. We are frequently willing to alter our circumstances, never our identities. The strength of our attachment to our own identities, the essayist points out, is inseparable from the intensity of our fear of death (xvii. 265). The progressive movement in the triad is inwards, each successive essay reiterating the leading idea—the barrier between self and other—of the first; in the third, social analysis gives way to philosophical realization.

Hazlitt's method as an essayist reflects the key premise of his metaphysics, the creative imagination's tendency towards self-affirmation, and its corollary for his theory of morals, a composite vision of truth. The manifold perspective of the essayist gives us a universal composed of individual particulars, and this perspective can not only be elicited from a comparison of separate essays, but is often manifested by the authorial voice within a single essay or even paragraph. Where Hazlitt is most apparently celebratory of solipsism and whimsy, we find an ironical undertone which debunks the very qualities he seems to exalt. The portrait of George Dyer in the essay 'On the Conversation of Authors' is an example of this; the account of Cosway's collection in the essay 'On the Old Age of Artists' is another:

His was the crucifix that Abelard prayed to—a lock of Eloisa's hair—the dagger with which Felton stabbed the Duke of Buckingham—the first finished sketch of the Jocunda—Titian's large colossal profile of Peter Aretine—a mummy of an Egyptian king—a feather of a phoenix—a piece of Noah's Ark. Were the articles authentic? What matter?—his faith in them was true. (*The Plain Speaker*; xii. 96)

The combination of affection and irony in the essayist's tone makes the passage at once a tribute and satire with regard to the intellectual solipsism which is here described. Equally, Hazlitt's numerous declamations of the unfitness of scholars and artists for love of society frequently win our sympathy for the very isolationism he affects to denounce. We can cite, for instance, the essay 'On the Disadvantages of Intellectual Superiority' in *Table-Talk*, or 'The Shyness of Scholars' in the *Uncollected Essays*.

The problem of solipsism is not only thematic, but also a generic issue in Hazlitt's conversational prose. If we recognize an autobiographical impulse in the whole notion of 'conversational' writing, there appear, in this regard, some grounds for comparison with *Liber Amoris*.

In an essay on *Liber Amoris*, Marilyn Butler argues that the extreme self-absorption of the main character in the 'novel' contains, in fact, a critique of romantic self-absorption. Butler finds that the stance of the novel is critical; it is 'itself introverted in pursuit of a critique of introversion.'[20] The categorical transformation of *Liber Amoris* from autobiography to critique and even to the further extreme of satire is open to question; the rawness of emotion in the book, emerging through all its self-consciousness and deliberately literary clothing, makes it impossible altogether to lose sight of the confessional aspect of the writing, and the cathartic urge that underlies this, as all confessions. Nonetheless, Butler's recognition in Hazlitt of an authorial voice that is at once critical and affirming of selfhood gives us a valuable insight, not only into *Liber Amoris*, but into the whole body of his conversational prose.

Butler aligns *Liber Amoris* with *Alastor*, *Endymion*, *Frankenstein*, and a host of other writings by Romantic authors which deal with the pitfalls of the self-reflecting imagination. The bitterness and unmitigated consciousness of failure of *Liber Amoris* makes it a strong indictment, she points out, of the self-absorbed condition of the Romantic artist. Moreover, if Hazlitt's 'novel' is the Romantic artist's expression of artistic failure, it is itself, from his own account, regarded by his contemporaries as an artistic failure, so that the 'critique of introversion' is doubly strengthened. The warning contained in the book is Hazlitt's familiar warning against *mere* abstraction; the emptiness of the ideal when it is severed from reality, rather than elicited from it.

---

[20] Marilyn Butler, 'Satire and the Images of Self in the Romantic Period: The Long Tradition of Hazlitt's *Liber Amoris*', in G. A. Rosso and D. P. Watkins (eds), *Spirits of Fire: English Romantic Writers and Contemporary Historical Methods* (London and Toronto: Associated University Presses, 1990), 164.

Yet qualifying this warning and rendering it ambiguous, there remains Hazlitt's commitment to his metaphysical and moral truth, that the object of the artist's self-absorbed pursuit *is* ideal, based on an idea of good that is independent of empirical considerations of 'interest'. Such a view of his own obsession is spelled out in the essay 'On Dreams' in *The Plain Speaker*, 'I conceive, . . . that this perseverance of the imagination in a fruitless track must have been owing to mortified pride, to an intense desire and hope of good in the abstract, more than to love' (xii. 23). The abstract hope of good redeems the principle of power—the self-affirming impulse of the mind—of mere selfishness, and even in its failure, attests to the possibility of a moral goal for humanity.

In the period in which he is writing *Liber Amoris*, Hazlitt is also preparing the second volume of *Table-Talk* for publication, and in the conversational prose, the ambiguity of the Romantic artist towards his own solipsistic condition is equally pronounced. Like *Liber Amoris*, the autobiography interwoven into the conversational essays stands as its own critique, because it tells a story of failure, of ideals that unfit the essayist for the real experiences of life. It is 'introverted in pursuit of a critique of introversion'. At the same time, its narrator stands vindicated precisely *because* of his pursuit of the ideal, and it is in this pursuit that he locates his whole moral ground.

Finally, the debate about the solipsistic ego is enacted also in the interplay between the autobiographical and conversational impulses in the essays. If the defining trait of the romantic autobiography is introversion, the whole notion of 'conversation' necessarily implies extroversion; the identifying characteristic of conversational prose, as Hazlitt himself tells us, is 'popularity and effect'. The egotism of the autobiographer is subsumed when his experiences are put to the illustration of a social or moral truth; equally, the conversational moralist frequently disappears into an overwhelming absorption with the events of his own life. In this way, conversation and autobiography are played off against each other in these essays.

The art of essay writing is one way in which Hazlitt's theory of the creative imagination is made concrete. Here, philosophy and practice are welded together, and the power of his authorial presence provides the strongest resistance to any attempt to impose upon him the criterion of negative capability. In the combination of the egotistical and the convivial, the particular and the universal, in the authorial voice that simultaneously exalts and debunks the pursuit of the ideal, and in the multi-facetedness of his vision, we find Hazlitt's personality as essayist and artist.

Bibliography

PRIMARY SOURCES

ARISTOTLE, *Poetics*, trans. I. Bywater, in *The Complete Works of Aristotle*, ed. Jonathan Barnes. Bollingen series no. 71.2. 2 vols. Princeton, NJ: Princeton University Press, 1984. ii. 2316–40.
BARNETT, E. S., and GIFFORD, W., 'Hazlitt's *Lectures on the English Poets*'. *Quarterly Review* xix (1818), 424–34.
BERKELEY, G., *The Works of George Berkeley, Bishop of Cloyne*, ed. T. E. Jessop and A. A. Luce. 9 vols. London: Nelson, 1948–57.
BURKE, E., *A Philosophical Enquiry into the Origins of our Ideas of the Sublime and Beautiful*. 2nd edn 1759; repr. Menston: The Scolar Press, 1970.
BUTLER, J., *Butler's Fifteen Sermons preached at the Rolls Chapel and A Dissertation of the Nature of Virtue*, ed. T. A. Roberts. London: Society for Promoting Christian Knowledge, 1970.
COLERIDGE, S. T., *The Complete Poetical Works of Samuel Taylor Coleridge*, ed. Ernest Hartley Coleridge. 2 vols. Oxford: Clarendon Press, 1912.
—— *Collected Letters of Samuel Taylor Coleridge*, ed. E. L. Griggs. 6 vols. Oxford: Clarendon Press, 1956–71.
—— *The Notebooks of Samuel Taylor Coleridge*, ed. K. Coburn. Bollingen series, no. 50. 4 vols published. Princeton, NJ: Princeton University Press, 1957–90.
—— *Lectures 1795: On Politics and Religion*, ed. L. Patton and P. Mann. Vol. i of *The Collected Works of Samuel Taylor Coleridge*. Bollingen series, no. 75. Princeton, NJ: Princeton University Press, 1971.
—— *The Watchman*, ed. L. Patton. Vol. ii of *The Collected Works of Samuel Taylor Coleridge*. Bollingen series no. 75. Princeton, NJ: Princeton University Press, 1970.
—— *The Friend*, ed. B. E. Rooke. Vol. iv of *The Collected Works of Samuel Taylor Coleridge*. Bollingen series no. 75. 2 vols. Princeton, NJ: Princeton University Press, 1969.
—— *Lectures 1808–1819: On Literature*, ed. R. A. Foakes. Vol. v of *The Collected Works of Samuel Taylor Coleridge*. Bollingen series no. 75. 2 vols. Princeton, NJ: Princeton University Press, 1987.
—— *Lay Sermons*, ed. R. J. White. Vol. vi of *The Collected Works of*

Samuel Taylor Coleridge. Bollingen series no. 75. Princeton, NJ: Princeton University Press, 1972.

—— *Biographia Literaria or Biographical Sketches of my Literary Life and Opinions,* ed. W. J. Bate and J. Engell. Vol. vii of *The Collected Works of Samuel Taylor Coleridge.* Bollingen series no. 75. 2 vols. Princeton, NJ: Princeton University Press, 1983.

GODWIN, W., *An Enquiry Concerning Political Justice.* 2 vols. 1793; repr. Oxford: Woodstock Books, 1992.

—— *A New Guide to the English Tongue,* in *A New and Improved Grammar of the English Tongue: For the Use of Schools. By William Hazlitt. To which is Added, A New Guide to the English Tongue, In a Letter to Mr. W. F. Mylius, Author of the School Dictionary. By Edward Baldwin, Esq.* London: M. J. Godwin, 1810.

HARTLEY, D., *Observations on Man, his Frame, his Duty, and his Expectations.* 2 vols. London, 1749.

HAZLITT, W. *The Complete Works of William Hazlitt,* ed. P. P. Howe. 21 vols. London and Toronto: J. M. Dent, 1930–4.

HUME, D., *A Treatise of Human Nature,* ed. L. A. Selby-Bigge. 2nd edn revised P. H. Nidditch. Oxford: Clarendon Press, 1978.

HUNT, L., *Leigh Hunt's Literary Criticism,* ed. L. H. and C. W. Houtchens. New York: Columbia University Press, 1956.

HUTCHESON, F., *An Essay on the Nature and Conduct of the Passions and Affections with Illustrations on the Moral Sense.* 3rd edn 1742; repr. Gainsville, Fla: Scholars' Facsimiles & Reprints, 1969.

JOHNSON, S., *Lives of the English Poets,* ed. G. B. Hill. 3 vols. Oxford: Clarendon Press, 1905.

—— *The Rambler,* ed. W. J. Bate and A. B. Strauss. Vols iii–v of *The Yale Edition of the Works of Samuel Johnson.* New Haven: Yale University Press, 1969.

—— *The Oxford Authors: Samuel Johnson,* ed. D. Greene. Oxford: Oxford University Press, 1984.

KANT, I., *Immanuel Kant's Critique of Pure Reason,* trans. N. K. Smith. London: Macmillan, 1929.

—— *Groundwork of the Metaphysic of Morals,* trans. H. J. Paton. 3rd edn 1956; repr. New York: Harper & Row, 1964.

KEATS, J., *The Letters of John Keats: 1814–1821,* ed. H. E. Rollins. 2 vols. Cambridge, Mass.: Harvard University Press, 1958.

LAMB, C., *The Works of Charles and Mary Lamb,* ed. E. V. Lucas. 7 vols. London: Methuen, 1903–5.

—— *Lamb as Critic,* ed. R. Park. London and Henley: Routledge & Kegan Paul, 1980.

LOCKE, J., *An Essay Concerning Human Understanding,* ed. P. H. Nidditch. Oxford: Clarendon Press, 1975.

POPE, A., *Pastoral Poetry and An Essay on Criticism*, ed. E. Audra and A. Williams. Vol. i of *The Twickenham Edition of the Poems of Alexander Pope*. London: Methuen, 1961.

PRIESTLEY, J., *Disquisitions Relating to Matter and Spirit*. London, 1777.

—— *The Doctrine of Philosophical Necessity Illustrated; Being an Appendix to the Disquisitions relating to Matter and Spirit*. London, 1777.

ROBINSON, H. C., *Henry Crabb Robinson on Books and their Writers*, ed. E. J. Morley. 3 vols. London: J. M. Dent, 1938.

SCHLEGEL, A. W., *A Course of Lectures on Dramatic Art and Literature*, trans. John Black. 2 vols. London: Baldwin, Cradock, and Joy, 1815.

SCHILLER, F., *On the Naive and Sentimental in Literature*, trans. H. Watanabe-O'Kelly. Manchester: Carcanet New Press, 1981.

SHELLEY, P. B., *Shelley's Prose, or, the Trumpet of a Prophecy*, ed. D. L. Clark. 2nd corr. edn 1966; repr. London: Fourth Estate, 1988.

SMITH, A., *The Theory of Moral Sentiments*, ed. D. D. Raphael and A. L. Macfie. Vol. i of *The Glasgow Edition of the Works and Correspondence of Adam Smith*. Oxford: Clarendon Press, 1976.

—— *An Inquiry into the Nature and Causes of the Wealth of Nations*, ed. R. H. Campbell and A. S. Skinner. Vol. ii of *The Glasgow Edition of the Works and Correspondence of Adam Smith*. 2 vols. Oxford: Clarendon Press, 1976.

STAËL-HOLSTEIN, G. de, *Germany*. 3 vols. London: John Murray, 1813.

TOOKE, J. H., *ΕπΕΑ πΤΕΡΟΕΝΤΑ or, the Diversions of Purley*, 2nd edn. 2 vols. London, 1798.

TUCKER, A., *An Abridgement of the Light of Nature Pursued*, ed. W. Hazlitt. London: J. Johnson, 1807.

WILLICH, A. F. M., *Elements of the Critical Philosophy*. London, 1798.

WORDSWORTH, W., *The Prose Works of William Wordsworth*, ed. W. J. B. Owen and J. W. Smyser. 3 vols. Oxford: Clarendon Press, 1974.

HAZLITT STUDIES

ALBRECHT, W. P., *Hazlitt and the Creative Imagination*. Lawrence, Kan.: University of Kansas Press, 1965.

—— 'The Tragic Sublime of Hazlitt and Keats'. *SIR* xx, no. 2 (summer 1981), 185–201.

—— 'Hazlitt's "On the Fear of Death": Reason versus Imagination'. *WC* xv, no. 1 (winter 1984), 3–7.

ASKE, M., 'Critical Disfigurings: The "Jealous Leer Malign" in Romantic Criticism', in J. Beer (ed.), *Questioning Romanticism*. Baltimore: Johns Hopkins University Press, 1995, pp. 49–70.

BAKER, H., *William Hazlitt*. Cambridge, Mass: Harvard University Press, 1962.
BATE, J., *Shakespeare and the English Romantic Imagination*. Oxford: Clarendon Press, 1986.
—— *Shakespearean Constitutions: Politics, Theatre, Criticism 1730–1830*. Oxford: Clerendon Press, 1989.
BATE, W. J., 'The Sympathetic Imagination in Eighteenth Century English Criticism'. *ELH* xii (1945), 144–64.
—— *John Keats*. London: Oxford University Press, 1967.
BLOOM, H. (ed.), *Modern Critical Views: William Hazlitt*. New York: Chelsea House, 1986.
BRATTON, E. W., 'William Hazlitt's Curious Concept of Taste'. *South Atlantic Review* lvii, no. 2 (May 1992), 1–9.
BROMWICH, D., *Hazlitt: The Mind of a Critic*. New York and Oxford: Oxford University Press, 1983.
BULLITT, J. M., 'Hazlitt and the Romantic Conception of the Imagination'. *PQ* xxiv, no. 4 (October 1945), 343–61.
BURWICK, F., 'Lamb, Hazlitt, and De Quincey on Hogarth'. *WC* xxviii, no. 1 (winter 1997), 59–69.
BUTLER, M., 'Satire and the Images of Self in the Romantic Period: The Long Tradition of Hazlitt's *Liber Amoris*', in G. A. Rosso and D. P. Watkins (eds), *Spirits of Fire: English Romantic Writers and Contemporary Historical Methods*. London and Toronto: Associated University Presses, 1990, pp. 153–69.
CARNALL, G., 'The Impertinent Barber of Baghdad: Coleridge as Comic Figure in Hazlitt's Essays', in D. Sultana (ed.), *New Approaches to Coleridge: Biographical and Critical Essays*. London; Totowa, NJ: Vision; Barnes & Noble, 1981, pp. 38–47.
CHANDLER, J. K., 'Representative Men, Spirits of the Age, and other Romantic Types', in K. R. Johnston, G. Chaitin, K. Hanson, and H. Marks (eds), *Romantic Revolutions: Criticism and Theory*. Bloomington, Ind.: Indiana University Press, 1990, pp. 104–32.
CHASE, S. P., 'Hazlitt as a Critic of Art'. *PMLA* xxxix, no. 1 (1924), 179–202.
COBURN, K., 'Hazlitt on the Disinterested Imagination', in J. V. Logan, J. E. Jordan, and N. Frye (eds), *Some British Romantics: A Collection of Essays*. Columbus, Oh.: Ohio State University Press, 1966, pp. 167–88.
DAVIES, R. T. 'Keats and Hazlitt'. *KSMB* viii (1957), 1–8.
DONOHUE, J. W. Jr, 'Hazlitt's Sense of the Dramatic: Actor as Tragic Character'. *SEL* v, no. 4 (autumn 1965), 705–21.
EAGLETON, T., 'William Hazlitt: An Empiricist Radical'. *New Blackfriars Review* (1973), 108–17.

ENRIGHT, N., 'William Hazlitt and his "Familiar Style"', in A. J. Butrym (ed.), *Essays on the Essay: Redefining the Genre*. Athens, Ga.: University of Georgia Press, 1989, pp. 116–25.

EPSTEIN, J., 'Hazlitt's Passions'. *The New Criterion* x, no. 3 (November 1991), 33–44.

FINNEY, C. L., *The Evolution of Keats's Poetry*. 2 vols. Cambridge, Mass.: Harvard University Press, 1936.

FITZPATRICK, M. A., 'The Problem of Identity in Keats's Negative Capability'. *Dalhousie Review* lxi, no. 1 (spring 1981), 39–51.

FOUCAULT, M., 'Power and Sex: An Interview with Michel Foucault'. *Telos* xxxii (1977), 152–61.

GARNETT, M. A., 'Hazlitt against Burke: Radical versus Conservative?' *Durham University Journal* lxxxi, no. 2 (June 1989), 229–39.

—— 'The Napoleonists'. *CLB* lxx (April 1990), 185–95.

GILMARTIN, K., 'Victims of Argument, Slaves of Fact: Hunt, Hazlitt, Cobbett, and the Literature of Opposition'. *WC* xxi, no. 3 (summer 1990), 90–8.

GROSS, J., 'Hazlitt's Worshipping Practice in *Liber Amoris*'. *SEL* xxxv, no. 4 (autumn 1995), 707–21.

HAEFNER, J. '"The Soul Speaking in the Face": Hazlitt's Concept of Character'. *SEL* xxiv, no. 4 (autumn 1984), 655–70.

—— '"Incondite Things": Experimentation and the Romantic Essay'. *PS* x, no. 2 (September 1987), 196–206.

—— 'Rhetoric and Art: George Campbell, William Hazlitt, and "Gusto"'. *CLB* lxiii (July 1988), 234–43.

HAMILTON, P., 'The Irritable Genius'. *CLB* xxvii (1979), 41–51.

—— *Coleridge's Poetics*. Oxford: Basil Blackwell, 1983.

HASSLER, D. M., 'The Discovery of the Future and Indeterminacy in William Hazlitt'. *WC* viii, no. 1 (winter 1977), 75–9.

HEINZELMAN, K., 'Self-Interest and the Politics of Composition in Keats's *Isabella*'. *ELH* lv, no. 1 (spring 1998), 159–93.

HELLER, J. R., *Coleridge, Lamb, Hazlitt, and the Reader of Drama*. Columbia, Miss.: University of Missouri Press, 1990.

HOUCK, J. A., 'Hazlitt on the Obligations of the Critic'. *WC* iv, no. 4 (autumn 1973), 250–8.

JACK, I. 'The Critic: William Hazlitt', in *Keats and the Mirror of Art*. Oxford: Oxford University Press, 1967, pp. 58–75.

JONES, S., *Hazlitt: A Life: From Winterslow to Frith Street*. Oxford: Clarendon Press, 1989.

KINNAIRD, J., 'The Forgotten Self', *Partisan Review* xxx, no. 2 (1963), 302–6.

—— *William Hazlitt: Critic of Power*. New York: Columbia University Press, 1978.

LEVIN, R., 'Hazlitt on Henry V, and the Appropriation of Shakepeare'. *Shakespeare Quarterly* xxxv, no. 2 (summer 1984), 134–41.
MACLEAN, C. M., *Born under Saturn: A Biography of William Hazlitt*. London: Collins, 1943.
McFARLAND, T., *Romantic Cruxes: The English Essayists and the Spirit of the Age*. Oxford: Clarendon Press, 1987.
MAHONEY, J. L. 'The Futuristic Imagination: Hazlitt's Approach to *Romeo and Juliet*'. *British Journal of Aesthetics* (1974), 65–7.
—— *The Logic of Passion: The Literary Criticism of William Hazlitt*. 2nd edn. New York: Fordham University Press, 1981.
—— 'William Hazlitt: The Essay as a Vehicle for the Romantic Critic'. *CLB* lxxv (July 1991), 92–8.
MARTIN, R., and BARVESIS, J., 'Hazlitt on the Future of the Self.' *Journal of the History of Ideas* lvi, no. 3 (July 1995), 463–81.
MUIR, K., 'Keats and Hazlitt', in K. Muir (ed.), *John Keats: A Reassessment*. Liverpool: Liverpool University Press, 1958, pp. 139–58.
MULVHILL, J., 'Hazlitt on Parliamentary Eloquence'. *PS* xii, no. 2 (September 1989), 132–46.
—— 'The Anatomy of Idolatry: Hazlitt's *Liber Amoris*'. *CLB* lxx (April 1990), 195–203.
—— 'Hazlitt and "First Principles"'. *SIR* xxix, no. 2 (summer 1990), 241–55.
MURAYAMA, M., 'The Function of the Imagination in Hazlitt's *An Essay on the Principles of Human Action*'. *Journal of the English Institute* ix–x (1979), 51–67.
NABHOLTZ, J. R., 'Modes of Discourse in Hazlitt's Prose'. *WC* x, no. 1 (winter 1979), 97–106.
NIBLETT, W. R., 'William Hazlitt as Critic'. *CLB* xxiii (1978), 137–44.
NOXON, J., 'Hazlitt as Moral Philosopher'. *Ethics* lxxiii (1963), 279–83.
O'HARA, J. D., 'Hazlitt and the Functions of the Imagination'. *PMLA* lxxxi, no. 1 (1966), 73–85.
—— 'Hazlitt and the Romantic Criticism of the Fine Arts'. *Journal of Aesthetics and Art Criticism* xxvii, no. 1 (1968), 73–85.
PARK, R., *Hazlitt and the Spirit of the Age: Abstraction and Critical Theory*. Oxford: Clarendon Press, 1971.
PATTERSON, C. I., 'William Hazlitt as a Critic of Prose Fiction'. *PMLA* lxviii, no. 5 (1953), 1001–16.
—— 'Hazlitt's Criticism in Retrospect'. *SEL* xxi, no. 4 (autumn 1981), 647–63.
PAULIN, T., *The Day-Star of Liberty: William Hazlitt's Radical Style*. London, Faber & Faber, 1998.
READY, R., 'Hazlitt: In and Out of "Gusto"'. *SEL* xiv. no. 4 (autumn 1974), 437–46.

—— 'Hazlitt as an English Comic Writer'. *WC* vi, no. 1 (winter 1975), 109–14.
—— 'The Logic of Passion: Hazlitt's "Liber Amoris"'. *SIR* xiv, no. 1 (winter 1975), 41–57.
—— *Hazlitt at Table*. London and Toronto: Associated University Presses, 1981.
—— 'Flat Realities: Hazlitt on Biography'. *PS* v, no. 3 (December 1982), 309–17.
REED, T. A., 'Keats and the Gregarious Advance of Intellect in *Hyperion*'. *ELH* lv, no. 1 (spring 1988), 195–232.
ROBINSON, J. C., 'Romanticism through the Mind of Hazlitt'. *Review* vii (1985), 65–76.
ROBINSON, R. E., *William Hazlitt's Life of Napoleon Bonaparte: Its Sources and Characteristics*. Paris: Librarie Minard, 1959.
ROOT, C., 'Jacobin Poetics and Napoleonic Politics: Hazlitt's Critique of Wordsworth'. *European Romantic Review* vi, no. 2 (winter 1996), 227–45.
RUDDICK, W., 'Artist or Novelist? Lamb, Hazlitt and the Nineteenth-century Response to Hogarth'. *CLB* lxi (January 1988), 145–55.
SALLÉ, J.-C., 'Hazlitt the Associationist'. *RES* xv (1964), 38–51.
SCHNEIDER, E. W., *The Aesthetics of William Hazlitt: A Study of the Philosophical Basis of his Criticism*. Philadelphia: University of Pennsylvania Press, 1933.
SIKES, H. M., 'The Poetic Theory and Practice of Keats: The Record of a Debt to Hazlitt'. *PQ* xxxviii (1959), 401–12.
STAPLETION, L., 'William Hazlitt: The Essayist and the Moods of the Mind', in *The Elected Circle: Studies in the Art of Prose*. Princeton: Princeton University Press, 1973, pp. 93–118.
STORY, P. L., 'Hazlitt's Definition of the Spirit of the Age'. *WC* vi, no. 1 (winter 1975), 97–108.
TRAWICK, L. M. III, 'Hazlitt, Reynolds, and the Ideal'. *SIR* iv (summer 1965), 240–7.
—— 'Sources of Hazlitt's "Metaphysical Discovery"'. *PQ* xlii (April 1963), 277–82.
VERDI, R., 'Hazlitt and Poussin'. *KSMB* xxxii (1981), 1–18.
WARDLE, R.M., *Hazlitt*. Lincoln, Neb.: University of Nebraska Press, 1971.
WHALE, J., 'Hazlitt on Burke: The Ambivalent Position of a Radical Essayist'. *SIR* xxv, no. 4 (winter 1986), 465–81.
WELLEK, R., *Immanuel Kant in England 1793–1838*. Princeton, NJ: Princeton University Press, 1931.
—— *A History of Modern Criticism 1750–1950*. Vol. ii: *The Romantic Age*. New Haven and London: Yale University Press, 1955.

WELLS, S., 'Shakespeare in Hazlitt's Theatre Criticism'. *Shakespeare Survey* xxxv (1982), 43–55.

WHITE, R. S., 'Hazlitt and Keats's attitudes to Shakespeare', in *Keats as a Reader of Shakespeare*. London: Athlone Press, 1987, pp. 31–55.

Index of Hazlitt's Works (P. P. Howe edition)

Abridgement of the Light of Nature Pursued, An:
  'Preface' 5, 10, 38, 147–9
Art and Dramatic Criticism:
  'On the Elgin Marbles' 60, 92
  'On Genius and Originality' 96
  'On the Ideal' 60, 92
  'On the Imitation of Nature' 136

Characteristics 37, 133
Characters of Shakespear's Plays:
  'Anthony and Cleopatra' 34
  'Coriolanus' 43, 119, 167
  'Hamlet' 117, 118
  'Lear' 23, 118, 122
  'Macbeth' 32 n., 117
  'Poems and Sonnets' 117
  'Romeo and Juliet' 89
  'The Tempest' 32 n., 143
Contributions to the Edinburgh Review:
  'Coleridge's Literary Life' 103, 158
  'Schlegel on the Drama' 34, 48–51, 142
  'Shelley's Posthumous Poems' 60
Conversations of Northcote 90

Essay on the Principles of Human Action . . . An 1–2, 9, 11, 17 n., 28–9, 33, 35, 53–4, 56, 60, 73, 78–83, 86–7, 90, 120–5, 127–31, 137, 148, 157, 164–5, 167, 173, 177
  Remarks on the Systems of Hartley and Helveticus 17 n., 53–4, 56, 60, 81–2, 120, 137

Lectures on the Age of Elizabeth:
  'Character of Lord Bacon's Works' 61, 126–7
  'General View of the Subject' 36, 95, 111–12, 121, 128, 157
  'On Ancient and Modern Literature' 101, 112
  'On Beaumont and Fletcher, etc.' 32, 65, 111, 113
  'On Lyly, Marlow, Heywood, etc.' 53, 65, 112–14
  'On Marston, Chapman, Deckar, etc.' 32, 113
  'On Miscellaneous Poems, etc.' 36–7, 65, 89, 112
  'On Single Plays, Poems, etc.' 114
Lectures on the Comic Writers:
  'On Cowley, Butler, Suckling, Etherege, etc.' 90
  'On the English Novelists' 23, 90, 92, 105
  'On the Periodical Essayists' 75, 118
  'On Shakespeare and Ben Jonson' 32 n., 65, 75
  'On Wit and Humour' 23, 72, 90
  'On the Works of Hogarth: On the Grand and Familiar Style of Painting' 32 n., 37, 59, 88–9
  'On Wycherly, Congreve, Vanbrugh and Farquhar' 65
Lectures on English Philosophy:
  'On Abstract Ideas' 136–40
  'On Liberty and Necessity' 26, 28 n., 108, 150, 152

Lectures on English Philosophy (cont):
  'On Locke's "Essay on the Human Understanding"' 17 n., 28 n., 33, 148, 159–60
  'On Self-Love' 80–1
  'On Tooke's "Diversions of Purley"' 5, 14–16, 27, 56–7, 140
  'On the Writings of Hobbes' 4, 139–40, 157

Lectures on the English Poets:
  'On Chaucer and Spenser' 38, 58, 101, 143
  'On Dryden and Pope' 58–9, 111, 133
  'On the Living Poets' 75, 88, 91, 99–100
  'On Poetry in General' 19, 20–1, 23–4, 27, 29, 33, 51–2, 65, 68, 70, 88, 91, 104, 122, 183–4
  'On Shakespeare and Milton' 45, 64, 101, 106, 117, 143
  'On Swift, Young, Gray, Collins, etc.' 63, 130
  'On Thomson and Cowper' 58, 62–3

Letter to William Gifford, A 1, 11, 20–2, 79, 81, 129, 165, 173
  see also Gifford, William in General Index

Liber Amoris 36, 176, 180–1, 188–9
Life of Thomas Holcroft, The 32 n.

Miscellaneous Writings:
  'Aphorisms on Man' 129
  'Belief, Whether Voluntary?' 126
  'Definition of Wit' 16
  'Madam de Staël's Account of German Philosophy and Literature' 5 n., 148, 158–61, 164
  'Outlines of Morals' 128
  'Outlines of Taste' 57, 91, 133
  'Spirit of Philosophy, The' 126

New and Improved Grammar of the English Tongue . . . 11–13, 16–20, 25, 41, 140

Plain Speaker, The:
  'Londoners and Country People' 143
  'Madame Pasta and Mademoiselle Mars' 35, 56, 62, 145
  'New School of Reform, The' 55, 74, 94
  'On Antiquity' 135
  'On Application to Study' 61, 68–9
  'On the Conversation of Authors' 143–5, 181, 187
  'On Depth and Superficiality' 93, 124, 134
  'On the Difference between Writing and Speaking' 65, 68, 93, 131 n., 135, 145–6
  'On Dr Spurzheim's Theory' 43, 55, 63, 93, 141, 145
  'On Dreams' 66, 145, 189
  'On Egotism' 45, 55, 125
  'On Envy' 1, 97, 124, 180
  'On Jealousy and Spleen of Party' 135
  'On Londoners and Country People' 35, 143
  'On the Look of a Gentleman' 144–5
  'On Novelty and Familiarity' 56, 61, 94, 96
  'On the Old Age of Artists' 32, 65, 145, 187
  'On the Old English Writers and Speakers' 61, 104–5
  'On People of Sense' 36, 61–2, 74, 131 n., 135, 145
  'On Personal Character' 93–4, 96, 134, 185–7
  'On the Pleasure of Hating' 124–5, 142, 181
  'On a Portrait of an English Lady, by Vandyke' 56, 60–1, 72, 95, 180
  'On the Prose Style of Poets' 45, 96, 143–5
  'On Reading Old Books' 146, 183, 185–6
  'On Reason and Imagination' 9, 132–4, 156, 163, 177
  'On Sitting for One's Picture' 33, 124
  'On the Spirit of Obligations' 124–5, 181
  'Qualifications Necessary to Success' 93, 124
  'Sir Walter Scott, Racine and Shakespear' 38, 41, 56, 68, 94, 119, 145–6, 172

Index of Hazlitt's Works

'Whether Genius is Conscious of Its Powers' 32, 45, 61, 65, 125, 168, 173

Political Criticism:
  'Arguing in a Circle' 171
  'Capital Punishments' 164
  'The Duke of d'Enghien II' 172
  'Illustrations of Toryism—From the Writings of Sir Walter Scott' 169, 172, 174
  'On the Spirit of Monarchy' 169–70, 176–7
  'The Political Automaton: A Modern Character' 169
  'Project for a New Theory of Civil and Criminal Legislation' 174 n., 178
  'The Treatment of State Prisoners' 175

Political Essays:
  'Character of Lord Chatham' 163
  'Character of Mr Burke' 44, 101, 105, 176 n.
  'Character of Mr Pitt' 173
  'The Courier and "The Wat Tyler"' 168–9, 172
  'Illustrations of "The Times" Newspaper' 170–1, 173, 175
  'Mr Coleridge's Lay Sermon' 60
  'On the Character of the Fox' 168
  'On Court-Influence' 77, 178
  'On the Regal Character' 170, 174
  'Pitt and Buonaparte' 167, 172–3
  'What is the People?' 150, 168, 174, 177–8

Prospectus of a History of English Philosophy 4, 28, 38, 138, 146–7, 152, 155–7

Remarks on the Systems of Hartley and Helvetius, see *Essay on the Principles of Human Action*

Round Table, The:
  'Observations on Mr Wordsworth's Poem The Excursion' 98, 180
  'On Actors and Acting' 180
  'On the Beggar's Opera' 180
  'On the Catalogue Raisonné of the British Institution' 180
  'On Classical Education' 180, 185
  'On Common-place Critics' 180
  'On Different Sorts of Fame' 180
  'On Gusto' 45, 47, 100, 110, 180
  'On Hogarth's Marriage à-la-mode' 180
  'On Imitation' 74, 180
  'On the Literary Character' 180–1
  'On the Love of the Country' 53–4, 122
  'On the Love of Life' 29, 31, 180
  'On the Midsummer Night's Dream' 180
  'On Milton's "Lycidas"' 104, 180
  'On Milton's Versification' 96
  'On Pedantry' 3, 34, 180, 185
  'On Poetical Versatility' 38, 180
  'On Posthumous Fame' 64, 109, 116, 180
  'On Religious Hypocrisy' 180
  'On the Tatler' 34
  'On the Tendency of Sects' 42
  'Why the Arts are not Progressive: A Fragment' 47, 180

Sketches of the Principal Picture Galleries in England:
  'The Dulwich Gallery' 33, 90–1

Sprits of the Age, The':
  'Lord Byron' 100, 143
  'Mr Coleridge' 93, 143
  'Mr Wordsworth' 107
  'Sir Walter Scott' 41
  'William Godwin' 100–1

Table-Talk:
  'Indian Jugglers, The' 52–4, 57, 74, 97–8, 168–9
  'On the Aristocracy of Letters' 107, 185
  'On the Disadvantages of Intellectual Superiority' 179, 185, 188
  'On Familiar Style' 183–4
  'On Genius and Common Sense' 9, 44, 64, 93–6, 98–9, 110, 170
  'On the Ignorance of the Learned' 185
  'On the Knowledge of Character' 128, 185–6
  'On a Landscape of Nicholas Poussin' 32 n., 75–6

Table-Talk (cont):
  'On Living to One's Self' 177
  'On the Past and Future' 52
  'On the Picturesque and Ideal' 89–90
  'On Thought and Action' 143
  'Why Distant Objects Please' 34–5, 38, 49, 96

Uncollected Essays:
  'Farewell to Essay Writing, A' 32, 184
  'My First Acquaintance with Poets' 17n., 44, 79
  'On the Causes of Popular Opinion' 3, 44, 183
  'On the Consistency of Opinion' 3, 44, 183
  'On Personal Identity' 63, 185–7
  'On Reading New Books' 185–6
  'On the Spirit of Partisanship' 175
  'Shyness of Scholars, The' 185, 188
  'Thoughts on Taste' 91

General Index

a priori principle 78, 121, 157–61
abstract/abstract ideas/abstraction 6–7,
    49, 94, 107, 108 n., 125, 128,
    134–41, 166, 170, 173–6, 183, 188–9
  Berkeley on 137
  Butler on nature of self love 81–2
  and concrete/experiential/particular 4,
    6, 9, 131–6, 161–4, 166, 173–4, 176,
    186
  Hobbes on 139–40
  Hume on 140 n.
  Locke on 15–16, 21, 136, 137 n., 174
  Tooke on 14–16, 18, 174
  see also aggregate; ideal; mind
aggregate 6–7, 132–6, 145, 177, 185
  see also abstract/abstract ideas/
    abstraction; association
Albrecht, W. P. 110 n., 123 n., 179 n.
Aristotle 88–9; Poetics 21, 24, 68
art 47, 94–5, 104
  imagination and 37, 47
  natural/nature in 33, 36–7, 47, 60,
    75–6, 95, 146
  power of 32–4, 62
association 7, 9, 17–18, 41, 55–6, 58, 94,
    146, 184–6
  and chain of being 46, 51–5, 58, 101,
    110–11, 146, 170, 182–4
  Hartley and 4, 54–5, 94
  imaginative 52, 58, 63–5, 75–6, 89,
    101, 104–5, 111–12, 173, 183
  mechanical 89, 172, 183
  of mind and nature 53 n., 58–61, 146,
    184
  of servility 169
  and sympathy 58, 64, 110, 120
  see also Hartley; mind

Bacon, Francis 61–2, 126–7, 138
  Advancement of Learning 61
Baillie, Joanna 75
Baker, Herschel 85, 99 n., 180 n.
Barnett, E. S., see Gifford, William
Bate, Walter Jackson 76 n., 109 n.
Beaumont, Francis 32, 113
benevolence/love of others/
  disinterestedness 9, 85–7,
    128–31, 136, 157–8, 165, 174
  and self-love 79–80, 82–3, 86, 124
  see also hatred; self-love
Bentham, Jeremy 31, 74, 168
Berkeley, George 33–5, 38, 56, 137,
    139–40
  An Essay Towards a New Theory of
    Vision (1709) 17–18, 31, 35, 72
  A Treatise Concerning the Principles of
    Human Knowledge 31–2
bias 89, 126, 166, 179, 183
  and genius 93–6, 108, 119
  rejection of mechanism 93, 130–2
  theory of 93–4, 107–8, 138–9, 175, 178
  see also abstract/abstract ideas/
    abstraction; mind
Bible 48–51, 83, 90, 128
Bloom, Harold 2, 7, 100 n., 176 n.,
    180 n.
Bonaparte, Napoleon 122, 176
Bromwich, David 7–8, 28 n., 40, 45 n.,
    94 n., 109 n., 140 n.
Bullitt, J. M. 6, 76 n.
Burke, Edmund 3, 24, 66, 172, 183
  genius 96, 171–2
  Philosophical Enquiry into . . .
    Sublime and Beautiful 5, 24–6,
    29–31, 34, 43 n., 96–7, 144
  prose style 44–5, 69, 96, 101, 105–6,
    143–4

General Index

Butler, Joseph: *Fifteen Sermons preached at the Rolls Chapel* 17 n., 78–84
Butler, Marilyn 188
Byron, George 99–101, 143

Caravaggio, Michelangelo 45, 65
'chain of being', *see* association; pantheism; Unitarianism
Chaucer, Geoffrey 101, 117
Christ 121, 128, 157
Christianity, *see* religion; Unitarianism
Coleridge, Samuel Taylor:
   compared to Godwin 143
   compared to H. 3, 6–9, 15–16, 20 n., 35–6, 40, 44–51, 54, 59, 66, 68–9, 72–3, 76, 84–9, 117–18, 121–2
   compared to Hogarth 59–60
   genius 91, 93
   and German idealism 3, 66, 160 n.
   organic form 73
   religious interpretations 7, 44, 48, 50, 53–4, 72–3, 85–8, 121–2
   the Unitarian 42–8, 72–3, 76, 79, 85–6
   WORKS:
   Biographia Literaria . . . 1, 15, 35–6, 45, 48, 72–3, 88–9, 103, 158–9
   'Eolian Harp, The' 87–8
   Friend, The 88 n.
   Lay Sermons 48
   Lectures 1795: On Politics and Religion 43
   Lectures 1808–1819: On Literature 44, 59, 69, 118, 122
   Letters 20 n., 46, 50
   Notebooks 121–2
   'Religious Musings' 44–5, 54
   'Rime of the Ancient Mariner' 44
   Watchman, The: 'On the Slave Trade' 85
Cosway, Richard, 32, 187

Davies, R. T. 109 n.
Dekker, Thomas 112–13
diction, *see* poetry
disinterestedness, *see* benevolence
duty, deontology, 155–7, 162–3
Dyer, George 182, 187

Eagleton, Terry 60 n., 170–1, 176, 178–9

Edwards, Jonathan 42
egotism, poetic 8–9, 93, 96, 98–101, 106, 109 n., 110–11, 117, 124–5, 169, 175, 180 n., 189–90
   see also bias; genius; power; solipsism
empiricism 4–5, 21–3, 26, 30, 79, 88, 106, 154, 162
   H.'s anti-empirical position 23, 26, 66, 106 n., 130, 147, 155, 157–8, 161, 165, 167, 176, 189
   Kant and 155–7, 165
   see also experience
epistemology 2, 6, 13, 16, 23, 43, 57, 74, 78, 120, 133–4, 136, 138–40, 148, 150, 154, 159–62, 166–7, 170–1, 173, 176
etymology, *see* language
experience 4–6, 17 n., 34, 36, 78, 92, 115, 117, 119, 121, 128–9, 131–3, 138, 154, 157, 159–64, 166, 174, 185–6
   see also empiricism

Fielding, Henry 40, 180
Finney, C. L. 109 n.
Fletcher, John 32, 113
Ford, John 65
Foucault, Michel 178
free will, *see* liberty; will
French, criticism of the 34–5, 56, 61–2, 112, 145

genius:
   and bias 93–6, 107–8, 138–9
   defeat of 172
   dramatic 111–13
   egotistical 96–9, 101–2, 110, 124, 126, 169–70, 175
   Keats on 108
   naïve 114–16
   nature and 60–2, 75, 95, 142, 146–7, 173
   ordinary 93, 110, 114–17, 119
   Schiller on 66–8, 114–16, 150
   sentimental 114–15
   Shakespearian 9, 107, 110–11, 114–19
   theory of 8–9, 23, 43, 57, 64, 69, 71, 74–5, 101–2, 108 n., 120, 126, 167, 171–2, 176 n., 184–5
   of various individuals 60, 65, 91, 98–9, 101, 112, 172, 183
   see also imagination; power

German idealism, *see* idealism
Gifford, William and E. S. Barnett:
  review of H. 22
  see also *Letter to William Gifford*, *Works* index
Godwin, William 86, 90, 100–1, 112, 143
  An Enquiry . . . Political Justice 86
  New Guide to the English Tongue . . . 12–13
good 37, 67, 79, 84, 94, 99, 122, 124, 150, 177, 179
  deontological 80, 127–8, 157, 162–3, 175–6, 189
  and power 127–8, 131, 174–7
grammar, *see* language; 'New and Improved Grammar of the English Tongue' in *Works* Index
'gusto' 9, 45, 47, 100, 110

Hackney New College 51
Hamilton, Paul 72–3
harmony 22, 26, 53, 58, 67, 70, 105, 146
Hartley, David 3–4, 66
  associationism 4, 54–5, 94
  criticism of 31, 73, 94, 137
  mechanism/necessarianism 4, 54–5, 66, 94, 168
  Observations on Man 42 n., 47, 55
hatred 124–5, 127, 129–30
  see also benevolence; love, general; self-love
Hazlitt, William (H.'s father) 42, 77
Heywood, Thomas 65
Hobbes, Thomas 3, 137, 139–40, 150–3
Hogarth, William 32, 36–7, 59–60, 88–9, 180
Homer 58, 116, 141 n., 181–2
Hume, David 3, 83 n., 139
  Treatise of Human Nature 21
Hunt, Leigh:
  on H.'s misanthropy 130
  review of *The Plain Speaker* 144 n.
Hutcheson, Francis:
  An Essay on the Nature and Conduct of the Passions and Affections . . . 156

ideal:
  abstract 6, 131–3, 135, 162, 166, 173–6
  artistic/poetic 7–8, 24, 33, 36–8, 59–60, 88–95, 100–1, 104–5, 107, 131, 143, 169, 183
  Kant on 162
  Keatsian 76, 107, 109, 179
  moral 125, 127–31, 145, 149, 166, 189–90
  and particular/experiential 4, 6, 92, 131, 135, 162, 166
  political 150, 166, 169, 175–7
  Reynolds on 92
  Schiller on 66, 91–2, 114–16, 130
  synonymous with 'idea' 88, 129
  transcendental 91–2
  see also idealism; truth, universal
idealism 3–7, 56 n., 66, 88, 93, 129–32, 135, 147, 166
  German 3, 5–6, 66, 91, 141, 146–7, 154
  see also ideal
imagination 1, 7, 21–7, 38, 40–5, 66, 69, 76 n., 92–3, 103–4, 110 n., 133, 135, 145, 173 n., 187–9
  analogous to deity 38, 41–2, 47–51, 53 n., 54 n., 83–4, 89–91
  associative 9, 51–5, 58, 63–5, 75–6, 89, 101, 104–5, 110–12, 120, 173, 183
  disinterestedness produced from 83, 86–7, 132, 136, 158, 174
  'gusto' of 47
  involuntary 21, 26, 65–7, 158
  lack of 35, 41, 65, 87–90, 106, 113, 135, 183
  morally neutral 121–3, 131, 152, 171–2, 174–5
  nature and 47–8, 54, 56–7, 59–63, 72, 95, 104–5, 111–12
  power 9, 23, 27–9, 32, 34–7, 42, 49–51, 53–4, 59, 62–4, 73, 76, 88–91, 96–8, 100–1, 106–7, 108 n., 110, 112–13, 115–16, 119, 122–4, 128–9, 136, 167, 169–71, 174, 176
  unity 41, 43–6, 51–2, 54, 67–8, 72–6, 105, 134, 144–5
  senses subordinate to 30–1, 34–8, 41, 43, 71, 82, 90, 123, 135, 158, 165
  sympathetic 58–9, 63–4, 101, 110–11, 120–1
  transformative 26, 29, 33–8, 60 n., 90, 93
  see also genius; mind; power

'Jacob's dream' 90–1
James, William 94 n.
Jeffrey, Francis 103, 158
Jenyns, Soame:
  Free Inquiry into . . . Evil, cited by Johnson 162 n., 163 n.
Johnson, Samuel 7, 74–5, 118, 180 n.
  on 'representative' metre 70–1
  review of Soame Jenyns 162 n., 163 n.
Jonson, Ben 65, 75
  Fall of Sejanus 113

Kant, Immanuel 3, 5–7, 67, 146–8, 153–65, 176
  Groundwork of the Metaphysic of Morals 67, 146, 153–7, 162, 164–5
  Critique of Pure Reason 5, 160, 164
  see also empiricism; ideal; idealism: German; will
Keats, John 8–9, 76, 105, 107–10, 116, 118–19
  Letters 8, 105, 107–9, 116, 119
  'negative capability' 108 n., 109 n., 179, 190
Kinnaird, John 2, 42 n., 83 n., 85 n., 99 n., 127–9, 130, 165, 168 n.

Lamb, Charles 52, 118
  'On the Genius and Character of Hogarth' 37, 51–2
  'On the Tragedies of Shakespeare' 118
  review of *Table Talk* 180, 184
language:
  etymology and grammar 11–20, 78
  mechanism of 139–40, 145, 172–3
  nature and 53, 57, 103–5, 146
  ordinary 11, 17–20, 65
  perversion of 172–3
  poetic 11, 19–20, 23–6, 38, 41–2, 65–72, 103–6, 150, 167
  and power 25, 41, 48–9, 78, 167–8, 172
  scriptural 23–4, 48–9
  syntax 19–20
  and truth 41, 68, 139–40, 145–6, 172–3
  and unity 68, 71–2, 146
liberty:
  innate love of 174
  and necessity 66–8, 150–4, 166
  and power 167–9, 171–2, 175–6
  see also mind; power; will; *Lectures on English Philosophy*: 'On Liberty and Necessity', *Works* index
Locke, John 3, 5, 37, 66, 140
  compared to H. 23–4, 48–9
  compared to Tucker 148
  criticized by H. 28, 31, 57–73, 84, 136–7, 168, 174
  theory of abstraction 15–16, 136–7, 139, 151–2, 174
  Essay concerning Human Understanding 17, 21, 23–4, 49, 136–7, 159–60

Mahoney, John L. 8, 100 n.
Marlowe, Christopher 112
mechanism 1–2, 40, 67, 90
  of Burke 30
  criticism of 31, 52, 74–5, 77, 81, 87, 93–4, 108, 135, 139–40, 146, 168–9
  of French 145
  of Hartley 4, 54–5, 94
  influences selfhood 2, 75, 123, 129, 131, 135, 174–5, 168
  of language 70, 140, 145, 172–3
  of Priestley 55
  see also association; mind
metaphysical poets 90
Middleton, Thomas: *Women Beware Women* 114
Milton, John 37, 45, 104, 172, 180
  genius 96, 101, 104, 117, 119
  influence 183
  intellect 112, 124
mind:
  active/anti-mechanistic 4–6, 16, 26–9, 52, 73, 78, 81, 84, 87–8, 93–4, 102, 104–8, 110, 140, 149, 152–3, 156–9, 161, 169, 183
  creates reality 31–8, 53, 62, 89–90, 95–6
  evil 122, 125
  free/independent of senses 2, 5–6, 11, 28–31, 35, 60, 71, 73, 81, 129, 151–3, 157–9, 161, 167
  genius 95–6, 120

language and 19–20, 68–72, 140, 145–6
  mechanistic models of 4, 15–16, 31, 52, 54–5, 74–5, 81, 87, 108, 139–40, 146, 168
  and nature/'relation' 7 n., 18, 18 n., 26, 33–4, 52, 53 n., 54 n., 56–64, 76, 84, 90–1, 95–6, 104, 114–16, 120, 131–4, 136, 138, 140, 142, 146–7, 161, 182, 184
  unity of consciousness 5, 43–4, 148–9
  unity of ideas 53–7, 76, 78, 134–8, 140–1
  see also bias; genius; imagination; power
Montaigne, Michel Eyquemole 75
Moore, Thomas 100
moral/morality:
  and abstraction 134–6, 140–1
  action 120–3, 125–7, 146, 157, 162–3
  and agency/freedom 131, 136, 150–3
  and alterity 81 n., 120–3
  Christ and 121, 157
  goal: unity 67–8, 131–2, 140–1
  ideal 127–32, 135, 166
  and imagination 121–3, 129, 131, 152, 172, 174–5
  and Kantian thought 67, 146, 154–8, 164–5
  non-empirical basis of 127–8, 154–8, 162–3, 189
  'practical' 128, 164–5
  symbiotic nature of 131–5, 150, 183
  romantic 141–6
  sense 132, 156
  see also good; ideal; liberty
Muir, Kenneth 109 n.
Mulvihill, James 176 n.

Napoleon, *see* Bonaparte
Nature, see genius; imagination; language; mind; truth
necessity, *see* liberty
Newton, Isaac 21, 23, 38–9
Northcote, James 65, 90, 124, 145

O'Hara, J. D. 6, 63 n.
Otway, Thomas: *Venice Preserved* 101

pantheism 46–7, 50 n., 53 n., 54 n.
Park, Roy 6, 40, 74 n., 108 n., 109n., 135 n.
Patterson, C. I. 92 n.
Pitt, William 167, 172–3
Plato 14 n., 160, 181–2
pleasure principle 29–31, 81 n., 143, 155
poet, *see* genius; poetry
poetics 2–3, 11, 20–1, 24, 33, 41, 78
  Aristotle's 24, 68
  Burke's 24–6, 34
poetry 8, 20–1, 34, 61, 72–3, 116, 118–19, 132–3, 141
  composition of 21–4, 32, 36, 51–2, 63–8, 88, 101–2, 107, 109–10
  diction 102–7, 184
  false 64, 89–90, 106, 112, 171–2, 176 n.
  Greek 49–50
  Hebrew 50
  ideal 7, 37–8, 59, 62, 88–9, 92–3, 105, 135, 143, 176 n.
  metre 70–1
  and power 9, 11, 20, 26–7, 32, 36–8, 41–2, 52, 58, 69, 75, 90, 99–100, 105–6, 111, 119, 133, 170–3, 176 n., 178
  and reality 33, 36–8, 41, 60, 62, 88, 104–5, 107, 143
  see also language: poetic
politics, *see* power: political
Pope, Alexander: *Essay on Criticism* 70–1
Poussin, Nicolas 32 n., 75–6
power 1–3, 7 n., 11, 16, 20, 23, 26–9, 32–8, 41–2, 48–59, 62–4, 66, 72, 74–6, 78, 112–13, 123, 127–31, 136–40, 143–4, 149
  Coleridge on 122
  and ego/self 8–9, 87–90, 93, 96–102, 105–8, 110–11, 115–16, 119–20, 124–8, 133, 163, 169, 175–6
  Foucault on 178
  innate 2, 9, 11, 27–9, 41, 49, 54, 73, 96, 106, 140, 152–3, 162, 166–8, 170, 172–5, 178
  Locke on 28
  political 2, 97, 166–73, 176–8

power (*cont.*)
  principle 2, 29–31, 38, 122, 124, 143, 155, 178, 189
  see also genius; imagination; language; liberty; mind; poetry
Priestley, Joseph 42, 50 n., 54 n.
  Disquisitions Relating to Matter and Spirit 42–3, 46–7, 50 n., 55
  Doctrine of Philosophical Necessity Illustrated 47, 51

Raphael 37, 45
Ready, Robert 7 n.
relation, *see* mind
religion 23–4, 35, 41–2, 48–51, 73, 76–7, 82–4, 90–1, 121–2, 128, 157
  see also pantheism; Unitarianism
Rembrandt 32, 61, 65, 90–1, 98–100, 124
Reynolds, Joshua: *Discourses* 92, 136
Richardson, Charles 183
Robinson, Henry Crabb: comments on H. 51, 142
Robinson, J. C. 70 n.
romantic/romanticism: general 2–3, 7–8, 34, 40, 65–6, 76, 141–2, 168 n., 181–2, 187–9
Rousseau, Jean Jacques 168, 183

Sallé, J.-C. 54 n.
Schiller, Friedrich:
  compared to H. 5, 66–8, 91–2, 114–16, 130–1, 141, 146, 150, 154
  on genius 66–8, 114–16, 150
  on the ideal 66, 91–2, 114–16, 130
  Kant's influence 67, 146, 154
  On the Naïve and Sentimental in Literature 53 n., 66–7, 91–2, 114–16, 129 n., 130, 141, 150
  on will 66–8, 114–15, 150
Schlegel, Augustus William:
  compared to H. 5, 141–2, 144
  Kant's influence 146, 154
  Lectures on Dramatic Art and Literature 48–9, 112, 141–2, 144
  'organic form' 73
Schneider, Elisabeth 6, 40, 48 n., 53 n., 4 n., 56 n., 63 n., 85 n., 133 n., 138 n., 160 n.
science 21–3, 38–9, 91, 140

Scott, Sir Walter 38, 56, 58, 94, 143,
self-love 79–83, 86–7, 120–1, 125, 129, 130, 132, 155, 170
  see also benevolence; hatred
senses *see* imagination; mind
Shakespeare, William 8–9, 73, 75, 90, 141 n., 143
  genius 9, 110–11, 113–19
  lacks 'gusto' 100, 110
  language 64, 68–9
  poet of nature 58, 111, 116–17
  WORKS:
  Anthony and Cleopatra 34
  Coriolanus 43, 119, 167
  Hamlet 118
  King Lear 23, 118, 122
  Love's Labour's Lost 69
  Macbeth 32 n., 117
  A Midsummer Night's Dream 32
  Othello 119
  Romeo and Juliet 89
  The Tempest 32 n., 69
  Troilus and Cressida 97
Shelley, Percy 60
  A Defence of Poetry 21, 26, 122, 132–3
  essay on the Colosseum 132
Sidney, Philip 112; *A Defence of Poetry* 21
Sikes, H. M. 109 n.
Smith, A.:
  Theory of Moral Sentiments 81 n.
  Wealth of Nations 95 n.
solipsism 181–2, 188–9
Southey, Robert 168, 172
  The Curse of Kehama 75
Spenser, Edmund 37–8
Spurzheim, Dr Johann 43, 93, 145
  see also *The Plain Speaker*: 'On Dr. Spurzheim's Theory', *Works* index
Staël-Holstein, Germaine de:
  Germany 154, 160–1, 164
Swift, Jonathan 129–30
sympathy 21–2, 25, 37, 75, 81 n., 83 n., 85, 87, 90, 117, 120–1, 123
  associative 53–4, 56–64, 95–6, 101, 110–11, 131–4
  see also imagination

Thomson, James 58, 62–3
Titian 72, 100

General Index

Tooke, John Horne 4–5, 66, 145, 175
  Diversions of Purley 13–16, 18–19
truth:
  and beauty 143–4
  imaginative/poetic 24, 26–7, 36–8, 59, 65–6, 73, 90, 93, 95–6, 98, 111, 113, 132, 134–5, 142, 171
  language and 41, 68, 139–40, 145–6, 172–3
  and nature 47–8, 56, 61–2, 95, 105, 111, 117
  plurality of 96, 126, 132–3, 185–7
  spontaneity test of 64–6
  universal 6, 24, 59, 89, 95-6, 117–18, 133–5, 147, 154, 174, 176 n., 177, 185, 189
  see also ideal
Tucker, Abraham *Light of Nature Pursued* 5, 10, 38, 147–50

understanding 7 n., 27, 43–4, 48, 57, 75, 97, 107, 136, 139–40, 152, 160–2, 169
  see also imagination; mind
Unitarianism 41–3, 48–51, 72, 76–7, 83, 86
  associationism and 51–2, 54–5
  deism and 41–2
  Coleridge and 42–8, 50–1, 72–3, 76, 79, 85–6
  H.'s father and 42, 77
  Priestley and 42–3, 46–7, 50 n., 55
unity:
  artistic/poetic principle of 40–1, 44–8, 51–2, 68, 71–6, 78, 144, 183
  of consciousness 5, 43–4, 148–9
  of ideas 53–7, 76, 78, 134–8, 140–1
  moral 67–8, 133–6, 140–2, 144–6
  of mind and nature 53–4, 56–9, 67–8, 87, 114–16, 138, 141–2, 146–7
  of natural creation 42–3, 67, 72
  see also association, imagination
universal 19 n., 61–2, 68
  ideal 58–9, 62–3, 72, 92, 95, 131–6, 146–7, 154, 166, 174–5, 177–8, 183

and individual/particular 24, 47, 84–7, 89, 92, 95–6, 111, 131–7, 139–41, 149–50, 154–5, 163, 166, 174, 176–8, 183–5, 187, 190
  see also truth
Utilitarianism 5, 20, 30–1, 74, 122, 135, 142, 157, 168

Vanbrugh, John 65

Webster, John 113
Wellek, René 40–1, 148 n., 159 n., 162, 164 n.
Whale, J. 3 n., 172 n., 173 n.
White, R. S. 109 n.
will 37, 46, 65–6, 80–2, 103, 123, 127–8, 150–1, 156, 169, 177
  biassed 94, 124, 126
  Butler on 81–2
  free/volition 19, 26–9, 31, 55, 66–8, 73, 81–2, 87, 94, 115, 123, 131, 150–3, 157–8, 178
  genius and self-will 93, 97–9, 117, 169
  of God 23, 46, 49
  Kant on 67, 153–4, 156, 158
  Locke on 151
  Schiller on 66–8, 114–15, 150
  Tucker on 149–50
  see also imagination; mind; liberty; understanding
Willich, A. F. M.:
  Elements of the Critical Philosophy 160–1
Wordsworth, William:
  H's criticism of 87–8, 100, 102–7, 109, 124
  genius 98–102, 110, 124
  on poetic diction 103–4, 106–7, 184
  WORKS:
  The Excursion 98–9, 180
  'Personal Talk' 32
  'Preface' to *Lyrical Ballads* 103–4, 106–7, 184
  'Preface' to *Poems* (1815) 51–2
  'Tintern Abbey' 55–6